99

Judging Evil

Judging Evil

*Rethinking the Law of Murder
and Manslaughter*

Samuel H. Pillsbury

NEW YORK UNIVERSITY PRESS

New York and London

NEW YORK UNIVERSITY PRESS
New York and London

Library of Congress Cataloging-in-Publication Data
Pillsbury, Samuel H., 1954–
Judging evil : rethinking the law of murder and manslaughter /
Samuel H. Pillsbury.
p.   cm.
Includes bibliographical references and index.
ISBN 0-8147-6665-X (alk. paper)
1. Murder—Philosophy. 2. Criminal intent. 3. Punishment—
Philosophy. 4. Consent (Law). I. Title.
K5172.P55   1998
345'.04—dc21   98-28137
                CIP

New York University Press books are printed on acid-free paper,
and their binding materials are chosen for strength and durability.

Manufactured in the United States of America

10 9 8 7 6 5 4 3 2 1

Contents

Preface

The Challenge of Criminal Responsibility

Twenty years ago, when I was a newspaper reporter in Jacksonville, Florida, I reported on a case that I have never forgotten. It was one of those cases that comes along every so often that affects everyone it touches. At times it seemed to touch the whole city.

The facts were horrific. A father was convicted of the terrible abuse of his four children, abuse so severe that it killed two of them and left another battered and nearly blind. During a six-month period when his wife—who had been the main target of his abuse—was in jail, the heavy-set man with a brutal temper kicked, punched, and slapped his children who ranged from three to eleven years old. As punishments he jammed their small heads in a flushing toilet, beat and kicked them, breaking their limbs and causing internal injuries; he scraped his fingernails on the insides of their mouths, and on and on. Two of the children died of the abuse. Finally the eldest boy escaped and the father fled the city, leaving his youngest daughter at a hospital with two dollars, her Teddy bear, and a note pinned to her clothes bearing the name and telephone number of her grandmother.[1]

At the time I was influenced by the liberal creed of the sixties which decried harsh punishment, but as I listened to this tale of horrors, so much worse than any fiction, I found myself agreeing with the state, that these acts deserved severe punishment. Surely if anyone deserved the death penalty it must be this Ernest John Dobbert Jr.[2]

Then I met Dobbert's defense attorney, one of the most perceptive observers of the criminal justice system I have ever encountered, and heard the testimony he offered at a resentencing hearing. Dobbert was the son of an abusive father who beat and degraded him. The son so feared his father that to avoid his learning about a bad grade, Dobbert Jr. once cut the telephone wires to the house. The defense evidence suggested that Dobbert Jr. was caught in a cycle of abuse far beyond his power to control. In a strange way

Dobbert loved his children. In prison he had shown himself to be a peaceful, even kind person. Given all this, how could we rage at him? What did he really deserve, this victim of abuse turned victimizer? But if Dobbert was not really to blame, how could we account for the deep sense of evil which his actions evoked? Why did his conduct seem so much worse than the sufferings wreaked by disease or natural disaster?

Florida's criminal justice system provided one answer to these questions. A jury found Dobbert guilty of first-degree murder, in a trial that focused entirely on what he had done to his children and not at all on what had happened to him as a child. At the sentencing phase of the case, the defense presented evidence of Dobbert's childhood abuse, but the judge did not find it significant. Disregarding a jury recommendation for life in prison, the judge imposed a death sentence. Years of appeals followed.

Meanwhile I left reporting and went to law school. The year after graduation I heard how the Dobbert case ended. My wife called me at work and said she had just heard on the radio that Dobbert had been executed. I was surprised by my own reaction. I was clerking for a federal judge at the time, and sitting in the elegant chambers office lined with bound reports of federal cases, I felt hollow and sick. I was certain Dobbert deserved severe punishment, but not death. I could not say exactly why, though.

I spent the next several years as a prosecutor and then became a law professor. I continued to puzzle over deserved punishment. I wanted to know what was right about the Dobbert case and what was wrong.

★

The question of what a person deserves for committing a harmful act represents an issue of central importance for our society. It is a basic question of moral responsibility, one important to any society. I think it is especially important for late twentieth-century America. Officially we put great faith in the universal principle of individual responsibility; in practice our commitment to responsibility is selective.

Increasingly fearful of crime, the public urges heavier and heavier penalties for a wide range of criminal offenses. Presidents, governors, and legislators compete to show their anticrime fervor by support for death penalties and draconian mandatory sentencing schemes. Everyone seems to agree that criminals must pay for their dastardly deeds; we hear cries of zero tolerance, no excuses. Yet this commitment to full individual responsibility falters when we confront defendants who do not fit the image of Criminal. When the "law-abiding" public encounters wrongdoers who look or sound like themselves, who tell stories of personal tragedies with echoes in the listeners' lives, excuses from responsibility suddenly multiply. Similarly, when some ask that society as a whole take responsibility for the features of that society that corrupt and destroy young lives, the idea of responsibility becomes controversial.

When critics complain that society itself inspires crime, that mainstream culture fosters greed and violence, responsibility becomes a catch-word for finger pointing. Politicians blame the entertainment media for corrupting the public with violence and graphic sex, while the media simultaneously cry free speech and blame the public because it likes sex and violence. All lament the violent nature of our society but few are willing to pay to change the society's taste for blood. The advocates of change nearly always point to some other group's behavior as the source of the problem.

Even within the criminal justice system, even in determining responsibility for the most serious of criminal offenses, we find major problems with the understanding of and commitment to moral responsibility. I can illustrate the problem by reference to a simply stated principle, one basic to criminal responsibility: we should judge the nature of human conduct, not human worth. If we punish Dobbert severely, we do so because of what he did to his children, not because he was a bad man. Criminal law judges conduct and not souls.

Like many moral principles, this notion seems both obviously right and impossibly vague. It is obviously right because how can any ordinary human being pass ultimate judgment on another's moral value? This is a task for God, not mortal man or woman. The principle seems impossibly vague because it seems to require a separation of bad acts and bad character, which our language conflates. A person who steals is a thief, just as the passer-by who braves an inferno to save a helpless infant is a hero. True, the "hero" may in the rest of his life be a thoroughly despicable person and the thief a dedicated public servant experiencing a personal crisis, but we need a shorthand for moral judgment. It's not practical to separate act and character.

In fact, we judge conduct apart from ultimate worth all the time. We simply judge what the person did in the situation. We judge the aspect of character revealed in the individual's specific conduct. We need not make any global judgments on the person's larger nature or worth.

The reason we often engage in global character assessment, in judgments of ultimate worth, is not that we must, but that it feels good. Such condemnation makes moral judgment simpler and more satisfying emotionally. By separating the world into good guys and bad guys, we can treat sympathetically the wrongs of our friends while condemning those of our enemies. The temptation to leap from judging conduct to ultimate worth is strong and not often resisted in a society where feeling often substitutes for logic in public discourse.

In my view, using criminal law to judge human worth not only distorts responsibility decisions; it is wrong in and of itself. Condemning a person as opposed to conduct contradicts the fundamental principle that criminal law defends: that all human beings have value. We have intrinsic moral value because we make moral choices. We can choose to do good, or to do bad. We can make a moral society, or an immoral one. We must take our choices seriously, by punishing the bad and rewarding the good, never forgetting that all persons have value.

In the legal system the tendency to judge individual worth is particularly prevalent and particularly dangerous. Police and prosecutors, among others, share a richly abusive vocabulary for offenders. They are beasts, rodents, insects, slimeballs, garbage, or containers of excrement. The most formal expression of these views is the death penalty. When the state of Florida killed Ernest John Dobbert Jr. it necessarily declared his life forfeit, his moral value nil. It condemned him as a worthless person. I think this condemnation was wrong and violated the essential principle that the criminal law should support.

★

The Dobbert case illustrates the significance of what might otherwise seem to be arcane matters of moral philosophy and legal theory. This book is not about the death penalty, or gun control, or the criminalization of drugs or mandatory sentences, or any other hot topic in criminal justice. Instead it focuses on matters generally removed from the public eye: what makes a person morally responsible for serious wrongdoing, and how our criminal law of homicide should be written and understood. These matters have broad implications within the criminal justice system and beyond, however. Our criminal code expresses basic public attitudes and values. It simultaneously reflects and shapes society in that it provides a basic template for individual responsibility. Criminal law constitutes our most fundamental rules of responsibility, and responsibility suffuses every aspect of human interaction.

This book argues for a particular theory of individual moral responsibility and its application to criminal homicide. As part of this argument the book espouses a particular style of moral reasoning based on a first principle of human value—of right in and of itself—rather than on a utilitarian calculation of the optimal consequences of a decision.

The book concentrates on the problems of the criminal law and in part 2 presents a number of specific proposals for legal reform. But whether the reader agrees or not with these proposals, I hope that she, or he, will find the ideas a stimulus to think about the kind of society we wish to have, and the kinds of lives we wish to live. Ultimately this is what individual responsibility is about.

I should offer a few words about my aims here—what I try for and what I do not. Although expressly philosophic in approach, I do not attempt to meet standards of academic philosophy in the rigor of argumentation and consideration of rival perspectives. Similarly, although this book is expressly legal in its concerns, it does not present the kind of close argument and detailed source attribution normally expected by the legal academy. I aim for a general audience of those seriously interested in morals, law, and criminal justice. Thus I do not presume extensive background in either philosophy or law, though I hope that those versed in law and philosophy will still find much to interest them here.

In part 1 I lay out my theory of deserved punishment, and consider a number of objections to it. Chapter 1 describes the difference between a theory of responsibility based on inherent human value rather than on calculations of the costs and benefits of responsibility decisions. Chapter 2 addresses one of the central challenges for any theory of deserved punishment, the causal explanations of the human sciences. Once we recognize that all human behavior has causes in genetics and the environment, what happens to the moral importance of rational choice? I argue that we need to distinguish scientific from moral questions and that we gain meaning from responsibility based on choice without regard to scientific explanations of genetic or environmental causes. Chapter 3 describes the essential components of my theory of deserved punishment: that persons merit blame for rational, uncoerced choices to disregard the basic worth of other human beings, regardless of what may be called their moral capacity to choose differently. Chapter 4 considers objections to the theory as it applies to a society with many unjust social conditions. Here I explore how social responsibility for crime should be considered independent of, but equally important as, individual moral and legal responsibility for crime. Chapter 5 addresses the concern that deserved punishment encourages cruel and excessive punishment by encouraging unrestrained anger. I argue that emotions have their own rationality, and that deserved punishment presents a set of emotional dangers no more or less significant than any other approach to punishment. The key to emotional regulation in criminal justice is the development of clear rules that express our best-considered moral intuitions concerning the morality of conduct.

Part 2 applies the theory of deserved punishment developed in part 1 to some of the basic doctrines of criminal homicide. Chapter 6 introduces the concept of *mens rea*, the mental element of crime, and defends the concept against several challenges, one from recent work in cognitive science, and another from a common understanding of the mind that seems to make proof of mens rea nearly impossible. Chapter 7 takes up the worst form of murder, critiquing current definitions based on premeditation and the commission of certain felonies, and proposing a new offense requiring a purposeful killing based on an especially bad motive. Chapter 8 covers the traditional doctrine of provocation and points to a number of problems with it, ranging from sexism to confusions concerning responsibility for emotion. I argue that killings done in the heat of passion deserve less blame if they come in response to serious wrongs and that we need to rethink the central examples of what such wrongs might be. Chapter 9 covers the main doctrines of murder and manslaughter that punish careless killings. Here I argue that culpability for careless homicide should turn on a demonstrated attitude of indifference to the lives of others rather than the definitions of recklessness and negligence normally used. In particular, I argue that we should blame for wrongdoing when the person adopts a self-interested philosophy of action that encourages disregard of risk, independent of actual awareness of risk.

★

In a society obsessed with violent crime and its punishment, in a nation where leaders in all fields call for increased personal responsibility, there might seem no need for extended discussion of deserved punishment for homicide. But in fact it is just because we say we are committed to principles of individual responsibility that we must look much harder at what those are and what they mean. The current discussion of violent crime tends to be a discussion of conflict, of fear and anger, of us and them. It tends to describe a war in which there is an enemy, an other, to be utterly vanquished. But moral responsibility is always about we, about us, about rules for the entire human community. It is about looking human evil in the face and not blinking. This proves to be much harder than it sounds.

Acknowledgments

Many people assisted with the research and writing of this book. I want to thank my research assistants present and past: Suzy Snyder, Karen Cox, Paige Ross, Ruth Pinkel, Hannah Irsfeld, Lisa Farrington, and Joseph Carlucci; the students of the three Criminal Law Seminar classes who read and commented on the book in draft form; and the staff, past and present, of the Loyola Law Library, in particular Bob Nissenbaum, Bill Mulherin, and Demetrio Orlino. My school, Loyola Law School, has provided generous research support through the Burns Foundation. I also must thank David Duffee and the School of Criminal Justice at the State University of New York, Albany, where I spent a sabbatical in the fall of 1992. Those who have read the manuscript or predecessor works and helped with comments include Peter Arenella, Anne Coughlin, Rebecca Dresser, R. A. Duff, Josh Dressler, Martin Gardner, Laurie Levenson, Tom Morawetz, Jeffrie Murphy, Rick Singer, Larry Solum, and George Thomas. Help here should certainly not be confused with agreement, however. Ideas contained in the book were sharpened by presentations to the law faculties of Rutgers-Newark, the University of Southern California, and Loyola. My special thanks to my colleague Lary Lawrence, who has always believed in this book and in my scholarly efforts; and to my wife, Linda, who has never allowed my work to become too academic, in the pejorative sense.

Portions of this book have been drawn from the following previously published articles by the author: *Crimes of Indifference,* 49 Rutgers Law Review 105 (1996); *The Meaning of Deserved Punishment,* 67 Indiana Law Journal 719 (1992); *Evil and the Law of Murder,* 24 U.C. Davis Law Review 437 (1990); and *Emotional Justice: Moralizing the Passions of Criminal Punishment,* 74 Cornell Law Review 655 (1989). Permission by the respective law reviews for the use of this material is gratefully acknowledged.

PART I

Deserved Punishment

1

A Question of Value

Americans do a lot of killing. Although we do not lead the world in homicide, our national rates far exceed those of any other industrialized nation. Indeed it is the violence of our crime rather than the overall numbers of crimes committed here that constitutes the special problem of American crime.[1]

The American homicide problem may be approached, truly must be approached, from a number of different perspectives. We need all of our collective skills: we need the work of novelists and movie makers and lawyers and police officers and social scientists and therapists and doctors and community activists and spiritual leaders, among others. Each asks a different question about crime that leads to different insights and suggestions for action. But what do we do with all these questions and answers? How do we reconcile the many truths that different approaches reveal? How do we decide on a course of action?

A typical criminal case will illustrate the challenge. Consider David, a young man who faces the judgment of a criminal court. David grew up in a chaotic family without much love and no parental guidance. In his early teens he developed a serious drug addiction and committed a series of burglaries and stole cars to keep himself supplied with drugs. Eventually he turned to armed robbery to support his habit. After several robberies he sought drug treatment, but found that all area treatment centers were full. He committed a final robbery, but this time his victim resisted and David killed her. What should we do with David? The answer to this question will depend at least in part on whom we ask.

The police officer who arrests David and the district attorney who prosecutes him will seek his conviction and incarceration. A psychiatrist called into the case will emphasize treatments to foster David's physical and mental health. A social reformer will take the case as an example of the need for better public support of families and more drug rehabilitation facilities. As long as all professionals work within their own area, their different approaches may not conflict. David may, simultaneously, be convicted and punished, receive psychological treatment, and find himself the poster boy of a social reform movement. Yet this neat division of professional turf will hold only as long as each professional agrees to respect the boundaries set by the other professions. In fact, the police officer may decry the treatment methods of mental health professionals on the grounds that these undercut self-discipline and moral principle; the psychiatrist may urge the judge to order treatment for David instead of incarceration, because treatment will produce better results for both David and society. For us to decide what we should do with David, we must decide whether we want to adopt the basic approach of the police officer, the psychiatrist, or the social reformer.

As law students learn in their first year of study, when professors ask the questions and they provide the answers, the most important part of any legal inquiry is how we frame the question. In this book I am primarily concerned with questions of legal guilt. I want to know how we should construct some basic rules of criminal liability. By virtue of asking this kind of question we focus on individual responsibility. The question leads us away from many of the concerns of nonlawyers, including the predominant concerns of the psychiatrist and social reformer.

This book pursues a particular kind of question about individual responsibility: I want to know whether David deserves punishment, and if so, how much. I want to determine the law's reaction to David's conduct according to moral assessment of his choice to rob and to kill, rather than according to the good or bad consequences of his punishment. This chapter begins by exploring some of the differences between the two main approaches to punishment: what I call the value approach (often labeled retributive) and the utilitarian. The chapter begins the argument, continued throughout the book, that the value method should provide central guidance to criminal responsibility because it best exposes and expresses the nature of our commitment to moral responsibility. Much of the chapter addresses objections from utilitarians and others concerning the subjectivity of the value approach. Many argue that value declarations represents nothing more than the personal preferences of a few powerful people. Indeed, the value approach meets neither of our predominant tests for the validity of public policy: scientific proof or democratic consensus. Value cannot be scientifically proven, because there are no objective indicators of value's existence, and it cannot be determined by a vote, because by definition, popular opinion cannot determine value. I argue that value remains a meaningful concept that we should debate in its own terms, according to our own experience of life. The value approach requires that we talk about right and wrong in some old-fashioned ways, but ways that remain vital to our modern well-being.

An Overview of Punishment Theory: Utility versus Value

Philosophers distinguish two general categories of moral reasoning: the utilitarian and the deontological. The utilitarian determines right conduct by what produces the greatest good for the greatest number. The deontologist determines right conduct by predetermined principles of right and wrong, judging that certain actions are right or wrong *in themselves*, regardless of their consequences. These two styles of reasoning produce similar results in most cases, but resolution of some of the hardest issues may depend on which approach we select.

Contemporary discussion of public policy issues often begins with value-style declarations, but the actual analysis and debate of issues is usually dominated by utilitarian considerations. Whether the issue is health care or criminal law, most of the detailed discussion will involve calculations of the consequences of a particular course of action. Who will be helped, who will be hurt: these considerations usually decide the question. We use the same analysis in private morality. We teach our children not to lie. When asked why, we may explain that lying hurts people and it never works. Liars are found out and punished. We say that the immediate personal advantage gained from lying will be greatly outweighed by the harmful results of that lie to the liar and others. The utilitarian approach to punishment similarly emphasizes the consequences of public action: we make perpetrators suffer in order to discourage the commission of future criminal harms.[2] English philosopher Jeremy Bentham put the basic case for a utilitarian approach to punishment as follows:

> The general object which all laws have, or ought to have, in common, is to augment the total happiness of the community; and therefore, in the first place, to exclude, as far as may be, everything that tends to subtract from that happiness: in other words, to exclude mischief.
>
> But all punishment is mischief: all punishment in itself is evil. Upon the principle of utility, if it ought at all to be admitted, it ought only to be admitted in as far as it promises to exclude some greater evil.

In other words, since the object of law is to maximize happiness and minimize pain, and since punishment involves the infliction of pain, punishment should be used only to the extent that its pain prevents other, greater pains. Bentham continued:

> The immediate end of punishment is to control action. This action is either that of the offender, or others: that of the offender it controls by its influence, either on his will, in which case it is said to operate in the way of reformation; or on his physical power, in which case it is said to operate by disablement; that of others it can influence no otherwise than by its influence over their wills; in which case it is said to operate by way of example.[3]

According to Bentham, punishment is justified to the extent that it alters the offender's desire to offend again, that it physically prevents him from further crimes, or that it deters others from criminal acts through the example of the offender's punishment. It is justified to the extent that it efficiently deters crime.

Returning to David's case, the classical utilitarian will likely urge significant punishment. David chose to inflict great pain on his victim and those who loved her and threatened the security of many, in order to gain a minimal amount of personal pleasure. We need to deter David and others like him from acts of such massive disutility. We need to devise a punishment that will persuade David that the likely rewards of the conduct are not worth the risks of punishment. Since robbery and killing are among the worst harms, which we want to deter most, they should receive among the most severe penalties. We should punish lesser harms to a lesser degree because we have a lesser need to deter them.

The utilitarian method can be constructed in many different ways, however. Sophisticated utilitarians may consider the basic pleasure/pain calculus insufficient, recognizing that determining the greatest good must take account of other considerations, including the long-term effects of many individual practices. Thus a sophisticated utilitarian might argue that David's punishment should depend not on a calculation of the costs and benefits of punishment in only his case, but we should look to construct rules that, applied over the entire set of similar criminal cases, produce the best overall outcome. Thus, even if David's incarceration would not by itself produce efficient specific or general deterrence, because the rule of incarcerating serious offenders produces efficient deterrence if applied generally, it should also be applied to David. A sophisticated utilitarian might even incorporate ideas about desert, saying that perceptions about the wrongness of David's conduct and accompanying intuitions that he deserves punishment must be respected by the law in order to maintain the system's legitimacy in the eyes of the public.[4] The public's belief in deserved punishment, even if erroneous, is a political fact the utilitarian must take seriously.

As the discussion of sophisticated utilitarianism should illustrate, the outcome of a particular policy decision may depend more on how the particular value or utilitarian theory is structured than on whether the decision maker goes the value or utility route. This does not make the choice of route unimportant, however. In practical terms, the value versus utility choice has important implications for how we approach moral questions and how we answer them. The most important difference may be in the extent of our commitment to determinate moral principles.

By contrast to the utilitarian method, which views every moral judgment as contingent on its expected consequences, a deontological approach to moral issues seeks to make decisions based on changeless principles of right and wrong. In this book I use a particular form of deontology that I call the value approach because it rests on an innate value that all human beings have because of their choosing ability. To contrast this approach with the utilitarian, recall the discussion of honesty. A value adherent might well agree with the utilitarian that we should not lie. The value adherent would argue for honesty not because honesty will promote general happiness, but because honesty is right-in-itself. Even if it provides no tangible, or even intangible good results, we should be honest. Taking a value approach does not mean that we necessarily treat a particular value as absolute, however. For example, I might value honesty but still recognize other competing values. I might value both honesty and human life so that, confronted by a situation where I must lie to save another's life, I might morally do so, deciding that the value of life outweighed the value of truth in this context.

In the legal context we often use the language of rights to express values. Declaring that every person has a right to equal treatment under the law is another way of saying that all persons have equal legal value. When we say that persons have a right to free speech, we mean that the law recognizes an inherent value in speech. As with other values, the rights to equal protection or free speech are not absolute. A constitutional right may be overridden by countervailing considerations, but the predetermined worth of the constitutional right must always be recognized.[5]

One of the most influential proponents of a value approach to punishment was the German philosopher Immanuel Kant. Kant argued that persons should be valued for their ability to choose for themselves. He wrote that this valuing requires that persons be treated as ends in themselves—as inherently worthy—and should never be used merely as means to an end.

When persons do not value others, punishment must follow. He argued that punishment valued persons for their choosing abilities, and so was a good in itself. Punishment should depend on the nature of the crime and not on the consequences that punishment may produce. Kant warned: "The penal law is a Categorical Imperative; and woe to him who creeps through the serpent-windings of Utilitarianism to discover some advantage that may discharge him from the Justice of punishment, or even from the due measure of it . . . for if Justice and Righteousness perish, human life would no longer have any value in the world."[6]

Modern philosophers have used Kant's approach to develop a theory called respect for persons, which holds that the individual's autonomy—his or her ability to make rational choices—must be respected. Under a Kantian approach to punishment, just punishment is what a person deserves according to the individual's choice to disrespect another. Deserved punishment for homicide respects autonomy in two ways: it respects the autonomy of the victim that was wrongly destroyed, and it respects the autonomy of the killer by taking seriously his or her choice to kill.[7]

Returning to David's case, the value approach would focus on the essential wrong of robbery and killing to further the robbery. David's chosen conduct violated human worth in several important ways. In particular, David disregarded his victim's rights to property, security, and life. A value adherent would argue that David should be severely punished not because of the goods that would come from his punishment, but because he deserved it as a result of his wrongful conduct.

At this point many readers may wonder: What's the big deal? We seem to reach the same conclusions regardless of the philosophic route we take. In our everyday lives we use both kinds of moral reasoning interchangeably. We teach our children: lying will only get you in trouble *and* it's just plain wrong. Indeed, most of the time both forms of moral reasoning do lead us to the same conclusion, especially considering the variations available in theoretical formulations. But as we move from the realm of theory to that of practice, a potentially significant difference emerges.

In criminal responsibility we must devise universal rules—rules that recognize only morally relevant distinctions between cases, not the personal (i.e., nonmoral) interests of the decision maker. And we must apply those rules uniformly. The value approach, with its strong statement of timeless principle, puts the challenge of universality and uniformity squarely to the decision maker. As a practical matter, the utilitarian approach provides less protection against self-interested, ad hoc rationalization of responsibility decisions.

As an example, assume one morning your supervisor comes in and asks whether a friend of yours has shown up for work yet. Although the workday has officially begun, your friend has not yet arrived. What should you tell the supervisor? Assume that (1) the supervisor will be angry to learn that your friend is late again, even though your friend always stays to work after hours and there is no need for him to be present when the workday starts; and (2) there is virtually no chance that the truth will come out later. Do you judge that a lie will produce the greatest good for the greatest number here—it will help your friend and will not hurt the company—or should you tell the truth because lying is wrong? Or, to extend the utilitarian calculation, perhaps a lie would produce the greatest good in this case, but the general rule of honesty is so important that it should be recognized even here—to produce the greatest goods over the long run. Again the two methods seem reconciled. But note what happens in human terms when you mull the issue.

If you view honesty as a fundamental value, a good-in-itself, a serious obstacle lies in the path of assisting your friend. Unless you value friendship so greatly that it overwhelms all other considerations, the rule of honesty precludes a lie. You need not ascertain what will produce the greatest good in the situation, you simply adhere to a preexisting principle. The challenge is less in determining what you should do than in mustering the conviction to abide by honesty's rule. By contrast, if you view honesty as a generally prudent policy whose particular application depends on the particular consequences, then you must calculate a wide variety of potential consequences, short and long term, personal and corporate in order to reach a decision. You must essentially reconsider the value of honesty in a particular situation—a situation in which strong personal considerations obtain. It will be much harder, psychologically, to weigh the importance of honesty as a general rule when the particular situation presents such strong personal reasons to create an exception. As a result, decision-making under the utilitarian method is more likely—as a matter of practice rather than theory—to be ad hoc and influenced by personal considerations.[8]

This comparison of value and utility should remind us that issues of moral responsibility involve more than an intellectual debate between rival policies. They engage our hearts as well as our minds. As we will see more clearly in later chapters, when we judge wrongly in the criminal field, the fault sometimes lies in our intellectual grasp of the situation involved; we miss some unusual aspect of the human interaction that should be vital to judgment. More often the failure stems from a lack of moral commitment, however. We do not care enough about justice in the situation to fully engage our moral faculties, or we balk at the cost of universal and uniform rules. We refuse to pay the price responsibility demands. It is in this regard, in hewing to the often difficult demands of moral principle, that the value approach presents the most significant advantage over the utilitarian.

Where Do These Values Come From?

Presented with the value approach to punishment the utilitarian will ask: Where do these values come from? Did the Almighty hand them to us engraved on a stone tablet? No?[9] Well then, are they a matter of universal and timeless human consensus? On hearing that the value consensus is neither timeless nor universal, the skeptic will conclude: value is nothing more than a fancy word for personal preference. It carries no more weight than one person's preference for strawberry over chocolate ice cream.

The value adherent's answer to this kind of skepticism will at first sound weak to modern ears. We find value in our experience of life. From a thoughtful, deeply felt examination of our own lives and those of all around us, we ascertain certain principles that resonate with moral truth. We find value in much the same way we find beauty or ugliness. These are not insights capable of scientific proof or universal affirmation, but this does not render them fictitious. Value is metaphysical; we can usefully discuss its dimensions, but we will find no impersonal, objective methods for proving or disproving its validity.

This response seems weak because it seems to challenge two of the most powerful sources of authority in contemporary America: science and democracy. We put greatest faith today in data supplied by either the scientific method or by public consensus. If we cannot test an idea by physical measurement or public referendum, we often dismiss it as personal opinion, something that counts for little in resolving questions of public policy. Such skepticism about subjectively derived ideas bodes ill for the value approach to punishment.[10]

Throughout contemporary criminal justice we find a tension between scientific understandings of the physical world and moral judgments of human conduct. We can trace this tension back at least as far as the ancient

Greeks, but the current dynamic stems from developments in the last two centuries. In pre-modern times, when the physical workings of the world remained fundamentally mysterious, human understanding of the physical and moral universe stood on an equal footing. Commonsense observations, tradition, and religious belief formed the basis for both kinds of understanding. With technological advances in many fields, most notably in the latter half of the nineteenth century, a distinctively scientific approach to truth emerged in public policy discussions. For the first time, scientists offered the general public tangible, useful proofs of how the physical universe worked. Transportation (railroad and steamship), communication (telegraph), and medicine (anesthetics and antiseptic methods for modern surgery and vaccines) were but a few of the fields transformed by scientific discoveries. Science's success in explaining and reshaping the physical world has been so dramatic that in this century it has come to overshadow all other forms of human understanding.

As we will see in chapter 2, insights from physical science challenge our common understanding of free will. In this and other aspects of morality, science presents an epistemological challenge: it raises doubts about whether the moralist's claims concerning human choice can be reconciled with scientific understanding of human behavior. The scientific method provides a tough test for knowledge: we should believe only what can be verified by independent observation. In other words, we should believe only what can be ascertained in a manner independent of the observer's identity and personal experience. The classic examples of scientific knowledge come from the so-called hard sciences: instrument measurements that verify the laws of physics, chemistry or biology. Data obtained in this way may be verified without regard to the national origin, politics, or personality of the scientific inquirer. The effects of gravity, the boiling point of water, these can be determined by criteria that do not require the application of personal thoughts, feelings, or experiences.[11]

No one claims, at least not explicitly, that the scientific method can provide moral answers. The scientific method seeks to explain human behavior (among other phenomena), while morality critiques that behavior. Science describes while morality prescribes. This means that if we want an objective test for morals, it will not come from science. Science may give us information highly relevant to moral decision making, but never moral answers. What the scientific method does suggest, is that even moral issues should be resolved according to objective criteria for decision making.

In a society deeply impressed by scientific thinking, and riven by disagreement about most issues of public importance, the lure of objective data is powerful, and the dangers of a subjective approach, like that of value, seem obvious. Once we look hard at apparently objective methods for moral decision making, though, the question of method becomes a much harder one. We see that, all too often, requiring objectivity is simply a way of avoiding responsibility for deciding moral questions on moral grounds.

Economic efficiency provides one apparently objective means of resolving public policy questions. In this capitalist society, the dominant norms are those of the marketplace. What is the best personal computer, the best automobile? The marketplace will tell us. But few argue that the laws of supply and demand should set criminal rules.[12] Criminal rules come prior to market concerns; the marketplace is in significant measure determined by criminal rules. Merchants may not compete by fraud or force because criminal law—on fairness grounds—declares these activities out of bounds.

Another form of objective data is direct measurement of public preferences. We could take a poll or have a vote. We recognize that only some questions are appropriate for majority determination, however. Even in this democracy, we find many issues where the majority's will does not and should not control. The general public decides which movies and books will make the most money, but not (at least not directly) who wins an Oscar or a Nobel Prize. Legislatures enact laws, but we rely on appointed judges to determine if these comport with certain antimajoritarian principles in the Constitution. We retain a strong sense that we can speak about right and wrong without reference to majority preference. As citizens we may have an obligation to obey democratically passed laws, but as human beings we retain the right and the obligation to criticize those laws when they are morally wrong. In this way, value analysis (and utilitarian analysis in many cases) stands apart from the democratic process.

Reinforcing the skeptic's doubts about the value approach is the fact that values depend on culture. A look at human societies around the world today, and throughout history, reveals that what many assume to be an unchanging and universal value in fact depends on the time-bound norms of a particular culture. To oversimplify considerably, the Japanese today value consensus, Americans value individuality, the English value respectability. Within a particular society, values may differ according to religion, ethnicity, race, class, and region. Even with regard to a harm as serious as killing, different cultural groups may have different values. For example, as we will see in chapter 8, norms of personal honor, important to determining whether a killing should be deemed provoked, may depend on sex, class, and even geography. Such norms may also change dramatically over time.

The cultural and historical contingency of value supports two different attacks on the value approach. First, it suggests that values are nothing more than collective preferences, and temporary ones at that. A value is like a rating for a TV show: it indicates popular support. If this is all that value entails, we should abandon our grand claims to ultimate judgment based on value and recognize that right and wrong are simply what a majority feel they are at a particular time. Second, the cultural contingency of value suggests that all efforts on its behalf are simply expressions of the will of the powerful. Thus the effort to base criminal justice on so-called shared values in fact represents an effort by a particular subculture within the society—the white, male, middle, or upper-class power elite—to impose its value preferences on the less powerful. Instead we should value diversity, even in the rules of criminal responsibility.[13]

To begin at the beginning, I agree that value is to some extent culturally dependent. We should not exaggerate the point, though. Compared to the overall similarity of moral principles recognized by many peoples over many centuries, the differences between groups seem less startling than they do at first. For example, virtually all organized societies recognize some form of murder and consider it a serious wrong meriting serious punishment. Most developed nations have a roughly similar law of homicide with basic distinctions between murder and manslaughter.[14] Within the United States, the law of homicide has changed remarkably little since the early days of the republic except in the realm of capital punishment. Nevertheless, consistent with our understanding that value comes from subjective insights, the value adherent must concede that understandings of value vary to some extent with changing times and cultures. The more important issue is what this variation in value means.

Critics often argue that the cultural contingency of value *disproves* the concept. Critics contend that if value were really universal and timeless, we would find a broad and unchanging consensus about its definition. Certainly changing definitions of human value appear unseemly, like a religious seer who disavows an earlier proclamation of divine, eternal truth in favor of a new and improved version. By definition, value should not be like a consumer product, constantly reshaped to meet changing market preferences. But this critique misconstrues the nature of human morality. A moral value represents an ideal of understanding and practice. We must struggle within ourselves and among ourselves to define our values. Because it is not objectively verifiable, value's definition will be both changeable and controversial.

The serious question is not whether value is provable—by definition it is not. The serious question is whether it is a meaningful concept. Do we need value? Does value improve our understanding and debate about moral issues, or will we do better if we dispense with it? A look at a controversial issue of public policy may help us decide.

Americans have been engaged for some time in a heated debate about the legality of abortion. Part of this debate concerns the value of human life and when that life begins. Although these questions are extremely difficult, they are not meaningless. To resolve the legal issue, we have to resolve whether a fetus shares the moral status, the value, of an infant. Many politicians would like to avoid this issue because it is the one that stirs passions and wrecks political compromise. As with many issues raised by medical technology, abortion is difficult to discuss for it takes us beyond the ordinary bounds of ordinary human experience. But the moral issue is too basic to avoid.

Some critics have argued that value is an important, meaningful concept but only within particular cultural bounds. This means that we should be more flexible in our moral and legal standards.[15] The effort to construct criminal law according to a single view of value represents an effort by the powerful to oppress the powerless. Just as nineteenth-century Western powers sought to subjugate foreign peoples and eradicate their native cultures by mandating new "moral" standards of dress, recreation, and sexuality, so the criminal justice system uses talk of "deserved" punishment to keep the have-nots in their place. This argument assumes that all value is relative, that we have no way of judging value across cultural lines. But does anyone really believe this? Remember that our main subject is criminal homicide and the value at issue is that of human life.

Consider the consequences if we could not make a value-based judgment across cultural lines. Confronted with white supremacists who lynch a black man in accord with a particular deep-rooted American culture, we could say that this conduct was dangerous, frightening, and destructive, but we could not say that it was wrong, in and of itself. We could not condemn the lynching as a repulsive act of racism, because this would amount to a critique of another culture. This is absurd. We can and do assess value without regard to culture. If we sometimes hesitate to make judgments across cultural lines it is because we have doubts about the moral issue, not because culture prevents judgment.

I can make the same point in a more positive way. Implicit in the commitment to have a nation, a state, a city, or any other formal political entity, is a commitment to establish certain fundamental rules of conduct. The nature of a community depends on what the community tolerates and prohibits, and also on how it views these standards of conduct. America as a nation strives to maintain the dignity and worth of the individual. We support individual rights because the value of the person was fundamental to the community envisioned by the framers of our Constitution, and this idea has persisted and grown along with the nation. This same value should inform our criminal law. Even in this polyglot society comprised of many different races, religions, classes, regions, ideologies, and other groupings, we may find common ground in the worth of every person.

The Importance of Value Talk in Criminal Law

Another way of addressing skepticism concerning value is to consider what would happen if we eliminated value concerns from our criminal law. Certainly both society and its criminal law would survive the change. Organized societies can function without either agreement about or commitment to ideas of human value. We could make all decisions about criminal liability by opinion poll or some other measure of collective preferences. We could accommodate group differences by providing for different rules of criminal conduct according to social group. In fact, both formally and informally we do each of these today. But in judging this way we strip the law of its most fundamental claim on citizen allegiance, its claim to do justice according to human value. The state could no longer argue that killing must be punished because it is wrong but only because it offends a majority of citizens. This would represent a major change from how we currently think and talk about criminal law. A brief look at the history of rape law should illustrate.

For centuries the Anglo-American law of rape made prosecutions for that offense a harsh test for the complaining witness. In order to win conviction, the state had to prove that the assailant forced the woman to have sexual intercourse, knowing that she did not consent, *and* that the woman resisted "to the utmost."[16] Most jurisdictions required that a rape victim's allegations be corroborated by a second witness.[17] Courts held that the woman's reputation for chastity in the community was relevant to the offense, which meant that defense counsel could freely question her about her previous sexual history. Through these doctrines the law demonstrated not only a distrust of women's complaints of rape, but also a judgment that most instances of co-erced sex did not involve severe harms to women. After all, the law rendered the majority of sexual assaults virtually unprosecutable.

In the last thirty years the American law of rape has changed significantly. The corroboration and resistance requirements have generally been abol-ished. New rape statutes have changed the definitions of nonconsent and force to permit rape prosecutions of attackers who use little overt force and who are negligent with regard to nonconsent. Rape shield laws now signif-icantly restrict the ability of defense counsel to inquire into the com-plainant's sexual history.[18]

This history of legal change can be understood in several ways. The clas-sical utilitarian may argue that earlier laws represented a poor utilitarian cal-culus because they improperly discounted the pain suffered by many women and exaggerated the pain of false claims of rape. The modern law maximizes utility better by reflecting a better understanding of the collective happiness of men and women. It also reflects an improved understanding of the dy-namics of male-female sexual relations. The social historian can explain the change in terms of workplace and private life alterations in gender roles. Each of these explanations is helpful, but I would argue none is sufficient, because none addresses the value question implicit in rape law. We cannot give a full account of what happened to the law of rape without speaking of how the law *values* women.

Traditional rape doctrines devalued women by devaluing their suffering and their testimony. The doctrines expressed social assumptions that sexual assault was either quite rare (and women who said otherwise were lying) or that it was not significant (because assaulted women either deserved their as-saults or suffered no real harm to their persons). The law devalued women as sexual choosers. The law disrespected women's ability to choose to tell the truth and to direct their own sexuality. The legal changes came not just be-cause they represented a change in collective preferences—which they clearly did—but because the old law rested on values that are anathema to modern society. Only by speaking in value terms can we express the full sig-nificance, the moral weight, of this legal change.

Conclusion

In this chapter I have introduced the argument that ideas of human value should guide the law of criminal homicide. I do not mean by this that utilitarian analysis should never inform legal decision making. The utilitarian's attention to the concrete consequences of punishment may serve as an important check on the metaphorical excesses to which the value approach is prone. My aim in this chapter, therefore, has not been to prove the ultimate superiority of value to utility, but to distinguish the two approaches and suggest a practical advantage to value in criminal decision making.

My other aim has been to defend the value approach against the concern, raised by many for many different reasons, that it is impossibly subjective. I have deliberately emphasized the subjective aspect of the value approach, because it is both the most important and most frightening aspect of its method. It requires a personal commitment to moral principle. The value approach reveals morality as a contest without an umpire, a clock, or a scoreboard. Each of us must decide for ourselves what is right and wrong and then persuade others.

Impressed by the often bloody failures of so many ideologies in this century, many Americans shy away from declarations of principle today. But we should not confuse content with method. That others have chosen the wrong first principles in the past, or failed to live up to them, does not mean that commitment to first principles of morality should be abandoned.

2

The Value of Choice

In the preface I raised a fundamental question about moral responsibility and punishment. I wrote of child-killer Ernest John Dobbert Jr. whose abusive tendencies were, in a sense, beaten into him by his own father. This fact might not be of great significance if we took a utilitarian approach to punishment. We could say that a harsh sentence might force Dobbert to change; it would at least prevent further harm to his children, and the example of his punishment might deter others from brutalizing their children. The problem comes if we insist that Dobbert must *deserve* his punishment. The word deserve seems to imply that Dobbert freely chose to harm his children. In what sense, if any, is this true?[1]

The problem of free will is one that humans have pondered for thousands of years. It has been a staple of philosophic inquiry since the beginning of that discipline. I do not claim to advance philosophic understanding of the problem here. My aim is pragmatic, to find a way to go forward in the face of philosophic controversy. I seek to structure the question of responsible choice in order to validate the most important aspects of our human experience. In this endeavor, I assemble a number of preexisting arguments about different perspectives on human behavior which support the special value of choice needed for deserved punishment. In chapter 3 I use the concepts of responsible choice developed here to form a theory of deserved punishment.

Responsible choice proves a deceptively difficult subject. Few concepts could be more familiar to us than the notion that we choose our actions for ourselves, and for these choices should be held responsible. All aspects of our lives reflect our faith in choice as the bulwark of responsibility. In work and play, in romance, in friendship and even in disputes, we expect ourselves and others to make choices that make a difference, that have consequences according to complex systems of responsibility. But when we view choice from the scientific perspective, this familiar and valued concept looks suddenly strange and frightening. Now human behavior appears as the product of genetic and environmental influences, most unchosen. Viewed from the scientific perspective, we miss what we care most about choice, but similarly, the familiar human perspective on choice obscures truths about human behavior readily apparent from the scientific. In this chapter I attempt a working reconciliation of these rival perspectives.

The Free Will Debate: Reasons versus Physical Causes

Consider the following marital dispute about an upcoming dinner party.

> *Wife:* "I don't understand. You promised not to invite the Caterwaulers. Don't you remember the last time they came over? We had to listen to Herbie go on for three hours about his baseball card collection. You promised me you wouldn't invite them again."
>
> *Husband:* "I know, but Herbie came in right when I invited Bill; I just had to, dear."
>
> *Wife:* "No you didn't. You could have made an excuse to Herbie or you could have just said nothing. You can't please everyone all the time."
>
> *Husband:* "Look, I feel sorry for Herbie, okay? I admit it—I'm a softie. It's just the way I am. It's the way I was brought up. I can't help it."

In this argument we find an introduction to the problem of free will, a problem in resolving the relationship between reasons, physical causes, and freedom. The wife believes her husband deserves blame because he rationally, of his own free will, broke his promise and invited the dreaded Caterwaulers. The wife identifies the husband's reason for the invitation but finds it morally inadequate. Meanwhile, the husband seeks exoneration from responsibility by claiming a lack of free choice due to physical causation. The husband says he should be excused because his action can be traced to "the way I am." In more sophisticated terms, the husband says his conduct is caused by genetics and environment, influences over which he has no control.

The law, which sets basic rules of responsibility, focuses almost entirely on reasons for conduct. Lawyers tend to speak as the wife does, assuming freedom to choose and judging based on the reasons for conduct. By contrast, scientists study the physical universe and focus on what I will call the physical causes of human behavior.[2] They focus on the genetic and environmental influences that make the husband "the way he is," to the exclusion of reason analysis. Each form of understanding seems unremarkable in context; the problem comes in trying to reconcile them. Once we understand the nature and importance of physical cause in human behavior, can we maintain the law's commitment to the importance of reasons? Even more important, once we understand the limits on freedom revealed by causal (i.e., genetic and environmental) explanations, can we still value rational, uncoerced choice in the way we must for moral responsibility?

Some believe that we must choose between reasons and physical causes. They argue that only one form of analysis can be valid in explaining human behavior. Some scientists, for example, deny the reality of reasons, arguing they are but a fiction of our consciousness, a convenient cover for the real workings of genetics and environment. To speak of the husband's reasons for breaking his promise makes as much sense, according to this view, as speaking of your car "deciding" to break down at a particularly inconvenient time. It may be emotionally satisfying but it interferes with real understanding of the phenomenon.[3] At the other extreme of the spectrum, some philosophers argue that reasoned action is not subject to the causal laws of the physical universe. That is, the way in which humans act is fundamentally different from, and incomparable with, the actions of other creatures or the occurrence of other natural events.[4] Increasingly, however, scientists and philosophers concede the reality of *both* reasoned and causal analysis. They agree that rationally chosen actions also have physical causes. The husband chose to invite the Caterwaulers because he felt bad for them and because of genetic predisposition and environmental—especially parental—influences. The question now becomes: Can a person deserve punishment or reward if her rationally chosen action can be traced to underlying circumstances (causes) she never chose?[5] If the husband felt badly because of genetic and environmental causes, does that affect his individual responsibility for what he did?

A Compromise Approach: Selective Causation

A tempting resolution of the tension between reasons and physical causes is to work a compromise between them. We are tempted to say: while reasons explain most action, in situations where causation is particularly strong, we must move to causal analysis and recognize at least a partial excuse from responsibility. For example, while most persons should be held responsible for their drinking and actions while drunk, alcoholics should have at least a partial excuse based on the dynamics of (the physical causation of) addiction. Take Sally, a severe alcoholic who is arrested for drunk driving. Assume that we have scientifically sound evidence that Sally's alcoholism is caused by a combination of genetic predisposition, her upbringing by alcoholic parents, and the malaise caused by a lack of jobs in her community. Sally did not choose her parents, her genes, nor the state of the local economy. Under the compromise approach this would lead to substantial, if not complete, exoneration from criminal responsibility.[6] Her drinking and driving may require society to take protective measures such as suspending her driving license and requiring alcohol treatment, but she would not *deserve* punishment. This approach builds on the common intuition that while persons are generally responsible for their own character, some unusually strong causal influences seem to overwhelm ordinary choice abilities.[7]

The compromise approach is appealing because it saves the general rule of individual responsibility while recognizing the importance of physical causation. The compromise approach accurately describes the way that many people actually view responsibility. Psychologists report that when we sympathize with others, we often attribute their problems to unchosen physical causes.[8] We say, Sally can't help being afflicted with alcoholism. (Of course if we feel less sympathetic to Sally, we readily switch to the responsibility side of the equation: we call her a drunk and say she needs to take charge of her life and sober up.) Arguments based on the compromise approach commonly surface at sentencing in criminal cases and in everyday moral conversation. The compromise approach has a fatal flaw, however. It misunderstands physical causation. All human actions are equally physically caused; causation in this sense is a constant.

The compromise approach assumes that the total amount of genetic and environmental influence on a person varies from situation to situation and person to person. The argument is that some human actions have strong roots in physical causes, but some do not. Thus we might assert that Sally's alcoholism should represent a partial excuse because it was causally exceptional. In contrast to the moderate social drinking in which most Americans indulge—and which seems chosen—Sally's drinking was predominantly caused by genetics and environment. Thus many will conclude that while moderate drinkers remain fully responsible for alcohol consumption, immoderate drinkers like Sally do not. But moderate drinking is just as much the product of genetic and environmental influence as immoderate drinking. Consider the differences in drinking norms from one ethnic group to another, one region to another, one generation to another. We have strong evidence of cultural, that is, environmental, causation, and often genetic dispositions as well. The exact nature of causation may change, but the fact of causation will not. Similarly, a behavioral scientist will have no more trouble explaining moderate drinking in terms of environmental and genetic factors, than excessive drinking. All drinking may be traced to genetic and environmental influences. The only difference in causation between moderate and excessive drinkers is what genetics and environment predispose for.

The compromise approach confuses the difficulty of a choice with its physical causes. Sally no doubt has more trouble making sensible decisions about drinking than most people do. She finds it hard to avoid drinking to excess. That does not mean that her drinking decisions are more closely linked to genetic and environmental influences than those of more moderate drinkers, however. It just means that with respect to alcohol she is causally unlucky. She was unfortunate in being born with certain kinds of genes, to certain kinds of parents. The majority of persons who experience fewer problems with alcohol were, by contrast, causally lucky. Their genetic and environmental influences did not predispose them to alcoholism.

In public policy, one of the most popular forms of the compromise approach in recent years has been to argue for excuse based on socioeconomic background. Since we know that racial discrimination, poverty, bad education, and a subculture of criminality dispose some persons to crime, we might excuse those persons for acting in accord with these unchosen influences. We should look beyond the immediate reasons for the individual's actions to the "root causes" of criminality. This approach suggests that if we just push hard enough for an explanation we will find who is *really* to blame and what remedial action will *really* make a difference. It suggests that people are like trees, with roots that can be excavated, treated, or severed.

Few who favor the socioeconomic excuse acknowledge the full ramifications of their argument, however. When we examine the causes of an action, we see an almost infinite chain of events and situations stretching back in time. No matter what cause we identify, we can always find an earlier, arguably more fundamental cause. If we are not satisfied with drugs, gangs, and lack of jobs as causes of urban criminality, we can add inadequate schools and poor family structure. Recognizing the importance of family structure, we turn to underlying causes of family disruption in economic change and in troubled relations between men and women. This search for ultimate causes does not end with the ultimately blameworthy, for it always ends with many causes, far removed in time, scattered among many persons and natural phenomena. Physical causation of behavior aids our understanding of that behavior, and is critical to devising methods of changing it, but by itself causation says nothing about blameworthiness.

The real problem with the socioeconomic causal excuse is that its logic extends far beyond socioeconomic disadvantage. If physical causation excuses here, then it must excuse wherever it is found. Studies of criminal behavior reveal that causal factors such as age, sex, intelligence, and even geographic residence influence criminality, and these are also largely unchosen.[9] Should these factors excuse or mitigate responsibility as well? Even the most privileged defendants can present plausible physical causes for their crimes. Clarence Darrow, in his brilliant argument to save the lives of Leopold and Loeb, demonstrated how they were the products of their inherited natures and upbringings, and thus their crime was as well. Convicted insider trader Michael Milken is as much the product of his family and social environment as any gang member. The scientific view holds that *all* action, including rational, uncoerced, and reflective decisions, can be traced to the unchosen influence of genetics or environment. Again—if physical causation ever excuses, it always excuses.[10]

Taken to its logical conclusion, the argument for excuse based on cause is the statement attributed to Madame de Stael: "Comprendre, c'est tout pardonner." To understand is to forgive. As soon as we understand why a person acted as he did, we must suspend judgment. This is a disturbing idea. I will argue that we should instead observe a distinction between physical causation and excuse commonly made in everyday conversation. In discussing another's callousness, an acquaintance might say: "Well, you have to understand that Steve acts like that because of the way his parents treated him." This sounds like an excuse until the speaker adds, as speakers in such situations almost always do: "Not that that's any excuse, of course."[11]

Compatibilism, Fairness, and Freedom

Most contemporary legal philosophers accept that human choices have physical causes, but hold that causation is compatible with moral responsibility.[12] As long as the individual makes a rational and noncoerced choice, the causes that underlie that choice are morally irrelevant.[13] Compatibilists argue that responsible choice need be free only in the sense that it is not forced on the person by other humans or by natural forces.[14] Under this view, as long as no outside force prevents the actor from doing as he wants, the actor has the freedom needed for moral responsibility.

The modern compatibilist generally views the difference between the reasoned approach to action and the causal approach as a matter of perspective.[15] We might imagine a kind of zoom lens that looks into the antecedents of human actions. The lawyer generally adjusts the lens to the everyday perspective of human experience, in which reasons for choice dominate the field. In litigating a case where a man is charged with stealing a shirt from a discount store, the lawyer will focus on the beliefs and desires that informed the man's conduct. The lawyer will want to know whether the man knew that he had the shirt with him on leaving the store and whether he realized that he had not paid for it. All of these considerations contribute to our understanding of the individual's action under what I have called reason analysis. The genetic and environmental causes of the accused's action—the physical causes that predispose persons to take items without paying for them—remain in the background. Perhaps they will be relevant if the accused must be sentenced, but even then their significance is highly controversial.

Meanwhile, the scientist, with her interest in physical causation, will adjust the lens to look beyond the reasons for action to the more distant physical causes of action. Assuming that the man intended to steal, the scientist may look for the predisposing causes of theft in genetics, family background, and in prevalent attitudes within the individual's subculture. The scientist will try to learn enough about the causes of the theft in order to predict and perhaps prevent future shoplifting.[16]

The compatibilist approach explains how we can maintain legal and moral responsibility in the face of scientific explanations of human behavior. It provides a means of distinguishing reasons and physical causes; in essence it holds that concern about free will stems from a misunderstanding about the freedom necessary for responsible choice. I agree with all of this, as far as it goes, but it leaves me dissatisfied. Compatibilism tells us how choice is useful—it connects norms of conduct to specific persons—but it does not say why we should value choice, why we should consider it the source of our greatest triumphs and failures. Compatibilism strikes a diffident note about choice that conflicts with our emotional experience. Free choice *matters* to us. I am reminded of the position adopted by many scientists: "Well, obviously there is no such thing as free choice *really*, but it is a very useful fiction and until we come up with something better, we should stick with it." This is like telling an author she has won the Nobel Prize for Literature, but this year the selection process was entirely random. We come away with something sought, but not what we wanted most.

To understand the gap that compatibilism leaves, we need to think more about why we desire the kind of freedom that compatibilism denies. Recall the husband's excuse for breaking his promise to his wife and inviting the Caterwaulers to dinner. He said: "I did it because that's the way I am . . . I can't help it." What are the implications of this kind of excuse? What does the husband's statement imply about the prerequisites of blame? The husband implies that free choice requires more than noncoercion; it requires the freedom to create oneself. He assumes that responsibility requires the ability to choose desires as well as actions. As Thomas Nagel put it: "I wish to be able to subject my motives, principles, and habits to critical examination, so that nothing moves me to action without my agreeing to it."[17]

The husband's argument draws on a widely shared concern with the fairness of moral responsibility. One reason we would like to believe that we can shape our characters independent of genetics and environment is that this would equalize the opportunity to do good or evil. It would mean that all persons would have equal opportunities to have good or bad desires and thus equal abilities to do right or wrong. But is this possible?

We readily acknowledge that nonmoral abilities are unevenly distributed. Some humans are prettier and some are stronger than others, due to genetics and, to a lesser extent, environment. Most of us readily acknowledge that we lack the genetic good fortune to have any hope of becoming another Da Vinci, a Beethoven, or even a Shaquille O'Neil. In fact, the uniqueness of these extraordinary talents seems to constitute a reason to praise their achievements. When it comes to morals, though, we worry that unless we have unlimited ability-to-do-otherwise, responsibility will lose its moral flavor. As a result we often assume that, in a moral sense, we *can* be whoever we want to be. But what makes us think that if we lack the "right stuff" to be a concert pianist, we have the essential ingredients to be a saint? Or to put it more realistically, why do we readily concede that some persons lack the fundamentals (i.e., genetics and training) necessary for even average athletic ability, but resist the notion that some persons lack the fundamentals for basic decency?

In his argument, the husband recognizes his own character limitations. He says he cannot change his horror of hurting others. His wife might contest this by observing that we can change a great deal about ourselves if we want to badly enough. She might recite the old clichés: Where there's a will, there's a way, or, You can do anything you set your mind to. These arguments miss the point, though. The husband acknowledges he could have done differently—if his desires were different. The point is that his desire to avoid hurting others is a basic feature of his character, one shaped by genetics and upbringing. We need not agree that this aspect of character is unchangeable; it is enough to see how important it is to the husband's choice, and that it originated in unchosen influences. Now we see the unfairness of a universal standard of individual responsibility.

As the husband's argument illustrates, we are *not* all equally equipped to handle moral problems. As it happens, the husband's character will generally keep him from hurting other persons. Only in this unusual situation where we find two moral principles in conflict—keeping a promise versus hurting another's feelings—does he find himself in a moral quandary. Others will have characters that dispose them to selfish and brutal conduct; they will have enormous difficulty avoiding wrongdoing. Given that these varying dispositions come from genetics and moral learning from others, we cannot say that they are chosen by the person. How many of us would have learned the importance of right conduct if not for those near to us who taught us by words and example?

We will return to concerns with the unfairness of moral responsibility in chapter 4. For now it should serve as a warning against a certain kind of self-righteousness in judging others. I mentioned in the Preface our tendency to judge overall character instead of merely conduct. Often we assume the moral question to be: If I were in the wrongdoer's situation, would I have done better? We assume that if we can answer affirmatively, we have established our essential superiority. If true, this may establish our superior moral character, but this seems a less impressive *personal* accomplishment when we remember the causal forces that shaped that character.

In the end the husband's argument appears silly. He reminds us of a child who wants every day to be Christmas or his birthday, not realizing both the practical and conceptual impossibility of the idea. Whatever freedom we have to choose does not, and can not, extend to shaping own characters independent of unchosen influence. As human beings we are creatures of the physical universe, subject to the same laws of causation as every other creature and object. Even our moral characters are subject to physical causation.

The real sticking point in the free will debate proves to be our ability to shape our own selves, including our moral characters. Philosopher Robert Nozick calls this "origination value."[18] I touched on it earlier in discussing the achievements of greatly skilled artists or athletes. We call such persons "gifted," acknowledging that they are the recipients of extraordinary abilities, and yet we treat their accomplishments as *theirs*, as something they have uniquely created. We view their works as specially valuable, as more than the sum of the physical causes that may have shaped their skills and motivation. We take a species pride in their achievements. In the same fashion we feel

ashamed at genocide and other human atrocities. We are horrified that someone like us—another human being—could do such evil.

Each of us wants to believe that we add something to the world. We take
pride in our own achievements, a pride of authorship that goes beyond our
environmental and genetic influences. We see ourselves as creative beings,
bringing value, and sometimes disvalue to our communities. But can this belief in value creation survive the scientific perspective? We may want to believe in it, but can our beliefs survive harsh reality?

When we adopt what Nagel calls the external stance, and look at choice
from an extrahuman perspective, we see immediate problems. Where does
our ability to create value come from? What is its concrete manifestation?
How does it fit into the causal scheme? At what stage in the causal process
does it operate? In fact, once we return to the realm of causal analysis, our
vaunted ability to create value seems just another fantasy of freedom from
causation.

We seem to have reached a conceptual wall, or more accurately, a gulf. We
have found strong evidence in favor of the causal understanding of human
behavior, and strong evidence in favor of reasoned analysis. It seems we
should be able to reconcile them, but so far we cannot. We will make one last
try, using a time-honored lawyer's technique: restating the question.

The Meaning of Choice

What must we know to justify the value that we commonly place on rational and noncoerced choice? As discussed in chapter 1, we do not need objective verification of value's existence. Value is a subjective concept. Thus we
need not try to find value via causation. What we do need is to find a way of
understanding how both the reasoned and causal approaches to choice might
be valid. We must ensure that the causal approach does not in some way undercut our commitment to responsible choice. To do this we must reexam-
ine the presumption, also discussed in chapter 1, that all truth comes from a
certain kind of scientific inquiry.

We begin with a common misconception about scientific inquiry: that all
scientific insights take the form of reducing complex phenomena to simpler
phenomena.[19] According to this view, understanding choice means reducing
it to its physical causes—the operative principles of genetics and environment—just as a true understanding of biology reduces biological workings
to rules of chemistry or physics. Taken to its natural conclusion, we should

end up with the ability to explain the world by understanding the behavior of subatomic matter.

In fact, science has accomplished very little of this sort of reduction. Biology remains a field distinct from both chemistry and physics, because even though biological phenomena must obey the laws of chemistry and physics, these laws do not fully explain biological phenomena. If we want biological answers we must ask biological questions. In fact, as we examine the advance in scientific knowledge generally, we see that it normally leads to a proliferation of fields of inquiry, not a reduction. Scientific understanding grows by adding different perspectives, not merging them.

Nor does reductionism generally obtain when we move between scientific and nonscientific fields. Consider the relationship between music and physics. Music obviously occurs in a physical realm and obeys the laws of physics, but if we want to know about music, we will not learn much from studying physics. If I want to understand the music of Charles Mingus I will have to learn about rhythm, harmony, and melody, not acoustics or acoustic theory. All this suggests that we should not assume that reasons will reduce to causes. Choice may occur within the constraints of physical causation, but if we want to understand choice, we will have to ask questions about reasons for choices, not their genetic or environmental causes.

This brings us to the fundamental problem of free choice: perspective. One of the hallmarks of modern thought in science, philosophy and many other fields has been the adoption of a detached, objective perspective. The inquirer begins by imagining herself entirely removed from the problem in order to gain a new and objective perspective on it. Philosophers devote a great deal of energy to developing such perspectives, with devices such as the "original position," a construct that imagines what rules we might create if we did not know what place in society we would have.[20] These constructs have great value in illuminating aspects of our world that we normally miss. But in gaining a new perspective, we lose an old one.

In recent years some philosophers have argued that our situation as humans constitutes an inherent limit on our ability to understand the world, one we should respect rather than try to overcome. There are some things that, because we are human, we cannot see or imagine. For example, humans live and die. Death is a fundamental part of our existence. Try as we may to remove its blinders, death severely limits our vision of the universe. We can wonder about immortality, but we can never really know what it might mean.[21] Thus some philosophers argue that the human perspective—the world as it makes sense to humankind—can provide a critical grounding to philosophy.

Adopting the human perspective on choice does not mean that we have rejected the truths of physical causation. Instead it means we recognize the limitations of those truths. Physical causation may tell us many important things, but it says nothing about value. Consider the event known as a wedding. If we take the extrahuman, scientific perspective, this ceremony may be explained by evolution. The human species needs to reproduce itself, and marriage, formalized by wedding ceremonies, represents an efficient means of reproduction. This hardly exhausts what we know of weddings and marriage, though. Most importantly, it says nothing of love. Love is the value on which the marriage ceremony is based. Love is enormously meaningful to humans, but understanding its meaning requires adopting the human perspective. It means taking the subjective experience of human life seriously.

Perhaps the strongest statement of the need to take the human perspective on choice comes from English philosopher Peter Strawson. Strawson argued that both sides of the classically framed free will debate have asked the wrong question.[22] Strawson maintained that we should not worry about proving the existence of free will (free choice as I have called it) because this assumes the possibility of its negation. In fact, we cannot live without it. He argued that our "reactive attitudes," the personalized, often emotional judgments of others' actions which play a critical role in our moral judgments, are fundamental to human nature. He noted that these reactive attitudes are so basic to our condition that they stand independent of the truth or falsity of determinism or free will.[23] These attitudes are a given, which "neither calls for, nor permits" rational justification.[24] In other words, our form of conscious, rational life commits us to a belief in responsible choice.

I agree with Strawson and others that our commitment to rational, noncoerced choice, and to responsibility based on that choice, is fundamental.[25] Still I want to know why. From our experience of life, why does choice have such a special value? The answer is strikingly simple. Choice gives meaning to our lives.

★

French novelist and existential philosopher Albert Camus began one of his most famous essays this way: "There is but one truly serious philosophical problem, and that is suicide. Judging whether life is or is not worth living amounts to answering the fundamental question of philosophy."[26] Camus' statement of the issue may seem far removed from our concern with criminal responsibility, but it is not. Responsibility for rational, uncoerced choice represents our basic means of constructing meaning.

At this point I make a major assumption. I assume that we can answer Camus' question in the affirmative. I assume that life has meaning. I assume that there is something more to life than the physical experience of pleasure and pain. I assume that we can experience more than sexual satisfaction, we can have romance and love; that we can do more than reproduce ourselves, we can have loving families; that in working we can do more than support ourselves, we can have fulfilling careers. These propositions are not wildly controversial; most Americans probably agree with them. As with other aspects of the value approach, though, their truth depends on personal experience, making objective proof impossible.[27]

The hoary phrase "the meaning of life" has been an object of ridicule in modern culture.[28] Even in modern philosophy the question has received scant attention. Most twentieth-century philosophers have treated meaning as purely a question of language, an inquiry into what words signify.[29] Still the search for meaning remains an essential part of every person's life, and a critical part of education. Robert Nozick argues that we find meaning in life by transcending the limits of individual physical existence. Each of us transcends our small, isolated situations by connecting ourselves and our actions to a wider context of value. The extent to which we find meaning depends on whether we connect our actions to larger values. A life devoted entirely to physical gratification (a limited existence) provides less meaning than one that includes the rewards of love and friendship (wider contexts of value).[30]

The argument from meaning, as I call it, shows how we can, and should, construct moral value in a morally indifferent universe.[31] The rest of the universe may not care that we value choice, we may not find any extrahuman evidence of the special worth of choice, but that should not matter. We value choice for our own, deeply important reasons. We value choice by moral responsibility—by caring for all choosers and by taking their choices seriously. In rewarding good choices and punishing bad ones, we reach beyond physical self-interest to achieve greater meaning in life. In that process we may find this meaning or we may not, but we have no hope of finding it unless we value choice.

Conclusion

The problem of free will sometimes reminds me of the 3-D cards that used to come as prizes in cereal and snack-food boxes. If you held the card one way you would see one image; if you tipped it slightly, a second image appeared. No matter how you held the card, though, you could not see both images at once. We have the same problem trying to reconcile the causal and reasoned views of choice. In this chapter I have tipped the card both ways and offered a way of dealing with the apparent conflicts between the rival perspectives. This gives us a way of going forward, but serious problems remain. The most serious is one introduced in the previous chapter, the problem of moral integrity, of practicing what we preach.

In this chapter I have argued that we are deeply committed to the value of choice. Unfortunately, this commitment often varies according to self-interest. Psychologists have observed that when persons receive praise they generally attribute the praise to their own chosen efforts, but when they're criticized for shortcomings, the same individuals attribute the shortcomings to external influences. In judging the wrongs of others we often fall into the same trap, emphasizing the physical causes of harms done by those we like, and emphasizing the responsible choices made by those we dislike. Avoiding this hypocrisy about choice represents the single most important challenge of criminal law.

3

Punishment as Defense of Value

In the spring of 1924, two young men in Chicago set out to commit the perfect crime. Richard Loeb and Nathan Leopold resolved to kidnap and kill a rich boy and then collect a ransom from his family.

For months the two had planned the crime. They rented a car under false names and prepared a ransom letter to "Dear Sir." On the afternoon of Wednesday, May 24, 1924, Leopold and Loeb drove by the private school Loeb had earlier attended, looking for an appropriate victim—a boy they could easily entice into the car, whose father was rich enough to pay a hefty ransom. Around five o'clock they spotted fourteen-year-old Bobby Franks and offered him a ride. Franks got into the car, and the three drove off. While one of the men drove, the other beat the boy on the head with a chisel, killing him. After disposing of the body, Leopold and Loeb sent a letter to Bobby's father, demanding a $10,000 ransom for the boy. The ransom scheme was abandoned the following day, when Bobby's naked body was discovered in a culvert by some railroad tracks.

Both Leopold and Loeb came from wealthy Chicago families. Both had already demonstrated unusual intellectual ability. Loeb was only eighteen, but he had already obtained an undergraduate degree from the University of Chicago and was in his second year of law school. Nathan Leopold, nineteen, had also pursued an accelerated academic career. He had just obtained his college degree from the University of Chicago and expected to attend Harvard Law School the following year. Leopold spoke many languages and was an accomplished botanist.

Soon after the murder, acquaintances remembered seeing Leopold at a party, in a jubilant mood. He said that if he were to be struck by lightning and die he would not be sorry, "because I already have experienced everything that life has to offer." On the Saturday night following the murder, Leopold and Loeb went to a nightclub with a University of Chicago classmate, Abel Brown. When Brown introduced Loeb to an acquaintance, Loeb shook the person's hand and said, "You've just enjoyed the treat of shaking hands with a murderer." Everyone took it as a joke.

Then Chicago police traced a pair of eyeglasses found near Franks's body to Nathan Leopold. Leopold and then Loeb were questioned by police; within a day both had confessed. Soon they were indicted for first-degree murder, a capital offense. The case became one of the most sensational in American history.[1]

Most Americans could not imagine a worse crime. The victim was a true innocent, a child chosen almost at random. The boy's killing was deliberate and well planned. It was motivated by money and the sheer fun of violating society's primal rule. It was accomplished by intelligent, well-educated, and wealthy young men who could have looked forward to a life of accomplishment and comfort. If anyone deserved serious punishment, it was Leopold and Loeb. Yet even Leopold and Loeb had an argument for mitigation of responsibility: they were young and they were sick. In a real sense they did not see the wrongness of their action. They could not help themselves.

In this chapter, building on the framework established in the previous chapters, I argue that punishment is deserved according to the wrongdoer's choice to disregard another's value. According to this approach, Leopold and Loeb met the basic requirements of deserved punishment because each of them purposefully, without external coercion and for rational, immoral reasons, participated in the killing of another human being. In so doing, Leopold and Loeb challenged the value of human life that society is formed, in significant measure, to defend.

The examples of Leopold and Loeb do raise an important issue in moral responsibility, however. They may have been psychopaths. If so, they likely lacked the capacity to feel for others and therefore could not see the wrongness of their conduct. Many legal commentators and moral philosophers have argued that without this moral capacity, a person may not *deserve* punishment. In this chapter I argue to the contrary. Leopold and Loeb may not have felt for Bobby Franks, they may not even have been *able* to feel for Bobby Franks, but still they were responsible. The moral principles that inform criminal responsibility deal with a person's obligations to a society, with choices about fundamental social norms. Leopold and Loeb acted out of cruelty and greed. For many reasons we should try to understand the sources of their motivations, but for purposes of criminal responsibility those sources are irrelevant. Even if they were psychologically unable to do otherwise than they did, they culpably chose to end another's life.

While rejecting the requirement of moral capacity, I argue that some cases require proof of an additional element beyond the standard requirements of deserved punishment: a minimum experience of choice in human interaction. The minimal experience of choice ensures that the person has enough of a history of seeing and feeling the connection between action and reaction, harm-doing and pain sensation, that he has the ability to understand the moral dimension of his conduct. With this element satisfied, in addition to the standard quartet of deserved punishment, we can judge that the doer of harm has seriously challenged the community's most fundamental moral values.

The Dialogue of Crime and Punishment

In his classic work on armed conflict between nations, Karl von Clausewitz described war as politics "by other means."[2] He meant that war represents the effort to resolve political disputes by military force rather than the usual techniques of politics. Clausewitz's remark remains startling, and enlightening, because we think of war as a singular in all respects, but in many cases the ends of armed conflict are essentially the same as in any political dispute—a redistribution or redirection of power. Similarly, criminal punishment may be described as moral argument by other means. While punishment necessarily involves coercion, even violence, and so seems incompatible with the notion of persuasive discourse, we should not confuse ends and means. Punishment is fundamentally a way of making public morality real. It is an argument, backed by force, that autonomy must be valued. Emil Durkheim put it this way: "To punish is not to make others suffer in body or soul, it is to affirm, in the face of an offense, the rule that the offense would deny. . . . Punishment is only the palpable symbol through which an inner state is represented; it is a notation, a language through which is expressed the feeling inspired by the disapproved behavior."[3]

Ideally, punishment persuades a whole society, from victim to offender to ordinary citizens, of the importance of the values attacked by the offender. Realistically, punishment represents a moral argument backed by force. If offenders, or others, are not persuaded by the rightness of the government's position, then perhaps they will be impressed by the force with which it is asserted. As in war, the object of government action is acquiescence to certain rules and power relationships. If the subject's acquiescence is principled, then victory is complete. Thus we feel best about punishment when the offender is personally convinced of his own wrongdoing. Yet we cannot expect this in all, or even most, cases. Persuading anyone of the error of her ways is difficult, and cannot be accomplished unless the individual is open to the message. In many instances, the best we can expect of the punishment "argument" is that it will impress the offender with the painful consequences of wrongdoing.

Under the defense of value approach, punishment is deserved according to the offender's choice to challenge human value. The most basic human value is autonomy: the ability to choose for oneself. Every person, as an individual capable of reasoned choice, has a basic ability to independently choose a life path which must be respected by every other person.[4] Respect may be too limited a term for this fundamental moral obligation, however. As we will see in chapter 5, much of our moral life occurs in our emotions. Emotions are one of the prime means by which we understand the moral status of conduct. For example, rape is not simply an act of disrespect for physical and psychic autonomy, it is also an act of hatred and cruelty because of the terrible and enduring pain it inflicts upon the victim. Thus our first principle should be described as moral regard—a caring for the moral abilities of others.[5] This principle expressly includes the emotional experience of others and, equally important, signals the importance of an active concern for others' welfare that will prove particularly important in culpability for careless acts. The principle of moral regard also encompasses self-regard, the idea that we may protect our own autonomy and worth from others' attacks.

Finally, criminal law may be used to defend the value of the moral community. This is the idea that we group together not just for self-interest, but because we find meaning in social interaction. Thus there is a value in the group's moral standards in addition to individual value. At least with regard to homicide in the United States, the central focus of this book, there is no significant difference between regard for the individual's value and the value of the moral community. For practical purposes, they are synonymous.[6]

Those persons who rationally resolve to hurt others in certain fundamental respects should be punished in order that they, and others, can see the moral significance of their actions. In this sense punishment completes an action-dialogue about basic morality. In committing a serious crime the offender inevitably expresses a moral philosophy.[7] By breaking into a home and stealing property, the burglar indicates that she cares nothing for the resident's private space and private property. The burglar may not want to make a public statement about personal autonomy and private property; in fact, she probably hopes her deed will go undiscovered, but her chosen action nevertheless presents a challenge to those principles. We punish, in part, to meet this challenge. Leaving the offense unpunished would undermine our commitment to the principles involved. It would indicate that, in a concrete sense, they do not matter.[8]

Much of this works on an emotional level. The burglar's disregard makes us mad; it challenges our fundamental beliefs about justice in the world, and this anger seeks relief in punishment. As will be discussed in chapter 5, to the extent that our anger is morally based, it provides a legitimate motivation for punishment.

The Basic Elements of Deserved Punishment

Most scholars of criminal law have argued that to deserve serious punishment, an offender must have met at least four criteria: that the person (1) acted to commit a serious harm; (2) with a culpable mens rea (sometimes called mental state); (3) without extensive coercion from external sources; and (4) was rational at the time of his action. Current criminal law sometimes punishes for less than this, and some have argued for additional requirements, but this quartet of concepts has received enough support to provide a useful starting place for a theory of deserved punishment.[9]

The most basic requirement of criminal law is that the person acted to cause a serious harm. To give a full account of what this involves would go well beyond the bounds of this book. Briefly, we need a theory of what constitutes an action—generally speaking, what kind of physical movement or nonmovement counts.[10] We need a theory of what kinds of harms should suffice to constitute a criminal offense.[11] We need a theory of personal identity that determines when bodily movements by a continuously existing physical being count—or do not count—as the conduct of the same person. For example, how do we handle persons with multiple personalities?[12] Finally, for a crime such as homicide, we need a standard to determine how much of a contribution the person must have made to the harmful result for him to be criminally responsible for the result.[13] For my purposes I will stick to the basic conceptions of current law here. In the case of homicide I assume that we may punish individuals for their willed bodily movements, or nonmovements, which cause or substantially contribute to another's death, when no extraordinary event disruptive of the individual's continuous rationality occurs between act and punishment.

More central to my concerns here is the law's requirement of mens rea. The law has traditionally categorized crime primarily according to the purpose, knowledge, recklessness, or negligence of the criminal actor—his mens rea.[14] Under the defense of value approach, mens rea is important because to determine just punishment we must assess the offender's attitude toward the harm done. As detailed in chapter 6, mens rea analysis involves determining why the individual acted as she did. The reasons for the conduct tell us to what extent the offender, in killing, made a commitment to moral disregard. Indeed, all of part 2 concerns mens rea definitions.

The law's requirement that the offender have acted without coercion from external forces is also consistent with the defense of value approach.[15] Persons who commit crimes because they are threatened with force by others, or while facing injury due to natural emergencies, do not challenge moral regard in the same way as the uncoerced. Those who act from human duress or natural necessity may be excused, partially or entirely, because they were not fully the authors of their own choices. Their decisions to harm stem from immediate forces not of their own making.

Finally, criminal law requires that the offender be a rational chooser. In assessing criminal liability we ask if the actor perceives the world and acts upon his perception in ways the rest of us can readily accommodate to our own worldview. We ask whether the individual displays cognitive rationality: Is he conscious? Does he see that he is the individual described on his driver's license and not Julius Caesar? We ask whether he works toward ends that we understand, such as the pursuit of money, physical pleasure, or career advancement, or ends that appear bizarre, such as preparing the planet for an invasion of space mushrooms. We ask whether the means he has chosen to achieve his ends make sense. Does he seek fame and fortune by such time-honored routes as playing in a rock band or writing a self-help book, or does he expect to achieve material success by constantly reciting prime numbers? We may finally look to personal identity: Is the individual sufficiently self-integrated that his conscious mind directs his actions?[16]

Punishment under the defense of value approach also requires basic rationality. Harmful acts by irrational persons do not challenge our basic values. We can understand the usual criminal motivations—the urges to violence and other forms of moral disregard resonate in the selfish drives of human nature—but how can anyone find satisfaction in basic delusion? Even if they are dangerous to others, crazy persons do not engage us in a dialogue about moral meaning. They seem to live in a different reality than ours, making communication by words or actions virtually impossible. In a moral sense, the actions of the crazy seem meaningless.

Further Requirements—Moral Capacity?

In recent years a number of lawyers, legal scholars, and philosophers have argued that criminal responsibility requires more than proof of harmful act, mens rea, noncoercion, and rationality. They have argued that the accused must also have had the capacity to choose morally. He must have had the psychological ability to do otherwise. In the Preface I suggested that child-killer John Dobbert may have lacked this ability. He learned family violence from his father. His environment—and perhaps his genetics as well—so strongly predisposed him to child abuse that, unless someone stopped him, we could predict with great accuracy that he would attack his own children at times of stress. He appears to have lacked the capacity to refrain from brutalizing his children in certain situations.

Leopold and Loeb present examples of another kind of moral incapacity. They were likely psychopaths.[17] A psychopath is a person who lacks empathy for others, an emotion probably essential to good moral character and good action. The psychopath is perfectly rational, however. Leopold was quoted by a reporter about the murder: "It was just an experiment. It is as easy for us to justify as an entomologist in impaling a beetle on a pin."[18] An examining doctor reported: "Leopold denies having any feeling of remorse at having committed this crime. He states that he has no feeling of having done anything morally wrong as he doesn't feel that there is any such thing as morals in the ordinary sense of the word. He maintains that anything which gives him pleasure is right, and the only way in which he can do any wrong is to do something which will be unpleasant to himself."[19] Another doctor quoted him: "Making up my mind whether or not to commit murder was practically the same as making up my mind whether or not I should eat pie for supper, whether it would give me pleasure or not."[20] Although codefendant Loeb was less forthcoming with the defense psychiatrists, their conclusions about him were similar. He also displayed a complete absence of remorse or compassion. As one doctor put it: "There became evident the absolute lack of normal human emotional response that would fit these situations and the whole thing became incomprehensible to me except on the basis of a disordered personality."[21]

Are individuals such as Dobbert, Leopold, and Loeb morally responsible? Current American law holds they are criminally responsible. Courts have uniformly held that psychopathy is irrelevant to guilt and may be an aggravating factor at sentencing.[22] Yet many have argued that criminal and moral responsibility have diverged here. Principles of blameworthiness that apply in other situations have been abandoned with regard to psychopaths because of the dangers they pose to society. For example, critics point out that a kind of emotive capacity sometimes is relevant to insanity. Under the prevailing insanity test, a defendant is excused from criminal liability if at the time of her act she did not know the difference between right and wrong. A long-term controversy in the law concerns how we define this knowledge: whether it is purely cognitive, like knowing someone's name, or whether it includes an emotive component, the kind of insight earned by personal experience. In instructing juries on this issue, most courts leave the definition of knowledge open to interpretation, permitting juries to take the broader emotive definition.[23] The same theory applied to psychopaths would result in an excuse from responsibility, because by definition psychopaths lack an emotive understanding of their own harmful conduct.

The excuse of infancy also seems to argue for the importance of moral-emotive capacity in responsibility analysis. At common law, children under the age of seven were deemed incapable of criminal choice, and those under age fourteen were presumed to be nonresponsible.[24] The infancy excuse overlaps somewhat with rationality: young people are not as good practical reasoners as older people. Even so, the rule seems to go beyond rationality. Many children, including those under seven, demonstrate good practical reasoning skills and commit harmful acts of their own volition. The fact that they might be excused from criminal liability suggests that the criminal law should recognize some further element of responsibility.

Building on these suggestions, a number of scholars have argued that moral responsibility requires an assessment of the individual's moral capacities. For example, Peter Arenella contends that moral responsibility requires certain moral-emotional capacities beyond practical reasoning, including the capacities to empathize with others, to internalize moral norms, and to be self-critical.[25] Other proponents define moral capacity differently, but all give a central place to the ability to empathize. Without an ability to care for others, proponents argue that a person cannot deserve punishment, even if her harmful act was rational, intentional, and uncoerced.[26] Capacity proponents argue, in essence, that we should excuse those persons who have not previously shown feeling for others, because such persons have no demonstrated capacity for moral concern, and if they lack capacity for moral concern, they also lack capacity for moral action.

The moral capacity approach comports with much of what we know about moral persons. We know that good character involves more than a working intellect. The person with good character empathizes with others and can view her own conduct critically. Since these qualities are needed to be good, and since we blame offenders for failing to attain goodness, it seems to follow that these qualities are a prerequisite for responsible choice.[27] The model also promises to broaden the law's understanding of persons and conduct. As never before, the law might fully consider the character insights of the novelist and the behavioral insights of the scientist.

For all of its attractions, however, the moral capacity approach is fundamentally misguided. It presents enormous pragmatic problems to criminal justice, and worse, it contradicts the central meaning of moral responsibility.

On a pragmatic level, declarations of nonresponsibility may easily lead to abuses of state power. If criminal punishment of the psychopath were not feasible, the state would quickly resort to preventive detention of such persons under civil law. Like other dangerous but nonresponsible individuals, psychopaths would be subjected to forcible confinement and, perhaps, "treatment." Experience teaches that this approach may be more destructive to individual worth than actual punishment.[28]

More related to our concern with deserved punishment is the problem of proof. How do we measure moral capacity? Generally speaking, the best way to tell what a person can do is to look at what he has done in the past. If we want to know whether a killer could have cared for his victim, we might look to prior, similar situations to see if he displayed empathy. But how do we know whether past situations are really comparable to the present situation? And even if they are comparable, the notion of *capacity* goes beyond proven ability. It includes the idea of moral potential—that the person could have done better than he did. How can we tell this based on the past? We could compare the person's present conduct with past actions by others, but how can we tell if different individuals and their situations are comparable? If I tell a student who has failed the California bar exam that she could have done better because I did, she can justly object: "Well, I'm not you. I wasn't born with your brain. I didn't have your education and I didn't have the support network you did."

Even if we can draw general distinctions between persons in moral capacity, the problems of determining capacity in a particular instance remain daunting. Assume that we could distinguish between three sorts of persons according to their levels of empathy. The first are the purely selfish: persons who have never shown concern for anyone but themselves. The second group, limited empathizers, have demonstrated concern for one or two other persons in their lives. The third group is comprised of full empathizers, those who have demonstrated concern for many persons in their lives. For each of these groups we must determine whether a member has demonstrated enough moral ability in similar, past situations to have had the ability to do otherwise in the criminal incident. Can we do this? Although we can say that a full empathizer has generally demonstrated more ability than a limited empathizer, this may not be true for all situations. How can we compare, for example, past interactions between a full empathizer and her professional colleagues, to a confrontation between the full empathizer and a longtime enemy? Is this latter situation different or the same as the limited empathizer encountering a person outside her limited empathy circle? Is it different than the selfish person encountering anyone else? Unless we have a good idea of what makes situations and persons similar for comparison purposes, this enterprise will be essentially speculative. Certainly it will prove impossible for American criminal law, which, as we will see, requires simple and universal standards of responsibility.[29]

The problems with moral capacity go beyond difficulties in proof, however. The requirement of moral capacity would violate the reconciliation of choice and physical cause reached in the previous chapter and eliminate a fundamental basis of moral responsibility. We are responsible for our chosen actions based largely on our *motivations* to do right or wrong. An excuse based on lack of proper moral capacity would excuse for lack of moral motivation and in so doing significantly diminish the scope of both moral responsibility and our conception of right and wrong.

As we saw in the previous chapter, the sticking point for the moralist in the science versus morals controversy is the individual's ability to control his own fundamental desires, his desires about his own desires.[30] We like to think that we decide for ourselves the kind of person we are, independent of unchosen influence, but this is absurd. Scientific explanations of the physical causes of human behavior indicate that no one acts free of unchosen influence. Taking unchosen influence into account, we cannot say with any degree of assurance that an offender like Dobbert could have done otherwise under the circumstances he faced. His genetic and environmentally inspired disposition to child abuse may have precluded any different choice, absent outside intervention. All we can say is that, *given proper motivation*, Dobbert could have chosen differently. If he had been more repelled by violence, if he had had less rage stored up from childhood, he could have chosen differently.

But assuming we could do so, why not judge what a person did in light of his motivational deficits? Why should we blame the psychopath for lacking a critical moral ability that is largely, if not entirely, beyond his own control? The answer is that the lack of moral capacity does not change the social meaning of the psychopath's action and social meaning is the subject of criminal responsibility. The psychopath's conduct represents the same fundamental challenge to human value that it would if we judged him to have empathy for others. In all cases the psychopath's conduct expresses a rational philosophy of disregard for human worth that requires formal, forceful response if society means to value human worth.

Every system of individual responsibility rests on a set of conditions or features for which individuals are assumed responsible. These conditions or features may not be—indeed usually are not—freely chosen, nevertheless we consider them integral to the moral person. They are part of the self for which the person is responsible. And nothing is more fundamental to the responsible self than that self's motivations. For example, we hold a mean person responsible for acting meanly, regardless of how he came by that meanness. A boy trained to cruelty by his parents will not be excused from responsibility for his own cruel acts as an adult on the ground that his parents "made him" cruel. Descriptively, the man may correctly attribute his mean disposition to his parents, but prescriptively—morally—he is wrong to seek an excuse on that basis. The motivation to cruelty shared by parents and child supports blaming both for their respective acts of cruelty.

The moral capacity approach asserts that responsibility requires that persons have the motivation to do good, but this motivation is exactly what we normally judge. When we describe wrongdoers as cold, sadistic, or cruel, we do not signify any excuse for their lack of moral concern: we blame them for it. Counselors who work with rapists report that many are "numbed out"; they have experienced so much horror and pain in their lives that they are desensitized to it in others.[31] This explains their behavior and allows us to sympathize with their situation. It does not amount to an excuse from liability, however. Regardless of how he came to be an uncaring, violent person, we blame the rapist for his uncaring, violent act. The cruelty of the rape is a moral fact that requires moral response regardless of origin. Similarly, when we tell someone that we think she could have done better, what we really mean is that *if the person cared more*, if she tried harder, she would have done better. If the student had studied harder she would have written a better exam. If the driver had paid more attention, he would have avoided the accident. In all instances we judge the motivation itself.

The moral capacity approach blurs the difference between the moral expectations that we create through responsibility and the predictions of human behavior that science offers. The fact that we can predict human behavior of a particular kind—for example, that psychopaths will hurt others unless stopped—does not mean that the behavior is nonresponsible. Prediction tracks physical causation; expectation constitutes our creative efforts to make the world a better place.

Moral responsibility involves setting standards—expectations—for ourselves, which will not always be met. We expect persons to behave better than they often do in fact. At the beginning of every semester, I tell my students that, barring unusual and unanticipated problems like illness or natural disaster, I expect them to come to class and to come prepared. This is not a prediction of what they will do. I can predict with great confidence that some students will miss class for trivial reasons and some will come to class unprepared. I still *expect* them to do better than this. If we had known enough about Leopold and Loeb as adolescents, we might have determined that there was a good chance they would become involved in criminal activity. This does not excuse them for their crimes, however.

One of the classic illustrations of the difference between moral expectation and behavioral prediction is the famous Milgram experiment. In this experiment, psychology students were instructed by authority figures to take actions that would apparently injure, even kill persons who were the purported subjects of a scientific test. Most of the students did as they were told. The test established that a high percentage of persons will harm others if an authority figure takes responsibility.[32] The test thus replicated in a laboratory setting a fact about human nature demonstrated in history many times over: that few people will raise moral objections to authority. Yet this is mere prediction; it does not change our moral expectations. The results of the Milgram experiments were, and are, shocking because we *expect* persons to behave better in the experimental situation: they were not physically coerced and they understood the harm they inflicted. Even though we could have predicted that most Germans would follow Nazi orders, however reprehensible (and could predict that a significant proportion of Americans would do the same under a similar regime), this prediction would not excuse. We still blame them for following immoral orders.

To adopt the moral capacity approach and to excuse for lack of empathy and other moral qualities would reduce the scope of right and wrong in society. Actions done by the most uncaring persons could not be described as cruel or vicious, only dangerous. They would not be the wrongful actions of responsible persons, but akin to the dangerous actions of the crazy, infants, or animals. This would transform conduct that appears to challenge our moral values into harmful but nonmoral activity. As we will see more clearly in the next chapter, this would diminish the meaning and importance of our moral values, for moral responsibility and moral values are intimately connected. Declarations that individuals attack our moral values will not carry moral weight unless we also hold such persons morally responsible.

Rejecting the moral capacity approach is a necessary but disquieting part of creating a strong system of responsibility. Its rejection should make us acknowledge some hard truths about ourselves. If we do not wish to excuse psychopaths for their lack of moral capacity, then we must acknowledge the implications for own moral status and abilities. We cannot reject moral capacity without also rejecting one of the most common and comforting truisms about individual responsibility, that it depends on our ability to do otherwise. If we blame psychopaths for acting in accord with motivations they never chose, then we must acknowledge the moral luck inherent in our own personalities.

A Further Requirement: Choosing Experience

For all my objections to the moral capacity approach, I agree that criminal responsibility requires something more than the basic quartet of harm, rationality, intentionality, and noncoercion. In the great majority of cases, proof of these four elements will establish that the individual has mounted a serious challenge to our basic moral values. There may be unusual situations where something more is needed for us to say that the accused truly challenged human value, however. In some cases we may have doubts that the offender has had enough experience of life to take a stand on basic human value. This additional requirement involves primarily the young, but might also encompass persons suffering traumatic mental injury. I will not explore this additional requirement in depth, for its consideration would take us beyond our concern with the core components of culpability; nevertheless, a brief explanation is needed to complete our basic responsibility picture.

In order to judge a person criminally responsible, she must have a basic conception of what makes humans valuable. She may not agree with our conception of value; she may even reject the idea that humans have any special value. What matters is that she know enough of life to take a serious position on the question of value. The excuse granted for youth provides the best illustration. Although rational, children are not criminally responsible because they have not experienced enough suffering from others' actions nor witnessed enough instances of others' suffering at their own hands for us to presume comprehension of human pain. Our blaming practices suggest that although young children have a cartoonish notion of the connection between act and consequence, they lack the experience to comprehend its real meaning.

An example from the movies illustrates the experience requirement in bright colors. In the movie *Terminator 2*, a boy becomes the focus of a deadly struggle between two killer-robots, terminators, that have been sent back from the future. As an example of the human–meets–alien/robot genre, the movie concerns (in part) the humanization of the robot, in this case the "good" terminator played by Arnold Schwarzenegger. Early on, when the boy protests the robot's willingness to kill, Schwarzenegger blithely explains: "I'm a terminator." When told that he cannot kill, the robot expresses complete bewilderment. At this point the robot displays rationality but lacks the experience of choosing and feeling necessary for moral agency. By the end of the movie, however, Schwarzenegger is transformed. By virtue of his own experiences, and those of the persons around him, Schwarzenegger comes to recognize and appreciate human value. With evident torn feelings, he sacrifices himself for humanity's survival.

Hollywood spectaculars notwithstanding, the experience requirement will only rarely make a difference in criminal adjudication. In addition to extreme youth, some instances of brainwashing or organic brain damage might represent claims under the requirement. Where an unchosen event so alters the choosing consciousness as to make the individual a different person, harmful actions by the person appear in a different moral light. The "new" person appears childlike in that she has not had a sufficient opportunity to experience life as a rational, feeling chooser. This approach puts a time limit on the excuse, however. If over a period of time the "new" person suffers from others' actions and sees others suffer from her own actions, then, assuming continuing rationality, the person again becomes responsible.

Conclusion: How Dobbert and Leopold and Loeb Deserved Punishment

In his repeated, brutal assaults on his children, Dobbert attacked the value of his children. He placed his own emotional self-satisfaction over that of his sons and daughters. He vented his rage on their bodies and souls, eventually destroying them as choosers. His intentional actions declared that he was their ruler, that they would have no separate existence from his, and, in two instances, no existence at all. Dobbert's murderous abuse spoke of a world without moral meaning, where autonomy held no special value. The state of

Florida punished Ernest John Dobbert to defend moral meaning against his violent challenge. The state, acting for society generally, sought to defend the possibility of moral meaning based on autonomy. Dobbert's case may have been tragic, his wrongdoing may have stemmed from his own victimization by his father, but his actions were still wrong. As stated in the Preface, I do not believe Dobbert deserved death, because such a penalty signifies the rejection of a person's essential value. Dobbert did deserve severe punishment, though, for his chosen acts of serious disregard for others.

Similarly, Leopold and Loeb, even if they were psychopaths, deserved serious punishment for their killing of Bobby Franks. Leopold and Loeb were rational, if highly unusual killers. In killing Franks they sought meaning in a readily comprehensible, morally challenging way. Each fed the other's worst tendencies. Together they may not have been able to avoid doing serious harms to others. Still, they chose to take a boy's life. Still, they chose to challenge society's rule that all life has value. Still, they deserved serious punishment.

4

Just Punishment in an Unjust Society

Virtually every Monday in virtually every major urban area in this country, criminal courtrooms fill up with those arrested over the weekend. In the milling confusion of these gatherings, as prosecutors review police reports and defense attorneys check files and clerks shout names and judges push through the calendar, the observer gains a good look at the criminally accused. The view may surprise. Can these really be the criminals we have heard so much about—this collection of mostly young men with tired eyes, dressed in rumpled street clothes or jail outfits, bound in chains, who scan the courtroom for family, or who know better than to look? They look more downtrodden than dangerous. Often their frames and faces bear the telltale signs of drug and alcohol abuse. Sitting in the waiting room of the public defender's office or touring a city jail or state prison will only reinforce the same impression. Disproportionate to the general population, the human face of those caught up in the criminal justice system is that of a poor, ill-educated, black or Hispanic young man.[1] This is justice in America? How can any legal system be just that so dramatically reflects society's social inequities? How can these persons deserve the punishment they receive?

Many criminal justice texts reprint a flow chart of the criminal justice system first created for the President's Commission on Law Enforcement and Administration of Justice in 1968.[2] The chart depicts the disposition of potential and actual criminal cases in the country. It looks something like a horizontal tree; at the left are broad roots depicting the actual crimes committed; from there the number of cases dwindle according to which crimes are reported to the police, those in which arrests are made, those in which charges are filed and so on. At the right of the page the tree ends in a thin strand of cases representing defendants sentenced to prison. The chart depicts a continuous winnowing of cases. At every stage of the process many are called but few are chosen. Only a few persons who commit crimes, and only a minority of those actually charged with crimes, receive the law's most serious penalties. On its face, this is unremarkable. Incarceration is hugely expensive in both economic and human terms; it should be used sparingly. But look at who is selected for this special treatment. Those sent to prison are primarily those who have already experienced the worst of life in America: the worst upbringings, the worst in schools, in housing, in health care, recreation, and job opportunities; they have grown up in the most violent, most drug-ridden, most despairing communities in the country. And now society sends them to prison? How can we say that such persons deserve this fate?[3]

Troubling for these reasons and others is evidence of enormous racial disparity in those punished. The most extreme disparities involve African Americans. For example, in 1994 blacks comprised approximately 12 percent of the nation's population, but almost 48 percent of the inmates in the nation's penal institutions were black.[4] Authorities attributed 55 percent of the intentional criminal homicides committed in that year to blacks.[5] This figure mirrors black victimization in homicide; consistent with the overall pattern of homicide as an intragroup crime, 54 percent of intentional homicide victims were black.[6]

Some studies have indicated that the criminal justice system discriminates on the basis of wealth, race, and class, treating cases of similar culpability differently according to these categories. Other studies suggest that disparities in punishment reflect disparities in offending; that is, the reason that most in prison are minority and poor is that most serious criminal offenders are minority and poor.[7] I do not enter into this controversy because its resolution does not affect the central problem of social injustice and criminal punishment. Even if the legal system does not discriminate—which would be extraordinary given what we know of human nature and the identity of most legal decision makers (neither poor nor minority)—the criminal justice system reflects deep-rooted inequities in society. Even assuming the legal system discriminates, treating poor and minority offenders worse than others because of their class and race, that discrimination explains only a small part of the class and race disproportion in our prison populations.

My concern here is with the impact of social structure on serious violent crime. We know today, as many realized two centuries ago, that those most likely to commit crimes are those with the least stake in the community—the poor and the socially ostracized.[8] We also know that social structure has a great deal to do with crime rates. Although American society takes many expensive steps to curb serious criminality, that same society promotes values that encourage criminal conduct. To cite just two examples of criminogenic influences, the modern United States celebrates the individual over the community and violence as a viable solution to serious conflict.

In America we value the individual most of all; we heap astonishing rewards on a select few who have demonstrated certain kinds of superiority over others. Our economic and cultural structures encourage, even demand, vigorous competition between individuals for limited goods. Cooperative efforts are widely praised but much less frequently rewarded. In all of these ways society suggests that individuals count more than the community. Meanwhile no activity celebrates the individual as much as criminal activity. The criminal offender takes the American dream to heart—that all should have their desires satisfied. The offender glories in selfishness, but does he do so more than the celebrities of entertainment, business, or politics who comprise our ever-changing national aristocracy?

Similarly, American society today displays a deeply ambivalent attitude toward violence. In our history and in our culture we place great value on violence to defend persons and community. In U.S. movies, television, literature, and news media, violence is ostensibly excoriated but actually celebrated. We rely on violence for an enormous amount of our entertainment. Any outside viewer of our culture would say that we are addicted to depictions of violence. More concretely, we permit widespread ownership of a variety of powerful weapons designed essentially for homicide. How can a society soaked in so much blood, both real and fictional, gain the moral authority to condemn violence by a few of its least-privileged members?[9]

These questions should disturb anyone who advocates the morality of criminal punishment in this country. Once we take the actual structure of society into account, the basic moral assumptions that inform criminal law seem much weaker than before. In this chapter I offer an uncomfortable answer to the problem of just punishment in an unjust and in many respects criminogenic society. I argue that deserved punishment for homicide bears no direct relationship to social structure. Punishment may be deserved even in an unjust society. Punishment may be deserved even in a society that indirectly promotes criminality. But none of this alleviates society's responsibility for injustice or crime promotion. Individual and social responsibility for violent crime are independent, and independently important constructs.

Social Contract and the Moral Authority to Punish

Many who argue that punishment may be deserved build their theory of punishment on the ideal of a social contract. They assert that all members of society consent to suffer punishment for fundamental rule violations in return for the benefits of life in a law-abiding society. Either citizens actually agree, or they tacitly acquiesce, in a mutual exchange of burdens and benefits. The penalties of criminal law are among the most prominent burdens, protection from other law-breakers one of the primary benefits.[10]

The social contract approach to deserved punishment holds several attractions. It anchors punishment in the moral rock of individual autonomy. Because individuals consent to the legal structure—or would consent if we put the question to them properly—they in effect grant government the right to punish violations of law. In essence, criminals consent to be punished. The approach also provides a social fairness justification: all individuals share the same basic benefits and burdens.[11]

The social contract approach inspires serious doubts about the possibilities of deserved punishment for many wrongdoers in America. Social critics correctly point out that we live in a deeply inequitable society. Opportunities for education, employment, and career satisfaction are distributed largely according to wealth. The real structure of American society contradicts oft-repeated claims that all persons are treated equal. Racism is a persistent and powerful force frustrating the efforts of many people to lead fulfilling lives. Our culture in many ways inspires selfish and violent conduct. For the poorest and most discriminated-against members of our society, the idea that the law functions by mutual consent sounds like a bad joke. Such individuals receive so few benefits from the current social arrangement that they cannot be said to have agreed to it. As a result, some have argued that even if such persons satisfy all the traditional elements of criminal guilt—bad act and mens rea—they do not deserve punishment because they stand outside the social contract.[12]

Some critics contend that society lacks the moral authority to punish members of the underclass. Taking an analogy from equity jurisprudence, a society responsible for unjust conditions has unclean hands, meaning that it cannot obtain the remedy of deserved punishment. Thus a society that promotes or condones racism lacks the moral authority to condemn acts by victims of that racism; a society that promotes greed and violence may not morally condemn acts of greed and violence.

Both arguments view justice as dependent on the moral authority of the punisher: unless the state has fulfilled its moral obligations, it may not morally condemn. The unjust state may use force against citizens, it may retaliate and coerce, but it may not impose deserved punishment. I disagree. The moral authority of punishment does not depend on the moral status of the punisher. Deserved punishment rests on a legitimate judgment of the accused's wrongdoing. With only a few exceptions, the moral conduct of decision maker and accused must be judged separately.

One exception is when the law being prosecuted is unjust. The Nazi law of race difference and the American laws of slavery and segregation are prime examples of legal systems that were formally legitimate but deeply unjust.[13] When individuals acted in ways that were morally justified, but condemned by those legal systems, they did not deserve the punishment they received. The American civil rights movement of the fifties and early sixties made this moral point by forcing authorities to jail protesters for what most Americans believed were morally legitimate activities, such as sitting without regard to race at a lunch counter or on a bus. The punishment the protesters received was viewed by many as undeserved, which helped undercut the legitimacy of the segregation system. Another exception is when the social or governmental structure effectively forces disobedience on persons. To survive in a truly oppressive state one may have to lie, cheat, or steal simply to survive. In these instances offenders might be convicted and punished for violating the criminal law, but they could not be said to deserve their punishment; in a moral sense they did not act wrongly.

Even in these exceptional situations, though, moral responsibility depends on the conduct of the accused, on whether she acted morally in the situation, not whether as a general matter the state is morally legitimate. Even in the antebellum South, even in Nazi Germany, some wrongdoers deserved punishment by the state. Like individuals, states have serious moral flaws, but in most cases those flaws do not affect the culpability of persons engaged in criminal acts.

The Unfairness of Deserved Punishment

There is a second dimension to the social critique of deserved punishment: the problem of inequity between citizens. Social critics are correct when they observe that those most likely to be criminally punished are also most likely to be the outcasts of society, the have-nots in all senses. I agree with social critics that in many basic ways the structure of our society is unjust and that this structural injustice causes crime. This frames the moral issue: How can punishment be deserved if its distribution depends in significant measure upon an unfair social structure?

In chapter 2 we saw that moral responsibility is unfair in the sense that it reflects variations in moral character that stem from genetic and environmental influence. To oversimplify, if our parents teach us brutality and dishonesty, we are likely to grow up to be brutal and dishonest adults. If our parents teach us compassion and honesty, we are likely to develop those traits instead. In neither event would we have chosen our basic moral disposition; that would depend on our luck in the parental sweepstakes. As we saw in chapters 2 and 3, the fact of such luck does not eliminate moral responsibility. It simply means that moral responsibility is not fair in the way that we normally assume.

I can illustrate the problem in another way. Imagine for a moment that we had some way of measuring basic moral character. Assume that we could determine the relative strengths of every person's inclinations to hurt others in different situations. With this information we might devise a handicapping system that would equalize responsibility. We might treat as equivalent a minor wrong by one who is basically compassionate and a more serious wrong by one who is basically hostile to others. Despite the differences in offense, we would impose identical punishments if we determined that the wrongdoers made choices of equivalent difficulty. That is, we would say it was just as hard for the hostile person to refrain from the serious offense as it was for the compassionate person to refrain from the minor offense.

The most obvious objection to such a handicapping scheme is its effect on deterrence. The handicaps would drastically reduce the threat of punishment of those persons most likely to offend, and thus those who most need to be deterred. Consistent with my concern with the value approach to punishment, though, I put this concern aside to focus on what such a scheme would do to our conception of right and wrong. Assuming we had no concerns about future dangerousness, what would such a scheme do to our understanding of basic value? Under this scheme an armed robber might receive a relatively light punishment if he had a severe moral handicap. We would explain the sentence to the robbery victim this way: "Don't misunderstand, the robbery was a terrible wrong; but given the defendant's moral handicap, it would not be fair to punish him the same as if you or I had done the same offense. He has a much harder time doing right than we do."

I doubt if the robbery victim, or the public, would buy this. They would resist because we indicate right and wrong, we *appreciate* right and wrong, through responsibility decisions. The link between judgment of wrong and consequence is fundamental and direct. Any significant disconnection between wrong and punishment diminishes our sense of what wrongdoing is. The handicapping scheme illustrates that, in a deep sense, fairness and moral standards are opposed; we must choose between them. Any move to improve the fairness of punishment by taking into account social inequities would diminish our valuation of right conduct. Since in fact we cannot measure moral disposition, and since we do and should care about right and wrong, we choose responsibility over equity.

Social unfairness should be treated in the same way. Just as the distribution of bad parents is an important factor in criminal behavior but irrelevant to criminal responsibility, so the inequitable distribution of wealth and social opportunity should not affect deserved punishment. In both cases we can trace wrongdoing back to unchosen influences and in the process identify systematic inequities, nevertheless we must set these aside to keep our commitment to moral choice. Unfairness of both varieties is tragic; it shapes who the person is, but does not change the person's responsibility for chosen action.

Here I need to add a reminder—my argument goes only to deserved punishment for serious violence. In the unjustified, unexcused killing of another we have a culpable wrong that we should agree merits legal punishment—assuming that legal punishment is ever merited. Where we have significant disagreements about the wrongness of the conduct, as for example with the criminalization of drug use, arguments about deserved punishment may follow considerably different routes.

Social Responsibility for Crime

To sum up the argument so far, deserved punishment for homicide does not require a just society. It does not require a state that cares about poverty, racial discrimination or other social ills. In fashioning rules of murder and manslaughter, we may employ the lawyer's technique of rigidly excluding the irrelevant, and focus entirely on an individual's chosen actions, regardless of social inequities that may have shaped his character. All this is true, and yet it is but half of the story. It is the half that the mainstream of American society—in the political and economic sense—self-interestedly emphasizes. Yet moral responsibility requires much more than this. The same human value that supports strong *individual* responsibility for crime also supports strong *social* responsibility for crime. It is moral hypocrisy of the first order to recognize only the former and not the latter.

The idea of social responsibility for crime will sound strange to those accustomed to the principles of liberal democracy. Why should we, the law-abiding, take any responsibility for conditions that shape others' characters? The whole point of America is that each citizen is responsible for himself or herself, isn't it? But this is nonsense. To be responsible means to take seriously the effects our actions have on other people. If our actions make the suffering and criminality of others more likely, we need powerful justifications for our conduct. Even if we have those justifications, moral responsibility requires that we engage in remedial and compensatory action. Responsibility for crime does *not* end with the punishment of wrongdoers.

What follows is a preliminary sketch, a set of suggestions for what a theory of social responsibility for crime might look like. Any serious effort along these lines would take us too far afield from the main project of developing a theory of deserved punishment for individuals, yet we cannot afford to leave social responsibility entirely unexplored. To do so would foster the common but fallacious notion that once we decide who deserves punishment for particular wrongs, there is nothing more to be said about responsibility for crime.

Like all forms of responsibility, social responsibility for crime involves four related decisions: a determination about a particular norm, conception of choice, time frame, and consequence. We can best understand the importance and interaction of these elements by first seeing how the elements work in the familiar setting of individual responsibility, and then applying them to social decisions. Consider the following situations. First, a friend who has had a great deal to drink at a party calls you (quite without justification) a fascist pig. Second, a young boy is caught stealing an expensive video game from a store.

We begin with a decision about norms. With regard to the drunken friend we might say that according to the norm of friendship, friends should not insult each other. Likewise, the boy's theft violates a basic principle of personal property. Each form of moral responsibility involves a particular conception of choice. We must decide, for example, whether the boy is too young or the friend too drunk for responsibility. Each form of individual responsibility has its own temporal framework, its own way of relating past, present, and future. In determining the consequences for action we must decide whether to emphasize desert for past wrongs or the need to change future behavior. Finally, determinations of responsibility vary according to the consequence that attaches to the finding. For example, we may decide that the light-fingered boy should be held responsible for purposes of parental reproval and not for criminal sanction. The determination of consequence range is closely tied to choice of norm. A judgment according to the norms of friendship implies friendship consequences; an application of criminal consequences implies a judgment according to criminal norms.

This review of individual responsibility reinforces a point made earlier, that responsibility comes in many different and independent forms. The review also reminds us of the creativity of responsibility. While we often talk about whether a person is or can be *found* responsible as if responsibility had some predetermined physical existence that awaits discovery, in fact the decision maker *determines* responsibility with every moral or legal judgment. With any form of responsibility we must decide on choice, norm, time, and consequence. We may be more familiar with individual than social responsibility for crime, but both forms depend on our own critique of the human world. There is nothing "natural" or inevitable about our current preference for individual responsibility.

What would social responsibility for crime look like? First, we must select a norm. Social responsibility for crime should follow the same basic norm as individual responsibility: the value of moral choice. If we value the individual's ability to make moral choices and to find fulfillment through a moral life, we should value these abilities in structuring society. Instead of focusing on individual choices to do right or wrong, we would focus on social choices: on the collective decisions that shape society. Here we must pay close attention to the unintended consequences of social decisions. As we will see in chapter 9, culpability can extend beyond intentional and knowing wrongs, to actions taken without proper concern for their impact on human value. We may not wish to help others become serious criminal offenders, but we make many decisions that will have this effect. We have an obligation to avoid this outcome where possible. In terms of time span, social responsibility must cover a longer period than individual responsibility. Social decisions taken today may have direct effects on two or three generations to come. Thus a society should take responsibility for past decisions as long as they continue to have an important effect today. The consequence of a finding of social responsibility should be the expenditure of social resources: money and effort. The society must commit resources in consequence of and to remedy criminogenic social choices.

All this will come clearer if we take a concrete example. Consider social responsibility for juvenile violence. In the last several years, while overall violent crime rates have declined, violence by young people has increased.[14] Throughout the country, in virtually all communities, Americans have been horrified by tales of utterly casual murders committed by teens and preteens. These killers do not care about our lives; they do not seem to care much more for their own. Many come from homes where parents are absent or abusive. Many have their own histories of serious drug abuse. All seem to have easy access to deadly weapons, from cheap handguns to powerful military-style assault rifles.[15]

One response to the problem of juvenile violence comes in the form of heightened individual responsibility. Certainly a serious review of juvenile delinquency laws and institutions is overdue. But what about social responsibility for this phenomenon? These new killers did not grow up in a vacuum. Their appearance in the United States of America at the close of the twentieth century is not a random event. Juvenile violence has increased because basic parts of our community have broken down, with youth bearing the greatest cost. Under the stress of great economic and social change, family structure appears weaker than at any time in modern memory. There are more single parent homes and more divorces. Other community institutions, especially schools, have fewer resources and less influence than before. Gangs, for both girls and boys, have often become more influential. National culture has become less judgmental about a wide variety of conduct previously considered immoral, including premarital sex. Births out of wedlock have increased dramatically. Drugs continue to plague many communities. More firearms, especially more handguns, are in private hands. These changes affect juveniles more than others because their characters are still malleable and they are more vulnerable to changes in their environment than adults who have the financial and other independence to create their own social situations. And we wonder why juvenile violence has increased?

The utilitarian argument for social change is obvious. Any reasonable method to reduce juvenile violence would greatly increase overall happiness. Not only would we save lives but we would restore a general sense of security. Taking the value approach, I believe we have a moral obligation to change that goes beyond collective self-interest. If we care about the value of young people, if we care about their ability to lead fulfilling and moral lives, then we should accept responsibility for collective decisions that affect their safety and their moral character. If we truly value our young, we should accept a number of painful consequences in the name of social change.

Some will object that I have left out a critical step, however. That social changes have had bad effects on the young does not mean that society made responsible choices to harm the young. Most often, social change is unintentional. Efforts directed at one social end often produce a much more significant, but entirely unintended and unanticipated effect on another facet of society. How can we hold society responsible unless we determine that society is in some sense culpable for its unintentionally harmful choices?

It often seems as if most of the recent changes in American society have occurred in a process beyond anyone's control or choice. Who can we say deliberately chose the particular direction that our society has taken in recent years? Is there anyone who is entirely satisfied with that direction? Yet the lack of a centralized, intentional decision maker does not end the social responsibility question.

Americans have made a number of public decisions that have had predictably criminogenic effects on young people. Among the most important have been decisions about taxes and government spending. For the last fifteen years, as a result of a number of voter decisions, local and state governments, and to a lesser extent the federal government, have had fewer resources with which to deal with all social problems, including those of youth. In California, voters in the late seventies changed the state constitution to put severe limits on any increase in general taxation at the state or local level.[16] This has restricted government resources and caused a steady deterioration in almost all government services, especially in urban areas. In Los Angeles, despite majority voter approval, efforts to increase the police force through new taxation have been defeated. The chronic shortage of police and other law enforcement personnel has meant that all law enforcement must engage in constant triage—decisions about which criminal violations will be ignored or handled perfunctorily.[17] This means that many early and relatively minor offenses by juveniles go unpunished, encouraging more offenses and discouraging those who would uphold the law.[18] In Los Angeles, juvenile probation officers carry an average case load of up to 180, making a mockery of their obligation to supervise closely all juveniles on probation. A lack of resources means that judges must often pass sentence without full information on a juvenile's criminal history, and that same lack of resources means that those repeat offenders who are sent to prison camps will serve only four to six months.[19] Meanwhile, government-funded social programs aimed at youth have been steadily cut. Even programs widely recognized as successful in keeping young people out of gangs have been cut or limited in scope. Resources for schools and public libraries have seriously declined.

It is impossible to quantify the contribution of taxation limitations on juvenile violence in California and elsewhere, but they have undoubtedly had a serious effect on the government's ability to respond to the problem. Although unintended, the effect was entirely predictable, and is today a matter of common understanding. Voters have made, and continue to make, policy decisions to further their own self-interest, which have a serious criminogenic effect on others. As a result of these decisions more youths will likely turn to violent crime and more youths will be injured as a result. Social responsibility for crime should create a social obligation to counteract these effects.

Complicating the responsibility question, of course, is doubt whether government programs to prevent crime actually work. The ability of government to affect citizen behavior in any form is limited, and to change the deep-rooted dynamics that produce large amounts of crime in certain communities is uncertain at best. But the same could be said for a wide range of government programs, including penal policy. We do not require powerful empirical proofs of the efficacy of increased punishment for a particular offense in order for government to declare it an important deterrent measure. The relevant question with respect to social responsibility for crime is whether society is putting the same effort, in terms of creative thinking and fiscal resources, into preventing juvenile delinquency as it does into addressing other social problems. Is the society as concerned with the social problems of the poor—which often produce street crime—as with the social problems of the middle class, which lead to less immediately threatening criminal activities? Or is it that the middle-class majority prefers to employ the model of individual responsibility for the poor, and employs social responsibility only when the subjects of judgment are middle class?

Social responsibility for crime involves more than a commitment of funds. It also implicates competing public values and interests. A determination of social responsibility for crime might mean giving up or restricting some currently treasured rights or privileges. To cite two particularly controversial possibilities, American society might be obliged to accept restrictions on general liberty in the form of gun control or restrictions on media depictions of violence.

Strong gun control—a nationwide ban on personal handgun ownership for example—might have a dramatic impact on juvenile homicide. If a large proportion of the public supported this change, we could dramatically reduce the availability of the most lethal and most common of all deadly weapons to the young.[20] Even if we assumed that young people inclined to violence would simply turn to other weapons, their violence would be less dangerous. Knives and clubs are less likely to kill, and rifles and shotguns are harder to conceal.

The reason we do not have strong gun control is that strong gun control involves too much political pain. Effective gun control would mean that many adult Americans would lose some or all ability to buy and own handguns. For those who view gun ownership as necessary to self-protection, strong gun control would mean trusting more in government and fate. For those who view gun ownership as an essential right, a basic part of the American way of life, gun control would mean a significant loss of individual liberty.

For those who do not see gun control as a civil liberties issue, social responsibility for crime may seem like a relatively painless program. But consider a program often promoted by conservatives: mandated change in our culture of violence. Either by direct government censorship, by indirect government pressure on the media, or by a set of voluntarily adopted standards, media might drastically reduce the violence content of current entertainment and news. We know that television has a powerful impact on the young. Young viewers, especially poor and ill-educated viewers, appear most vulnerable to television's pernicious influences. We know that young people today spend a frightening proportion of their lives in front of a video screen. We know that American television is saturated with violence. Many studies indicate serious effects on the young from watching violent programming.[21] Overall, the impact of television and movie violence on killings by the young may be as significant a factor as the easy availability of handguns. To do something about it would involve serious pain, though: either a modification of current First Amendment standards, or a voluntary restriction of artistic license. It would also mean that adults might have to suffer duller entertainment, for we can make no neat separation between adult and youth programming—and violence is exciting.

Again this is only a suggestive account. Social responsibility for juvenile violence does not necessarily mean raising taxes, banning handguns or censoring television. Social responsibility might, in fact, involve none of these. My point is that social responsibility would involve significant and painful obligations, and it is because those consequences are painful that we avoid them. My point is that if we as a people consider ourselves obligated to foster the development of nonviolent youth, we should be willing to do much more to change the current structure of society.

Scapegoating

Social responsibility is by definition self-responsibility; it involves placing negative consequences on ourselves for our own shortcomings. Individuals do not often do this; societies prove even more reluctant to do so. The great moral danger we face—and the moral wrong we have too often committed—is making the criminal offender a scapegoat for social ills. The structure of criminal law tempts us to do exactly the reverse of what social contract proponents suggest: instead of making social responsibility swallow individual responsibility, we make individual responsibility swallow social. If the poorly educated, unskilled, angry-at-the-world wrongdoer may be blamed for his violent acts, then why not blame him for being angry and unemployed? If we believe that violence on TV and at the movies provides no excuse for crime, then why blame its producers and disseminators for its general effect on society? We can just blame the offender for everything. If we disregard the difference between act and actor, we can label the offender a Criminal, as distinguished from the rest of us, the Law-Abiding. Now the problem looks simple: eliminate the Criminals from our midst and peace and justice will reign.

This kind of scapegoating is both wrong and stupid. It is wrong because it distorts the meaning of deserved punishment and ignores the importance of all the other forms of responsibility that coexist with individual criminal responsibility. We can impose social responsibility for the promotion of greed and violence without affecting the individual responsibility of those who actually steal and rob. This kind of scapegoating is stupid because however much we would like to believe otherwise, society constitutes one of the most powerful influences on criminal activity. The reason that some American cities have far higher homicide rates than others is not that more "Criminals" live in one place than the other, but that political, economic, and other social differences make one community more conducive to homicide than the other. Similar differences explain the huge disparity between American homicide rates and those of other industrialized democracies. If we want to reduce violence in this country we will have to take seriously social as well as individual responsibility for crime.

Conclusion

The social critique of deserved punishment grows out of the urge to find some clean starting place, some place of absolute equality from which all moral judgment may flow. It fails because there is no such place. We all have dirty hands, and all societies are unfair. The social critic asks: How can punishment be deserved if the offender is the victim of an unfair social structure? I answer: Because deserved punishment is not about social fairness. Deserved punishment does not aim to restore a fair social arrangement, nor to restore an equilibrium of moral burdens and benefits. Deserved punishment forms part of our ongoing struggle to impose moral structure on a morally indifferent world.

The social critique should remind us of several important truths about moral responsibility, though. It reminds us that deserved punishment speaks to the nature of the wrongful act and not the ultimate worth of the person. With a change in social structure or family, the identities of punisher and punished would also change. It reminds us that the basic structure of American society is flawed, and the criminal justice system reflects those flaws. As a result, deserved punishment neither establishes the basic virtue of the law-abiding, nor the essential evil of the offender; it simply identifies and responds to particular acts of wrongdoing.

The social critique should also remind us that responsibility does not end with criminal guilt. We may simultaneously hold individuals criminally responsible, regardless of social wrongs, while we place time and energy consequences on society for righting those wrongs. We can change our culture of greed and violence without affecting the punishment of thieves and killers; we can alleviate economic inequities without altering the deserved punishment of individuals. We should do all of these things if we are committed to human value.

5

Moralizing the Passions
of Punishment

Issues of criminal responsibility inspire powerful emotions. The outcome of a single case can set a city on fire or change the nation's law. In recent years the rage and fear generated by criminal offenses has strongly influenced American politics, from city council and judicial elections to campaigns for the presidency.[1] Sometimes we see these passions as a positive force, galvanizing the public and government to action in defense of individual value. At other times the passions seem ugly, revealing a bigoted, fearful, and mean-spirited side to American society.

I remember a capital murder trial I covered as a reporter in Florida. A teenager was charged with stabbing a woman to death in an effort to rob her of the cash she had on hand as she opened her restaurant in the morning. I remember the trial because of the victim's husband, an older man who came to court every day and stared with unrelenting venom at the defendant. His eyes were dark holes of rage and despair.

The man's life had been destroyed by his wife's murder and now he directed all his remaining energies to the defendant's destruction. Whenever someone is about to be executed in this country, we see the same look and hear the same voice on the news. Reporters seek out relatives of the deceased, knowing they will make a good story. Most of those willing to speak to the press have been consumed by the victim's killing. Their hurt has no limit and neither does their need to see the killer suffer.[2]

What should we do with all this passion? We must hear these survivors, for they remind us of those murdered, but their vitriol is disturbing. We know justice should not be this personal, this primitive, this bloodthirsty, for just punishment is not revenge.

The justice of criminal responsibility depends in large part on our ability to moralize the passions of punishment. Some have argued that this is impossible under a theory of deserved punishment, that emphasizing what the offender deserves for a past wrong only exacerbates the human tendency to excessive, immoral rage. Critics argue that it brings out the worst in human nature and leads to cruel punishments. The chapter opens by considering this objection, but we soon see that the problem of emotive influence goes beyond punishment theory. Judgments of deserved punishment may be distorted by excessive anger, but estimates of deterrence may be similarly distorted by excessive fear. Each theory of punishment has its own emotional dangers. The solution to the problem involves a better understanding of the relationship between reason and emotion.

We see that emotion has its own rationality which cannot be ignored, even in deliberative decision making. Emotions may assist moral judgment, or hinder it. We need to recognize when emotions have moral content and when they do not. In particular, we need to recognize the special moral dangers of self-deceptive emotions—when we may deceive ourselves about our own biases toward a person or situation. Particularly because of the formal structure of American criminal justice, which gives a central place to the jury, the decision maker most prone to emotive influence, we need criminal rules that meet certain criteria for emotive regulation. We need rules that are clear, morally evocative, and based on conduct rather than general character. These will help curb, although they certainly will not solve, the problem of amoral emotive influence on criminal judgments.

Reason, Passion, and Theories of Punishment

Some have argued that the main task of criminal law is to suppress anger. As one scholar put it:

> When a reprehensible crime is committed, strong emotional reactions take place in all of us. Some people will be impelled to go out at once and work off their tensions in a lynching orgy. Even the calmest, most law-abiding of us is likely to be deeply stirred. . . . It is one of the marks of a civilized culture that it has devised legal procedures that minimize the impact of emotional reactions and strive for calm and rational disposition.[3]

Proponents of deterrent theories often argue that a focus on the future effects of punishment reduces the temptation to anger that comes from dwelling on past wrongs. They argue that emphasizing the concrete goods of punishment makes the punishment decision more deliberative and less emotional.[4] This critique misconceives the problem of emotive influence.

Judgments of deserved punishment often do rest on anger. Anger is based on a judgment of wrongdoing and inspires an urge to punish, both of which reflect different aspects of formal judgments of deserved punishment. Indeed, we cannot judge that a person deserves punishment without also expressing the basis for anger at the offender's deed. If we judge that a person shoplifted from a store and so deserves punishment, we have stated the basis for someone—the store owner at least—to be angry with the person. The problem with the overlap between anger and moral assessment is that anger is morally unreliable.

Anger can be moral or immoral. Our anger may stem from petty jealousy, bigotry, or from a sense of injustice. While anger may support the moral judgment that the offender deserves punishment, it can also drive revenge, the urge to inflict suffering on another according to a purely personal sense of wrong.[5] Anger may be shaped by shared norms about the severity of wrong done, or it may depend on the individual's unique perception of wrong.[6] We may become angry at another shopper in a store because she selfishly pushed to the front of a long line or because we are offended by the grating sound of her voice. We cannot say, as a general rule, whether anger should influence decisions about deserved punishment because we cannot say, as a general rule, whether anger has moral content.

Nor is the problem of emotive influence limited to anger. Even sympathy, that most benign of emotions, may distort judgments of criminal responsibility. Sympathy for a person accused of a crime may make us more sensitive to the nature of the choices she made and so more careful in our assessment of her culpability.[7] To this extent sympathy greatly assists proper moral decision making. But sympathy can also distort moral judgment. A judge or jury may sympathize with a defendant because they share the same race, class, or gender—factors irrelevant to culpability. In California, judges commonly tell jurors: "[You] must not be influenced by pity for a defendant or by prejudice against him. . . . You must not be swayed by mere sentiment, conjecture, sympathy, passion, prejudice, public opinion or public feeling."[8]

Nor does the problem of emotive influence disappear if we change punishment theories. Consider what happens when we try to assess punishment according to deterrence principles—the punishment that most efficiently deters future criminality. Now the problem of amoral anger seems to diminish, because we no longer ask an anger-inspiring question. No longer concerned with deontologic blame, we turn to the future: What kind of punishment will do the most good? This sounds like a less personal and thus less emotional question, a matter of balancing individual and social interests in objective fashion. But here appearances deceive.

Decisions about whether, or to what extent, punishment will deter future criminality directly implicate another of our strongest passions: fear for our own safety. Like anger, fear may or may not have moral content. We may reasonably fear for our lives or the lives of others and so act in justifiable self-defense. Or we may fear based on prejudice. Generally we fear most what we understand least. For example, residents of relatively safe suburbs often have much greater fear of crime than do those who live in more dangerous urban areas.[9] We tend to fear certain highly unusual crimes of violence, like stranger kidnappings of children, than the much more common crimes of domestic violence. We often exaggerate the dangers posed by those of different races and classes.

To sum up: regardless of punishment theory, decisions about proper punishment are likely to be influenced by emotions, and those emotions are morally unreliable. Sometimes our feelings direct us toward justice, other times they do not. As a result, emotions may distort judgments of criminal responsibility, whether the measurement of responsibility is according to desert or utility. The solution to the problem of emotive influence lies not in punishment theory, but in a better understanding of the complex relationship between reason and emotion.

Understanding Emotion—A Different Kind of Rationality

The distrust of emotion displayed by many critics of deserved punishment has much wider echoes in law and philosophy. Courts generally distrust the influence of emotion because they, like many philosophers, view emotion as an opponent of reason.[10] Likewise, many moral theorists have held that right depends on moral reason uninfluenced by feeling. They have argued that emotions are passive, irrational occurrences that undermine the person's rationality and responsibility. Thus important moral decisions, especially the sort that the criminal law involves, should be reached in an entirely dispassionate way.[11] I disagree on several grounds. First, the argument implies the impossible—that important moral decisions can be properly made without emotive influence. Second, the argument misconceives the tension between reason and emotion, seeing them as irreconcilable opponents when in fact they represent rival but closely related modes of human understanding, including understanding of morality.

The experience of emotion is basic to human life. It cannot be wished away. Emotions help us make sense of the world. Our feelings connect our inner life to events in the world beyond us.[12] I can describe a friend in terms on which independent observers could agree—tall or smart or funny—but what my friend means to me is more personal. It has to do with the emotional ties between us. In this way emotions ground meaning. We cannot imagine achieving a personal goal without experiencing an emotional lift, or experiencing a personal failure without feeling hurt. Without an emotional reaction, we cannot honestly say that these events mean anything to us.[13] Nor does emotion's importance end as we move from the personal realm to the more public. Our emotions are involved in virtually all significant decisions. Feelings signify significance. In this sense, emotions bring responsibility to life. They represent the electric current that connects normative theory—general ideas about right and wrong—to personal experience: how we feel about a particular issue.

Emotions serve as an important, though partial, guide to rational inquiry. Initially they provide a pattern of salience which helps order our thoughts and actions.[14] In our lives we accumulate enormous quantities of data, and every day we confront new information. Emotions direct our attention to particularly important aspects of a situation. They also suggest certain rational approaches. Even philosophers often begin work on a difficult problem with a gut reaction. All this suggests that emotions are both more rational and more complex than has been generally recognized.

Philosophers and psychologists in recent years have developed so-called cognitive theories of emotion as a way of understanding the particular rationality of emotional reactions.[15] Such theories come in many varieties, but all share the idea that emotion depends on a perception of some aspect of the world that can be judged correct or incorrect according to rational principles. Emotion under this view involves a rational assessment of a person or situation, associated with a physical sensation, normally accompanied by a desire to undertake a particular kind of action.[16] If you return home tomorrow to discover a shattered bedroom window and papers scattered around the room, you may experience shock at the discovery. A perception that you have been burglarized will inspire fear, anger, and disquiet at the invasion of your private space. But if you discover that the window was broken by a tree limb and the room disordered by the wind, you will feel relief. The fear and anger will dissipate because the assessment of violation needed for these emotions will have disappeared.

This approach gives us another way of understanding anger, the emotion so important to deserved punishment. In the burglary example, the first step to anger is the rational assessment of wrong, of the burglar's deliberate and selfish invasion of the home. This assessment sparks a sensation of heightened tension, or, in psychological terms, arousal. Finally, the emotion of anger characteristically involves a desire to engage in denunciatory and punitive action, in this instance to find and punish the burglar.[17]

Emotion and Legal Decision Making

From this overview of emotion, we may identify specific dangers in emotive influence on criminal responsibility decisions. First, *emotions are personal*, but law consists of universal rules. Second, *emotions are prereflective*, meaning they depend on unarticulated premises, but law requires deliberate decisions based on articulated reasons. Third, emotions usually involve *simple judgments*; decisions about guilt and innocence are usually complex.

Philosophers of emotion describe emotions as profoundly personal. Whether a driver becomes furious at being cut off on the freeway, or can laugh it off, will depend significantly on personality type, on what the action signifies to the driver's self. The person who views the world with distrust, who resents his position in society and feels threatened by many others, will likely react more angrily than one who shares none of these traits. While the individualization of emotion can be exaggerated—there is a universality of feeling upon which much of our culture depends—the personalization of emotion makes its influence on moral judgment problematic. In a moral sense, we can rely on our feelings *only* when we are sure that they rest on rational assessments that accord with general moral principles, and not just our own preferences or experience.

Similarly, the rationality of emotions is prereflective and intuitive.[18] We do not feel sad, for example, because we: (1) observe that certain logical prerequisites for sadness are present, and then (2) decide to feel sad. Instead, following some triggering event, we just feel sad. The rational assessments of emotion require no conscious effort; instead, they tend to come ready-made, fashioned by past experience. As a result, emotions can surprise and confuse us. We may feel sad and have a hard time figuring out why. Nor do emotions always respond to reflective judgment. Hours after determining that the bedroom window was broken by a tree, you may still feel jumpy as a result of your initial belief that you had been burglarized. The adrenalin generated by the shock of discovery may cause longer-lasting physiological and emotional changes. Or consider phobias—the unreasoning fears that govern some persons' lives. A person may live in terror of ants, believing that even a single insect may devour him. Given this belief, the individual's fear on seeing an ant is eminently rational: we all fear sudden, violent death. Yet the fear is absurd because the assessment of danger on which it rests is unfounded: no single ant, or even horde of ants, presents this kind of danger. Unfortunately, even if the antophobe intellectually realizes that he is safe, he still experiences panic.

In legal decision making, obviously irrational emotions are not our major concern, though. In a deliberative setting, such irrationality can be identified and corrected for. The more serious problem for the law lies in the hidden biases that distort moral judgment. It is the problem of self-deceptive emotions.[19] As a general matter we know that emotions often distort others' judgment, but we often fail to recognize its similar influence upon ourselves. Assume that I say something hurtful to a colleague because I am angry with her. Although the real reason for my anger is jealousy of her recent accomplishments, I may not want to acknowledge this, even to myself. Instead I focus on all the ways the colleague may have deserved my annoyance, elevating trivial complaints into apparently significant grievances. If I am good at manipulating cognitive assessments, I will soon have justified my initial anger, and perhaps increased it. Since this process operates at the prereflective level, my conscious mind may be unaware of the deception involved. Unless forced to careful reconsideration, I can sincerely state that I spoke out of righteous indignation for wrongs my colleague did, and not out of jealousy.

Finally, feelings tend to be simplistic. The translation of complex reality into emotional myth or paradigm usually involves a considerable simplification of the situation.[20] Feelings often turn the complicated human drama of our world into a melodramatic conflict between good guys and bad guys. In criminal justice decision making we commonly oversimplify the subject of our judgment by exaggerating the evil of the offender. Avoiding the hard work of evaluating the many interrelated and conflicting aspects of the conduct, we see the harm done and jump to a condemning conclusion. Instead of recognizing the many shades of gray, we see only black and white.

The emotional tendency to oversimplify does not always work against the defendant; its direction depends on the decision maker's personal situation with respect to victim and accused. The Ventura County jurors who decided the first trial of the police officers who beat Rodney King, or the New York jurors who sat in the Bernard Goetz case, almost certainly identified with the defendants in those cases. When it came to crime and race the jurors saw themselves on the same side as the defendants, and so found it hard to convict them of wrongdoing. Their emotional mythology would not permit them to see these otherwise law-abiding whites as committing acts of brutality on black men. Instead they saw law-abiding (white) persons defending themselves and others against the threats posed by fearsome young (black) men. Those who speak for an offender at the time of sentencing provide another example of this dynamic. Relatives of an offender often plead for mercy on the offender's behalf while denying the evil of which the offender stands convicted. They cannot admit the seriousness, or sometimes even the bare facts, of the offender's wrongdoing because such an admission contradicts the pleader's emotional mythology. The offender cannot be a Criminal, because he is a cared-for Husband or Son.

In the case of a serious crime, decision makers are often tempted to condemn beyond what is deserved. When called upon to judge a stranger who is to some extent responsible for a serious harm, the decision maker's temptation is to ignore moral complexities and declare the person and his act entirely evil. The decision maker labels the offender a Criminal, remaining indifferent to the person—the being capable of both good and evil—behind that label.[21] In this way the offender is designated as "other." The more we can designate a person as different from ourselves, the fewer moral doubts we have about condemnation and punishment.[22] We assign the offender the role of Monster, a move that justifies harsh treatment and insulates us from moral concerns about the suffering we inflict.[23]

In our private lives, the fact that we otherwise value those we judge checks the temptation to exaggerate their wrongdoing. The people who hurt us are often friends, relatives, colleagues—individuals whose good points we acknowledge and value. Our judgment takes place within a context of caring, limiting the tendency to exaggerate evil. This emotional check is weaker in criminal justice decisions, where offenders are normally strangers to the decision maker, and appear more strange because of social, economic, and racial differences.

Differences between offenders and those who sit in judgment on them leads to what I call the otherness temptation. This is the inclination to feel hostile to those who appear different from us. It is what makes whites judge crimes committed by blacks against whites more harshly than if they were committed by blacks against blacks.[24] As we will see, in modern America the otherness temptation presents the most serious challenge of all.

Passion, Diversity, and Juries: The Modern American Context

As a nation with an extremely diverse population, committed to a form of criminal justice that gives a central role to nonprofessional decision makers, the United States today has particularly acute concerns with emotive influence on criminal law. The great American challenge in criminal law, as in so many other areas of public policy, is to forge community rules to serve a people with many different group affiliations. Especially in its urban areas, where a large proportion of criminal activity takes place, the population of the nation is diverse by any definition. This diversity is not a singular feature of the present age; it has been a defining feature of the "nation" since the arrival of European settlers. Today the nation's population contains large numbers of every race and virtually every ethnic group in the world, with increasing proportions from Asia and Latin America. Americans practice a wide variety of religions. The United States today, although it lacks the class consciousness of many other Western nations, has among the widest wealth differentials— the gap between rich and poor—of any Western democracy.

The diversity of the American population means that the otherness temptation in American criminal adjudication must always be a major concern. The diversity also means that criminal adjudication will be especially controversial. In the United States the criminal law must take the lead in defining the moral community. In other nations particular religions or social traditions may effectively define the moral community; criminal law only reinforces judgments made by other institutions. In the United States, where those other defining institutions are weaker, the criminal law's message must be proportionately stronger.

The challenge of diversity in American criminal justice is further magnified by our commitment to jury trial. Even in the context of Western democracies, the American jury trial represents a strikingly populist method of adjudication. All persons charged with serious criminal offenses have the right to a trial before lay members of the public.[25] Unless the accused waives the right by pleading guilty, he may not be convicted of a significant crime without the agreement of lay jurors.[26] American judges have quite limited power over the determination of guilt or innocence in a jury trial. Judges may rule on the minimum amount of evidence necessary to convict, but may never order a conviction.[27] Judges are required to instruct juries on the law, but generally they are not permitted to comment on or "sum up" the evidence in the way that English jurists do.[28] Judges are excluded from jury deliberations.[29] If the jury resolves to acquit the defendant, that decision is absolutely irreversible, even if clearly erroneous.[30] If the jury convicts, the judiciary reviews the merits of that decision by a highly deferential standard.[31]

We should not exaggerate the commitment to jury trial in present day criminal justice, however. Whatever rights to jury trial American law formally recognizes are often undercut by the practical realities of the system—which demands more efficient case processing than jury trials permit. The enormous press of cases, the limited number of courtrooms, judges, and public defenders and the considerable power of prosecutors to threaten harsh sentences mean that most cases are resolved by a plea of guilty—and waiver of jury trial right. Only a small minority of the criminally accused ever face a jury.[32] Those cases that do go to jury trial have a significant impact on the everyday charging and bargaining process, though. The perception of what a jury might do plays an important role in the negotiations between prosecution and defense, and sometimes the judiciary, over case dispositions.

The point is that as a matter of formal structure, the American criminal justice system gives lay members of the public a critical role in legal decision making, much more of a role, with less regulation, than is true in most comparable systems. Adjudication of criminal law in this country is thus designed for direct appeals to the public's inchoate sense of justice. By design, the system permits more emotive influence than systems that feature more judicial control.

Moralizing the Passions of Criminal Responsibility

Recognizing the problem of emotive influence, the criminal justice system has devised two basic methods of emotive control: regulation by role and regulation by rule. Employing these strategies, the legal system seeks to force decision makers to reach beyond their own personal situations and gut reactions to the universal standards of moral responsibility.

Perhaps the simplest way to regulate emotive influence is by role. In essence, modern law seeks to depersonalize, and thus de-emotionalize, litigation by taking it out of the hands of the parties. In contrast to earlier forms of adjudication, which featured direct confrontations between victim and the accused, modern criminal trials are waged by legal intermediaries.[33] Lawyers, with only their professional pride at stake, act out the conflict. Similarly, the decision makers—lawyers transformed into judges and citizens transformed into jurors—act according to certain formal, publicly declared expectations. By placing the judge on a high bench in a black robe and asking jurors to take an oath and sit in the jury box, we ask these citizens to abandon their normal biases and judge according to legal standards. We ask them to decide by law and not by instinct.[34] Jurors promise to follow the judge's instructions; trial judges promise to follow the law as written by legislators and interpreted by other judges.

The emotions inspired by crime are too strong and too subtle for control by role alone, however. We must also regulate by rule. Traditionally, lawyers have thought that the maximum control of emotion comes with hard-edged rules—rules with relatively clear, nonnormative criteria. The tax code, or the requirement that a person be at least thirty-five years of age to be president, are examples of such rules. Although there will be hard cases under each, involving normative decisions, most cases can be resolved without resort to complex moral judgment. Many lawyers believe that hard-edged rules like these engender less uncertainty, and thus less room for emotive influence, than more soft-edged rules. Soft-edged rules employ relatively vague and explicitly normative criteria, for example the rule that custody decisions should be made "in the best interest of the child," or that punishment not be "cruel and unusual." Clear, fact-oriented rules allow for impersonal justice; they permit the goddess of justice to balance her scales blindfolded. Vague, normative standards play to personal emotions.

Unfortunately, as we will see throughout the remainder of the book, most important rules of criminal law involve direct moral assessment. Determinations of an offender's mens rea, for example, involve moral assessment of the offender's criminal choice. Justice requires that the law remain open to explicitly normative concerns. This means that our best hope of controlling emotive influence is to make that influence self-conscious—to provide a means for public discussion and reconsideration of personal and prereflective intuitions about a case. We cannot expect the criminal law to somehow override emotions, but rather to indicate which emotions have moral content and which do not.

In order to moralize the passions of punishment, criminal rules should meet three criteria: (1) they should be clearly stated; (2) they should be morally evocative; and (3) they should be act and not character based. An ideal criminal law would provide a clear and complete statement of the moral principles relevant to the assessment of a particular form of wrongful conduct.

The easiest of these criteria to satisfy is that the criminal law be act based. As I have argued throughout, culpability should depend on the nature of the wrong done and not the character of the accused. We should do this because criminal law defends the fundamental value of all persons, including wrong-doers. To paraphrase St. Augustine, we should love the offender even while we hate his offense.[35] We should also follow this principle because it checks the natural tendency to make criminal judgment depend on how much we identify with the accused or the victim.

The line between an act-based and a character-based rule can be difficult to draw, however. Often it is a distinction more of degree than kind. After all, in order to assess the act we must pay considerable attention to the actor. We need to know whether a killer was crazy or sane, whether he killed deliberately or by accident. In assessing criminal conduct we necessarily assess a human actor, but only as revealed by the action. What we should avoid is a broader judgment of the person. As we will see in part 2, several kinds of criminal rules violate this principle. Traditional doctrines of common law liability that rely on allusive descriptions of evil-doing present significant dangers of character assessment. While such evocative language brings the advantages of flexibility and moral suggestiveness, it can also encourage the decision maker to focus on the individual's moral dispositions generally. Similarly, modern rules that emphasize the quality of an individual's choice-making or his ability to choose direct attention away from the actual conduct. Instead of focusing on what the person did, the decision maker becomes caught up in a complex psychological and moral assessment of general choice-making by the person, which often turns into a larger assessment of his character—whether the person is fundamentally good or bad.

The goal of clarity means that rules of criminal law must be stated in simple, public language. Legal jargon and complex phrases should be avoided whenever possible. As long as our prime decision makers are legal novices, the rules of criminal law must be stated in public terms, in words with common meanings, though necessarily more precisely defined than they are in ordinary usage. Strangely, courts and legislatures seem to balk at the idea of clear, modern language. The traditional terms of the common law exert an almost magical hold over many in the legal profession, and even new enactments are frequently burdened with unnecessary and often unexplained technical terms. In murder cases, judges frequently instruct juries that guilt depends upon a determination of "malice aforethought" even though the term has virtually no public meaning—these are not words common to public discourse—and their legal meaning cannot be derived from dictionary definitions. Even lawyers recognize that the phrase is misleading. By employing it in our basic law of murder, we increase the risk of juror confusion and resulting injustice.

Hardest to define and achieve is the requirement that criminal rules should be morally evocative. By this I mean that for the most serious offenses, rules should address the most important moral considerations involved in the wrongdoing. While this would seem an obvious point, it is not, for as we will see in the next chapter, sometimes we may wish to limit the scope of offense definition in order to minimize the risk of overbroad interpretations. But unless the law encompasses our best moral intuitions, it loses its best opportunity for emotive regulation. When the law articulates our otherwise inchoate moral sensibilities, it provides a way of questioning less worthy emotions. It provides a basis for discussion of feelings and the connection between those feelings and proper judgment. What we must always try to avoid is leaving the powerful passions aroused by punishment issues hidden. Then their influence depends only on the self-awareness and moral strength of the individual decision maker.

Conclusion

In the last chapter I rejected the idea that deserved punishment somehow restores a fair moral balance in society. I argued that offenders do not deserve punishment because they have disturbed the equitable distribution of burdens and benefits among citizens, but because they challenge our basic moral values. The idea that punishment restores balance may be correct in another sense, though. The passions inspired by criminal wrongs can be so strong they unbalance individuals and even societies. Recall the husband described at the beginning of this chapter who lived only to see his wife's killer dead. He had lost (or had taken from him) the balance of values and interests that makes a meaningful life possible. Obsessed by a single goal whose achievement will bring only small satisfaction, he represents another kind of homicide victim.

The same dynamic can be seen in the larger society. We see a nation obsessed with harsh punishment, with the death penalty and mandatory sentencing schemes of unprecedented scope and severity. We see a society willing to spend billions on new prisons, even at the cost of public education and health. We see a society emotionally unbalanced.

In criminal justice we must balance reason and feeling. We do, and should, care about criminal responsibility. The wrongs of murder and manslaughter merit outrage. In determining deserved punishment we should consult our hearts as well as our heads. In the end, we must have a reason for our judgments of culpability, though. We may begin with a feeling but we must end with reasons. In this respect deserved punishment differs not at all from rival theories of punishment.

PART II

Defining Murder and Manslaughter

6

From Principles to Rules
An Introduction to Mens Rea

Now we move from principles of deserved punishment to rules
of law, from generalities about blameworthiness to defining and grading different categories of homicidal conduct. In a sense we move to more familiar
territory, for the basic considerations involved in defining homicide offenses
are the same as we use in everyday human interaction—considerations of intent, awareness and motive, calculation and accident, passion and dispassion.
But here we also enter the realm of lawyers and the particular traditions of
Anglo-American criminal law. We enter a linguistic thicket, in which special
historical and legal meanings about terms like malice, premeditation and
provocation, must be considered. Almost as troublesome, though, will be the
ordinary language of blameworthiness, which for all its suggestive power
contains many traps for the conceptually unwary.

My task in this chapter is threefold: (1) to introduce the concept of mens
rea as it applies to murder and manslaughter; (2) to introduce some of the
competing criteria for mens rea rules; and (3) to defend basic mens rea analysis against two fundamental objections, one arising out of new work in cognitive science, and another that comes from a common misconception about
how we understand and judge each other's choices.

As a preliminary matter, we need to canvass the variety of different rules
that come under the heading of mens rea—all the different principles involving intent to harm and awareness of harm, culpable risk taking, motive,
and quality of decision making that form the core of the law of murder and
manslaughter. Once these basics are in hand we turn briefly to considerations
of rule drafting. Not only must we decide what kinds of culpable conduct an
offense should cover, but we also must decide how to express our judgment
in mens rea rules. This proves to be a matter of both substance and style. The
broadest and most nuanced rules tend to be those in which aspects of mens
rea are defined by allusion to character traits. But these same allusive forms
of mens rea suffer most from the ills of vagueness, threatening to violate the

criteria for rule drafting set out in the previous chapter. Meanwhile, analytic forms of mens rea, whose definitions rest on states of awareness or desire, often prove underinclusive, that is, too narrow. Finally, we consider briefly the politics of rule drafting, which favor overinclusive rather than underinclusive rules.

The second half of the chapter concerns not the particulars of mens rea rules, but objections to the whole mens rea enterprise of assessing criminal culpability based on reasons for conduct. We consider the objections of some cognitive scientists, who have argued that because it appears that the brain does not process information in discrete stages of beliefs and desires, that assessing conduct according to beliefs and desires is nonsense. Again we see the need to respect the differences between the scientific and moral projects, to understand that scientific explanations of physical dynamics do not necessarily undermine our judgments about the meaning of conduct. We can blame or praise action based on reasons even if those reasons do not describe a particular physical state of the brain.

Finally, we take up the common concern that judgments about criminal culpability are difficult and unreliable because they depend on evidence that is largely hidden from view. According to this argument, only the chooser really knows his own choice; the rest of us are limited to educated guesses. This notion rests on a controversial and ultimately untenable view of the separation of mind and body that makes evidence about choice seem more mysterious and less accessible than it really is. In reality, we have two potential sources of information about choice—the chooser's subjective reports and witnesses' observations of conduct—each with their own evidentiary strengths and weaknesses that must be considered in drafting mens rea rules.

Mens Rea

At the heart of criminal law lies the concept of *mens rea*, a Latin term variously translated as "evil mind," "evil will," or "guilty mind."[1] Mens rea refers to the requirement that, to be guilty of a crime, a person must have made a bad choice, not just a choice that had harmful results. As Oliver Wendell Holmes Jr., put it: "[E]ven a dog distinguishes between being stumbled over and being kicked."[2] For the most part, criminal law focuses on kicking rather than stumbling.

As I use the term here, mens rea refers to the basic culpability language of criminal law, that is, the words that establish the general wrongfulness of particular conduct. It does not include what are usually termed affirmative defenses, those justifications or excuses that may render noncriminal otherwise criminal acts. For example, a person who purposely kills another commits no crime if the killing was in self-defense. Similarly, a purposeful killing may be excused if the killer was motivated by a crazy reason and so was insane at the time of the homicide. Such affirmative defenses form a critical part of the responsibility rules of the criminal law, but in accord with the basic structure of the book, I concentrate here on the doctrines of mens rea that provide the primary test of culpability.

Two hypothetical homicide cases will help illustrate the many forms of mens rea used in American criminal law. In our first case a professional killer is hired by an embittered husband to kill his wife. The husband pays the killer $10,000 at the outset and promises another $10,000 on completion of the execution. After several days of surveillance and preparation, the hit man kills the wife by a single gunshot from a high-powered rifle, and receives full payment.

In our second case a woman directs her tractor trailer truck down an unobstructed state highway under optimal driving conditions. She drives at or under the speed limit. Suddenly a young child runs out from behind a parked car into the roadway. The driver instantly slams on her brakes, but it is too late. The truck strikes the child and kills it.

These are not hard cases, either for morals or law. The truck driver appears an innocent actor—she bears no fault in the child's death, even though her uncoerced, rational act of driving caused the child's traumatic death. The hired killer, by contrast, has not only committed a crime, but one that we will probably classify at the highest level of culpability. Nevertheless, the cases illustrate the many different kinds of mens rea rules that the criminal law employs.

Among the most important category distinctions made by mens rea rules is that between an intentional and an unintentional wrong.[3] The hit man's case illustrates the classic pattern of intentional criminality, where the offender seeks to harm the victim. We ask a very limited why question about the accused's conduct: Why did he fire the gun as he did? Did he intend to kill someone? The facts indicate he did intend to kill: he wanted to kill in order to collect his second payment.

By contrast, the truck driver did not intend to kill the child. Instead we will characterize the incident as an accident; to use Holmes's terms it appears that the driver stumbled rather than deliberately kicked. But the lack of intent to harm will not be definitive as to guilt. As we will see, we may still blame the truck driver according to other forms of mens rea.

Moving beyond intent to harm we find a set of mens rea distinctions that turn on awareness of harm. We may ask about the truck driver: Was she aware of the danger to the child before she hit the brakes? In this case, the facts indicate no prior awareness. If for some reason the driver had realized, prior to the incident, that her driving posed a significant risk to persons like the child who was killed, she might be found guilty under a standard of either knowledge, or more likely, recklessness.[4]

If the driver was not aware of the danger until too late, we still might raise culpability questions about notice of danger and general attitude toward endangering others. Assuming that the driver only spotted the child at the last second, was she paying enough attention to her driving? Did she miss seeing the danger earlier because she was listening to the radio or talking on a cell phone? Did her conduct prior to the accident indicate that she acted with general disregard for the welfare of others? These considerations inform the oft-used mens rea of negligence and another form of mens rea called indifference which is discussed at length in chapter 9.[5]

In American homicide offenses, we find several unique forms of mens rea that analyze the emotional and deliberative quality of the accused's choice. In the next chapter we see that many jurisdictions ask decision-makers to determine whether the purposeful killer premeditated about his homicidal act in order to judge liability for first-degree murder. Here the law seems to address not just what the individual chose to do, but how he chose—whether the homicide was carefully and coolly considered. The hit man's conduct exemplifies this kind of mens rea: his crime was well planned and efficiently, presumably calmly executed. Similarly, we see in chapter 8 that most jurisdictions provide a special category for heat of passion killings, those homicides committed under specially provoking circumstances. Here the spontaneous and emotional quality of the homicide contributes to the classification of the killing as a less severe offense.

Finally, mens rea may address the motive for the conduct. Motive addresses the underlying reason for action. For example, assume an offense that requires proof of intent to kill. Intent to kill involves why the person acted as he did—why did the accused pull the trigger while holding the gun as he did. If, as in our hit-man example, the answer is that the accused sought the victim's death, the intent question is answered affirmatively. But in some cases we might want to know more than this. We might ask a further why question, about motive. Why did the accused want to kill the victim? We know that the hit man made a financial arrangement to kill, thus profit was the motive for the crime. For reasons explored further in the next chapter, this motive should constitute an aggravating factor in our assessment of the offense. But as we will see in chapter 8, motive may also represent a mitigating factor. When the accused had good reason for great anger at the victim, this motivation, in combination with sudden passion, may convince the decision maker to convict of a lesser offense.

The nonlawyer may ask at this point: why do we need all of these different rules? Why don't we just stick with the biblical commandment, thou shalt not kill?[6] The reason is that even with a deed as harmful as homicide, our moral code is complex, and we need legal rules to express important moral distinctions. We need to distinguish homicide cases, not only as to guilt or innocence, but as to degree of offense. The serial killer and the barroom brawler who kills his opponent should not be punished alike. Some will respond—Why not leave those distinctions to sentencing? Certainly many important moral distinctions are left to sentencer discretion rather than being written into law. The real issue here is division of power. Who do we want to make the most important decisions about culpability—judge or jury? If the jury only makes a crude decision about liability, then the most important legal decisions, even in cases that go to trial, will be left to the sentencing judge.[7] The formal structure of American law has always given the jury a more central role than this, asking that jurors set the basic parameters of punishment by resolving the category of offense, with the fine-tuning of punishment left up to the judge at sentencing. The same presumption guides my arguments for legal reform.

Rule Drafting: Allusive and Analytic Styles of Mens Rea

Determining the proper mens rea definition for criminal offenses requires more than conceptual analysis; it requires effective expression. As we saw in chapter 5, American criminal law requires rules that clearly and completely express our best moral intuitions about the wrongdoing involved in the offense. Unfortunately, in drafting mens rea rules, the aims of clarity and complete expression stand in considerable tension with each other. If we define wrongdoing broadly in order to encompass all relevant moral considerations, we also increase the hazards of vagueness. If we define the wrong narrowly so as to reduce vagueness, we increase the chance that important moral considerations will be excluded.[8] This tension becomes clearer when we examine the two dominant styles of mens rea expression—the allusive and the analytic.

The allusive style of mens rea as I call it defines wrongdoing according to a general moral characteristic revealed by conduct. The mens rea expression alludes to the central wrong by moralistic description rather than by defining the particular features of the choice or conduct involved.[9] By contrast, the analytic style defines wrongdoing by describing particular aspects of harm doing, such as the actor's goal or state of mind, usually without explicit moral language. The analytic style aims to divide wrongdoing into component parts; if the requisite parts are present, the conclusion of legal and moral condemnation should follow automatically.

English common law relied heavily on the allusive style. Mens rea requirements were often described in vague, moralistic and emotive terms such as "malicious," or "depraved," "willfull" or "wanton." The language was that of character judgment, and courts assumed that in judging the criminal conduct they were making character assessments as well. For example, in determining that malice aforethought was proven in a case, a Pennsylvania court held that the homicidal act was "without any just cause of provocation to take life, and, therefore, evidenced a heart malignant, and ready to execute vengeance even upon a friend, in a moment of wicked passion."[10] Later the court distinguished between mental or emotional disturbances that constituted mitigation from what it called "evil passions" in this way: "Evil passions do often seem to tear up reason by the root, and urge on to murder with heedless rage. But they are the outpourings of a wicked nature, not of an unsound or disabled mind."[11]

In the nineteenth century, and continuing into the twentieth, Anglo-American law turned away from overtly moralistic standards of mens rea in favor of definitions that categorize behavior according to particular beliefs or desires, especially with respect to intent and awareness.[12] The most noted analytic definitions of mens rea are the basic culpability definitions in the Model Penal Code (MPC), a draft code published in 1960 by the American Law Institute, a group of practicing lawyers, judges, and legal academics. The MPC contains a hierarchy of four basic forms of culpability: purpose, knowledge, recklessness, and negligence. The MPC, which has influenced legal reforms in many states, exemplifies the modern trend in Anglo-American criminal law to define mens rea according to the offender's conscious desire for or awareness of the harm involved.[13]

The MPC also contains mens rea provisions that may be characterized as allusive, however. Although lacking the colorful moral language of the common law, these provisions similarly rely on general principles of morality to guide decision makers. For example, the code defines a form of reckless murder that requires proof of "extreme indifference to the value of human life." Indifference represents a moral characteristic not defined by specific conduct, intent or state of awareness. Recklessness under the code also contains allusive elements. In order to be found reckless a person must disregard a risk so substantial and unnecessary that "its disregard involves a gross deviation from the standard of conduct that a law-abiding person would observe in the actor's situation."[14] Here the decision-maker's main guide is the character of a law-abiding person. Similarly, the code provides that a person acts with criminal negligence if "considering the nature and purpose of his conduct and the circumstances known to him," the individual's conduct "involves a gross deviation from the standard of care that a reasonable person would observe in the actor's situation."[15] Here the reasonable person's characteristic perceptions and actions provide the legal test.[16]

All this brings us to the critical drafting question: which of these approaches should we prefer? Unfortunately, there is no general answer because the advantages and disadvantages of each will be inextricably intertwined with the particulars of the offense they are employed to define. Thus in homicide, the question of mens rea style must be answered individually with respect to each of the major forms of murder and manslaughter.

Nevertheless, there are some general considerations we should keep in mind with respect to the drafting of criminal law. Preliminarily we need to review the idea of risk of error—the extent that rule drafting must take into consideration the potential for erroneous interpretations and applications by decision makers. And then we must acknowledge the eight-hundred-pound gorilla in the matter of rule drafting: public opinion.

No matter how much effort we put into their wording, no matter whether we prefer allusive or analytic styles, mens rea rules will produce morally wrong results in some cases. The mistakes may stem from an error in the rule's wording, or in the way the decision maker applies it; but like all other human rules employed by human decision makers, mistakes about mens rea are inevitable. Granting this, the question becomes, What can we do to minimize the worst kinds of mistakes?

In criminal law, mistakes come in two varieties: erroneous convictions and erroneous acquittals. The Anglo-American legal system, with its emphasis on individual liberty and rights, frequently expresses a greater concern with erroneous convictions, thus the famous saying "better that ten guilty men go free than that one innocent be convicted." Applying this adage to criminal law, we should err on the side of underinclusiveness—rules that are too narrow—because this minimizes the chance of erroneous convictions. This would seem to favor the analytic as opposed to the allusive style of mens rea. But the reality of criminal justice is opposite: politicians strongly favor overinclusive rules, because they know the public prefers rules that may punish too much instead of rules that may punish too little.

In the modern United States, elected politicians make criminal statutes, often in a highly partisan, politicized manner. This means that criminal rules must win popular approval, or at least avoid popular condemnation. And the worst flaw that a criminal law may have in the modern public's view is not overbreadth but underinclusiveness. The public fears a law that may punish too little far more than one that punishes too much.[17]

The public readily assumes that even if the law is overbroad as written, its overbreadth will be cured by the exercise of police and prosecutorial discretion. Governmental authorities will assure that only the true "bad guys" will be prosecuted. The public assumes that if the executive authorities fail to exercise adequate discretion, then judges and juries will fill the gap. These assumptions about the legal process are almost certainly naive, at least with regard to poor and minority defendants, but that does not change their political power. The bottom line is that for political reasons, offense definitions are far more likely to be overinclusive than underinclusive. No proposed change in the criminal law that risks significant underinclusiveness will be taken seriously. This limits how far we can go in replacing allusive mens rea with analytic, and broad rules with narrow ones.

Again this discussion must remain preliminary. The critical analysis of mens rea must await the consideration of specific homicide offenses. Only one other matter lies between us and that consideration: meeting the general objections that have been raised to the whole idea of mens rea as the basis for criminal judgment.

Understanding Reasons and Choice—The Challenge of Cognitive Science

All forms of mens rea discussed so far assume that we can understand human behavior according to the beliefs and desires of the individual involved. In this respect mens rea analysis employs the same background assumptions and analytic methods of ordinary life. We normally assume that if a person desires strawberry ice cream, and is offered such a treat, she will accept it. We say that she had a reason for acting as she did—she wanted a strawberry cone with sprinkles, believed that she was being offered one, and so jumped at the chance. This method of analyzing conduct, which cognitive scientists often term folk psychology, provides a generally reliable way of interpreting human behavior in our everyday interactions. In recent years a number of philosophers and cognitive scientists have raised serious doubts about the validity of such reason analysis, however. They contend that new insights into how human intelligence works show that reasons as we normally understand them do not exist. If such objectors are right, the long-standing effort to draft mens rea rules in criminal law according to reasons for conduct must be abandoned.

The concerns raised by cognitive science about reason analysis start with our physical understanding of the human brain. Most who study human behavior today reject the dualist argument of René Descartes who maintained that the mind, which governs choice, is an organ entirely separate from the physical body. Instead, nearly all scientists and philosophers assume that the brain is the locus of choice. All mental activity occurs within the physical brain, therefore all choice must be in some sense reducible to physical processes. This means that our understanding of brain dynamics has important implications for our understanding of responsible choice.

In the last thirty years, research in computer science, neurobiology, and psychology have produced many new insights into how the human brain works. Where before we had to rely on human introspection—thinking about our own thinking—to understand human intelligence, now we have reliable data from objective observers in neurobiology, computer science, and other fields to tell us about the functioning of human intelligence. The new data about human intelligence describe a different kind of process than reason analysis presumes. While some cognitive scientists have theorized that brain states correlate with the beliefs and desires of ordinary understanding, current research into the brain has not produced much evidence to support this position.[18] Scientists cannot tell from electrical, chemical, or other examination of the brain whether the individual has a particular belief or desire. There seems to be no physical dimension to reasons.

Equally challenging to traditional moral thinking is the dynamic of brain activity that cognitive scientists report. We often presume that human choice is a linear process of information perception, organization, and finally decision. We presume that it has a determinate beginning, middle, and end. Many scientists now believe that the brain functions as a neural network, in which brain cells make complex, interactive, and overlapping connections with one another to process information and produce decisions. Instead of a central intelligence unit or brain core that organizes conscious thought in a single, linear, chronological decision process, scientists see a highly competitive, ever-changing interaction of rival perceptive and analytic processes. There is no central intelligence and no single definitive view of what the person knows or desires. At best, we can speak of particular perceptions, ideas, and desires that predominate at particular times.[19]

For my purposes I assume this new picture of brain function is accurate. The question now becomes: What does this do to culpability based on reason analysis, with its presumption of discrete and ascertainable beliefs and desires? Some cognitive scientists and philosophers insist that the new understanding of human intelligence makes reason analysis as obsolete as phrenology, the nineteenth-century "science" of categorizing intelligence and personality according to skull configuration.[20] I disagree. While cognitive science provides a corrective to some sloppy tendencies to which we are prone in reason analysis, we should not confuse explanations of the mechanics of mentality with judgments about the meaning of choice.

We can start by asking whether anything in the new understanding of the brain contradicts reason analysis. Have we learned anything that makes talk about beliefs, desires, motives, and the like fundamentally ridiculous? The answer is no. Return to our original mens rea examples. Nothing cognitive science has shown us in recent years invalidates our judgment that the hit man had a particular understanding about money and killing that provided the motivation for his action. Cognitive science may make us more careful in our description of the hit man's choice, making us more aware of the complexity and contingency of his decision-making process, but it does not preclude the concept of acting for a reason, nor does it undercut the normative significance of reason analysis.

As we did in chapter 2, we have to distinguish the aims of responsibility analysis from those of scientific explanation. In criminal law we are not concerned with the most accurate description of the physical mechanisms of mental decision making. For example, we could imagine a criminal law system that would apply to several different intelligent species, each with different brain systems. In criminal law we are concerned with responsibility for the use of intelligence. We are concerned with the meaning of choice.

In law we care about the reasons for human action because reasons provide the action's human meaning. The truck's fatal collision with the child has a very different meaning for us if we understand that it was accidental— that the driver was conducting herself safely and the child suddenly and unpredictably ran into her path—than if we believe that the driver deliberately steered toward the child in an effort to kill it. The driver's beliefs and desires matter because they relate to our norms of conduct. In terms of the neural networking of the brain, this analysis is no doubt simplistic, but it is simplistic to a purpose. It focuses on the aspect of the choice process that we care about most—and that the driver should care about most.

Again we see the importance of perspective, of the difference between moral analysis that starts with the human experience of choice, and scientific analysis that seeks observer-independent criteria. Science seeks to understand human intelligence by "taking the top off" and watching it work. With new forms of brain scans and computer modeling, among other research techniques, such observation is now feasible. But the fact that we can learn about intelligence in a different, physicalist way does not mean that all understanding about intelligence must reduce to physicalist explanations. If love cannot be reduced to biology and biology cannot be reduced to chemistry, then why must we assume that human choice is reducible to neurochemical brain states?

As in chapter 2, we see that the moralist and the scientist pursue different questions, based on different basic assumptions, which lead to different answers. The moralist assumes that life has meaning and devises responsibility rules accordingly. Desiring to know how the human world should be ordered, she makes normative judgments about human conduct. By contrast the scientist assumes that understanding comes from verifiable observation of the physical world. She seeks explanation through physical causes. The two enterprises overlap and interact, but we court serious confusion if we think them essentially the same.

To put this another way, the most radical critics of reason analysis argue that we should stop talking about reasons and speak instead of the actual physical dynamics of brain activity. Yet such a language would be fundamentally inadequate to our everyday human needs. Even if we understood perfectly the physical mechanisms of the brain, we would still have to take a normative stand on human behavior. We would still have to decide what we think of it. We may want to revise the terms of reason analysis, but by virtue of our commitment to choice and meaning, we are fundamentally committed to normative assessment of reasons.[21]

The separation of scientific and normative realms is by no means complete, however. Properly understood, cognitive science can play an important role in responsibility theory. Cognitive science sets important constraints on our conception of responsible choice. For example, in the next section we consider a common metaphor for choice that describes it as the product of an internal chooser within the mind. Cognitive science helps us see the absurdity of this conception of choice and so helps prevent some common misconceptions about the assessment of others' choices. In chapter 9 we will see that cognitive science provides new insights into perceptive processes, which in turn informs our concept of responsibility for perception, an important element of responsibility for carelessness. Cognitive science may well inform our understanding of the relation between dispassionate and passionate decision making, an important issue in both chapters 7 and 8. In each instance, scientific understandings of the brain do not eliminate reason analysis but allow us to conceive of it in a different way.

Assessing Chosen Action: The Proof of Mens Rea

Having defended reason analysis against its scientific doubters, we must now mount a defense to critics who employ so-called common sense to question its reliability. We must rebut the notion that judging another person's reasons for acting is a fundamentally hazardous task, because it involves guesswork concerning internal mental events that only the chooser can assess directly. If this is true, it would render nearly all forms of mens rea unprovable.

In all homicide cases, to win conviction the prosecution must prove beyond a reasonable doubt that the offender acted with the required mens rea. Normally this is the hardest part of the prosecution's case. The accused may know why he acted as he did, but how can anyone else? As one nineteenth-century jurist wrote concerning a claim of self-defense: "The prisoner says he believed his life was in danger. Who can look into his heart? If the *law* allows *him* to judge, who can contradict him? The [physical] circumstances are nothing; it is his *belief* that justifies him."[22] Modern lawyers commonly speak of the difficulty of reading another's mind in order to determine mens rea.[23] All of this suggests a nearly impossible task for the prosecution. But once we have cleared away the misconception of choice that drives this objection, we can see that assessing reasons for others' conduct requires no special powers. It simply involves another instance of applying our general understanding of human behavior to a particular situation.

The reading-minds objection, as I will call it, is based on a common misconception of choice. In philosophic terms, it expresses a dualist view of the relationship between mind and body. It assumes, as Descartes argued, that mind and body occupy separate realms. Descartes asserted that because mind is separate from body, and is uniquely the realm of the self, that only the self has direct access to its workings. Each of us may introspect directly and accurately about our own choices. Others may make inferences about our choices, but only the chooser knows for sure. This means that, absent sincere confession, proof of mens rea will always be problematic.

Of course one need not have heard of Descartes to be a dualist. In fact, the most common understandings about what choice is and how it works reveal dualist assumptions. Witness the metaphor of the internal chooser, a metaphor that informs a great deal of thinking about choice. According to this metaphor, our choices are the work of minichoosers in our minds. We imagine a tiny human agent, a "humunculus" or "ghost in the machine" who directs all mental activity. This internal chooser operates something like an air traffic controller directing airplane landings and takeoffs: she absorbs information from a variety of external sources and, exercising her own considered discretion, produces decisions to act. Or perhaps the internal chooser operates more like a computer following a program that prioritizes actions depending on the situation and a list of operative desires.[24] In accord with its dualist assumptions, the metaphor suggests that the choosing person may accurately recount the decision process of her own internal chooser, but that outside observers will be limited in their assessment to educated guesses based on the person's observable behavior.[25]

I call this vision a metaphor for choice because it does not purport to supply a literal description of choice, but provides an analogy for its workings. The metaphor gives us a way of imagining how choices are made. As with any metaphor, the question we must ask is whether the metaphor assists our understanding of the underlying phenomenon. Does the metaphor of the internal chooser illuminate choice? Or does it obscure more than it reveals?

Philosophers, legal scholars, and others have long recognized the absurdity of this conception of choice. Its very description reveals its incoherence. No one really believes that we have within ourselves another little person who makes all the decisions. Moreover, the conception is obviously incomplete. The metaphor does not explain what needs explaining—how choices are actually made. The metaphor just transfers the problem from the whole person to the person's internal chooser. It does not explain how the internal chooser chooses.[26]

Work in cognitive science has further undercut the metaphor's claim to useful guidance. We have seen that conscious thought seems to emerge from a never-ending, interactive process; it does not represent a particular stage in thinking, and does not occur in a particular place. There is no central processing unit or consciousness center that works in the way we imagine an internal chooser might. Similarly, cognitive science casts serious doubt on the metaphor's picture of mentality divided into stages of passive perception and information organization followed by active decision making.[27]

But despite all the evidence against it, the metaphor of the internal chooser still influences our understanding of choice. Even as we reject it on logical grounds, we unconsciously return to it in our language. The problem is that we have a hard time imagining choice in any other way. As discussed in chapters 2 and 3, we recognize and value each other largely according to choices—what we choose to say and do. Indeed, we distinguish humans from all other creatures and things based on the ability to choose. Therefore choice is quintessentially human—and hard to imagine without a human face. We also know that choice occurs inside us, within the mind. And our experience of choice suggests an internal dynamic in which a variety of inputs and priorities are sorted to produce a decision. The internal chooser metaphor simply combines these notions into a dynamic image: that of a minihuman who absorbs, sorts, and decides.

Even the most sophisticated views of culpability are susceptible to the influence of the internal chooser metaphor. Without any explicit articulation of the metaphor, legal doctrines may reflect its basic conception of choice. For example, juries are commonly instructed: "The intent of a person or the knowledge that a person possesses at any given time may not ordinarily be proved directly because there is no way of directly scrutinizing the workings of the human mind."[28] Here we see the standard dualist suggestion that evidence about choice lies uniquely in the mind of the accused. Unless the accused tells us, we will have no "direct" evidence of mens rea.

Courts have solved the apparent problem of proving mens rea by special evidentiary instructions. First, courts urge juries to employ "indirect" evidence of mens rea. Thus jurors may be told that "[i]ntent is a subjective matter which can seldom be proven with direct evidence. Rather, you may infer the defendant's intent from all the surrounding circumstances of the case."[29] Second, courts instruct juries that they may presume mens rea from proof of certain probabilities. Juries have traditionally been told that "[u]nless there is evidence presented to the contrary, the law presumes that a person intends the natural and probable consequences of his actions."[30] Thus mens rea may be proven by a probability calculation. If the defendant's action was likely to cause the particular result, then the jury may presume, in the absence of contrary evidence, that the defendant sought that result. The problem with this instruction is that while it states a general truth, it does not cover all relevant situations. While most who commit acts likely to harm others also desire this result, or at least realize the result will likely follow, the trial of a criminal case is not concerned with "most" people. A trial concerns a particular defendant and a particular event. The case may present the unusual situation of an act likely to harm done by a person who neither desired nor realized the likelihood of this result. In such a case the natural and probable consequence instruction effectively requires the defendant to prove that his case stands as an exception to the standard rule. Requiring such proof by the defendant contradicts the constitutional requirement that the prosecution prove all essential elements, including mens rea, beyond a reasonable doubt.[31]

From this we see that the internal chooser metaphor does more harm than good. We should banish it from our thinking about choice. But how? The solution comes not in devising a new metaphor for choice, but in shifting attention from the internal dynamic of choice to its meaning in context. Instead of concentrating on what transpires within the chooser's mind, we should concentrate on the accused's conduct and the surrounding events that permit us to make interpretations about the reasons for that conduct. Our concern here is with the meaning of conduct—why the person acted as she did, not how she arrived at the decision to act in this way.

Determining reasons for conduct may be hard in many cases, but not because it relies on specially mysterious, hidden evidence. We require neither Godlike insights into the human mind nor documentation of brain activity. Based on our extensive background information about human behavior, we can observe conduct and reach relatively reliable judgments about why the person acted as she did: what she sought, what she realized might occur, and how much she looked out for the welfare of others. We can make these judgments because from our own personal experience of human conduct, and the collective observations of humankind, we know a great deal about the range of human motivations, intentions, attitudes, and awareness. In the courtroom as elsewhere, we can make sense of conduct by seeing if it fits a recognized pattern of human conduct.

To return to our earlier examples, when we see a man receive a significant sum of money from another and later point a deadly weapon at a third person, a stranger to the man but a person with whom the payor had a dispute, and the weapon discharges, killing the third person, are there any great mysteries as to why the shooter acted as he did? It certainly looks like a contract killing. We will have to consider alternative interpretations of these events, but there will be few stories that make as much human sense of this situation as that the shooter purposely killed the victim in order to fulfill his homicidal contract.

This does not mean that assessment of reasons for conduct will be easy or noncontroversial. Such assessment involves the decision maker's individual experiences and sensibilities, which vary from person to person, meaning that decisions will often be disputed. It also means that the accuracy of such decisions cannot be independently verified. There is no way to determine that a mens rea decision is right or wrong by purely objective means. Finally, assessment of reasons can prove difficult because we often lack sufficient information about individuals and context. The less we know about the persons involved and the context of the interaction, the less chance we have of making sound judgments about the conduct. If all we know of the hit man offense is the split second interaction between shooter and victim, all kinds of scenarios are plausible—among them self-defense, heat of passion, and even some form of accident.

Reconciling Chooser and Observer Points of View: Further Considerations in Drafting Mens Rea Rules

An important practical problem in the proof of mens rea remains. Even assuming we focus on reasons for conduct rather than the internal choice process, how does the decision maker synthesize information received from two different sources: the chooser and the observer of the choice? If we hear rival accounts of an incident from the accused and from a witness to the accused's action, how do we reconcile them? And what happens if we have information only from one kind of source? These are important questions for the criminal process, and if we can adequately address them, we will go a long way to curing some basic misconceptions about mens rea.

As an example, assume that a mother is charged with child abuse for hitting her toddler with a frying pan. A neighbor who witnessed the incident states that the mother deliberately slung the frying pan at the child after the child spilled her milk. But the mother testifies that the greasy pan slipped from her hand and accidentally struck the child. Who should we believe? How can we assess the relative strengths and weaknesses of these accounts?

As we have seen, the internal chooser metaphor emphasizes the first-person perspective: only the mother truly knows the reasons for her choice. This means that as long as she does not lie about her perceptions, we must believe her account. Yet we have rejected the internal chooser metaphor, finding that it distorts our picture of choice more than it reveals. Does our new focus on the accused's reasons for action mean that we should now emphasize third-person information? In many cases the answer is yes, but here we have to be cautious about general rules. Assessment of reasons for action requires careful attention to all sources of information, including first-person and third-person accounts. As we will see, each kind of source has unique evidentiary advantages and disadvantages.

The chooser has one great evidentiary advantage over all other sources of information about her behavior: she has superior access to subjective data about the incident. Only the accused mother can provide an authoritative account of the subjective experience of her handling of the frying pan and her child's injury. She can tell us what she recalls seeing, understanding, and feeling. This does not mean that the chooser is necessarily the most reliable reporter, however.

In most cases the chooser's account will be affected by her desire to justify her conduct to herself and others. This desire for self-justification may inspire the chooser to lie about feelings and thoughts. Or the desire for self-justification may operate at a less conscious level, influencing the chooser's own understanding of the event. In reconsidering the event, the chooser may engage in self-deception. What the chooser wants to believe about herself becomes what she actually believes. The mother may now sincerely believe that the child's injury was accidental, even though at the moment she slung the frying pan, she wished to hurt the child. Finally, we have to recognize that persons vary enormously according to their powers of self-insight. Some people devote considerable time and energy to understanding themselves and can provide elaborate and articulate explanations of conduct. Others display relatively poor self-understanding. They do not wonder why they acted in a certain way; they avoid introspection. As a result, such persons will not be able to provide much information about their behavior.

What about the observer of conduct? How reliable is her information about the chooser's reasons for action? Obviously the observer of another's conduct lacks access to the actual experience of choice. The observer must read emotion from facial expression, body language, and context. The observer may be fooled by individual peculiarities of the chooser; for example, she may interpret an habitual scowl as evidence of rage. And the observer will have her own individual biases that can affect perception and recall.

The observer has other information advantages, though. The observer sees things the chooser cannot. For example, the chooser will not likely see or sense her own facial expression, and may not hear the tone of her own voice. Along these lines, a colleague once told me that in teaching a legal writing class he made a great blunder in providing his students with individual cassette tapes containing his recorded comments on their papers. He provided the tapes to save time, not realizing that his frustration with their writing problems made him sound angry and even disgusted on the tapes. He was astonished by the student resentment which resulted, and believed the students were overreacting until he was confronted by the tape-recorded evidence. When he listened to the tapes and became a third-party observer to his own conduct he realized what he had done. This underscores the observer's greatest advantage in culpability assessment: an independent stance that generally permits less biased interpretation of conduct.

The tension between observer and chooser reports provides a last set of general considerations for the drafting of mens rea requirements. In addition to the broad rules versus narrow rules and allusive versus analytic tensions considered earlier, we now must consider the extent that the rule probes the internal choice process versus focusing on the external characteristics of choice. The more the mens rea rule requires judgments about the internal dynamics of decision making, the more that first-person accounts will be privileged or that decision makers will have to rely on indirect inferences to make critical judgments.

The mens rea's of premeditation, and to a lesser extent provocation, provide the clearest examples of rules that require judgments about internal mental dynamics. As we will see in chapter 8, a murder is premeditated if the decision to kill was coolly and calculatedly made. The theory is that the homicidal decision is worse if the person clearly considered the consequences of his action before the deed. While there are many external criteria from which we may infer premeditation—planning activities, speech, facial expressions—the real test must be what occurs within the chooser, leading us back to the objection with which we started—the need to be a mind reader. Here the mind-reading objection has real force. The mens rea does require an examination of information directly accessible only to the chooser. Similarly, some forms of provocation mens rea also require the decision maker to assess the emotionality of choice and degree of internal self-control. As we will see in chapter 9, such mens rea's also place untenable demands on the readily available evidence.

Conclusion

When I was younger I thought that the most significant device human science could ever produce would be a machine that would allow an individual to experience life as another person. If each of us could, just for a brief while, enter into the thoughts and feelings of another human being, then return to our own identity with a complete memory of the experience, we might attain a new level of human understanding. If whites could live for a while as blacks, and vice versa, if women could sense life as men, it could change the world. We would go from imagining another's experience to *knowing* it as our own.

I still think such a device would be beneficial, but I no longer believe it would change the world. Right now we know more than enough to understand each other's experiences. Without any special machinery or training we can empathize with others' situations and assess others' reasons for conduct. We can do these things because we share the human condition. What prevents us from accomplishing these ends is not ability, but desire. We find it easier to make simplistic, biased judgments than to exercise our best judgment and recognize the moral complexities or hard moral truths involved.

In this chapter we have reviewed the many potential forms of mens rea and reviewed some of the general considerations relevant to drafting mens rea rules. We have addressed two basic objections to the whole enterprise of judging others' conduct based on assessment of their reasons for action. We have, in other words, laid the basic moral and legal foundation for the work still to come. Now we must apply the theory of responsibility developed in part 1 and general concepts of mens rea developed here to the particulars of our most serious category of violent offense: homicide.

7

The Worst Crime of All

On the night of January 15, 1978, Ted Bundy went hunting. He had done it many times before. He was good at it. He wore several layers of clothes so he could change quickly. He carried at least three pairs of knotted pantyhose that he could use as a mask or a ligature. And he had a club that he had fashioned from a tree branch wrapped with cloth. This made a deadly weapon which could not be traced to him as a gun might be.

Bundy had arrived in Tallahassee, Florida, a few weeks earlier, after having escaped from jail in Colorado, where he faced a murder charge. He found lodgings in a rooming house near the campus of Florida State University. He liked college campuses. He had a college degree and had attended law school for a while. But mostly he liked college campuses because he liked to hunt women students.

That night he hung out at a bar frequented by Florida State students. Later in the evening he apparently tried to attack a young woman nearby, but she ran from him and escaped. Later Bundy went to a campus sorority house, that of Chi Omega. It was early in the morning when he entered the sorority through a door with a bad lock. Once inside, he went wild. He entered the room of Lisa Levy. As he had done many times before, he smashed the woman in the head with a blunt object, this time his club. The crushing blow laid open her skull. He raped her and sodomized her with an aerosol can. He bit her buttocks, leaving a deep mark in her flesh.

Bundy then went across the hall and attacked Karen Chandler. His blows broke Chandler's jaw, fractured her skull, the bones surrounding one eye, both her cheekbones, and opened deep cuts in her face. He also attacked Chandler's roommate, Kathy Kleiner, again smashing her in the face. Her jaw was broken and some of her teeth were knocked out. Blood from the two women spattered everywhere, even on the ceiling. Bundy moved on.

In another room he found Margaret Bowman, who he clubbed and strangled to death. Then he heard the sound of someone coming into the sorority and he fled. On his way back to his rooming house, Bundy stopped to break into the apartment of Cheryl Thomas, a twenty-one-year-old dance student. While she slept he smashed her jaw. Police later discovered a pantyhose mask and a large semen stain on Thomas's bloody bed.

Thomas and two of the Sigma Chi victims survived Bundy's attacks. Levy and Bowman died. Before he was caught, Bundy killed one more time: twelve-year-old Kimberly Leach. He took Leach from the grounds of her junior high, then raped and killed her.[1]

After his Florida arrest, Bundy became one of America's best-known serial killers. Until the day he was executed in the state's electric chair eleven years later, he made local and national news. The press and public were fascinated with the contrast between Bundy's social persona and his crimes. Why would a handsome, well-educated, and intelligent young man commit such vicious crimes? I pursue a related, but slightly different question here. Many will agree that Bundy's crimes are among the most heinous imaginable. But why? What is the evil of these deeds and how should it be legally defined? What is it that makes some criminal killings worse than others? What is the hallmark of the worst wrongdoing?

In contemporary law, the worst form of murder takes two basic forms: premeditation and felony murder. In most jurisdictions a homicide will be first-degree murder if it was either premeditated, usually meaning that the killing was in some sense calmly considered, or if it occurred during the commission of a serious felony. Thus under the law of most American jurisdictions, Bundy was guilty of the first-degree murder of his Sigma Chi victims both because (1) the killings were purposeful and premeditated, and (2) they occurred in the course of committing the felonies of burglary or sexual assault.[2]

In this chapter I argue that the doctrines of premeditation and felony murder are seriously flawed. In practice, both concepts are overbroad, permitting the classification of too many killings in the worst offense category. Both doctrines rest on flawed moral theory as well. Premeditation assumes that the worst wrongs involve the most extended, dispassionate consideration of wrongdoing, and while this is often so, it is not always. Meanwhile, the felony murder doctrine draws on the common view that we can categorize humans into Criminals and Law-abiding and should apply different rules of responsibility to each, such that any homicide committed during certain felonies automatically becomes murder. I argue that as a matter of theory this approach is morally indefensible, but has survived in practice because it produces morally justifiable results in many cases, and in the remainder our instinctive antipathies to the felon outweigh our moral reservations. In place of these doctrines I argue for a new offense definition based on purpose to kill and certain especially bad motives for killing.

The moral argument developed here is one that will be repeated through-out the remainder of the book—that we should look harder at the many forms of human evil. In offenses like those committed by Bundy, we con-front the darkest side of humanity, and our tendency is to be satisfied with vague moral and legal language that expresses our instinctive repulsion. We assume that we know such deeds when we see them and do not need to ex-plore their sickening details. But as we will see, the task of separating the "av-erage" murder from the worst is subject to all the otherness temptations dis-cussed in previous chapters, and has important implications for our own moral conduct. Whatever is worst in these homicide offenses may give us im-portant clues to what is worst in other human conduct. We need to look hard even when we would rather turn away.

Before introducing the basics of the premeditation and felony murder doctrines, I should note one important limitation on the chapter's scope. This chapter concerns the definition of the most aggravated form of murder, that which merits the law's most severe sentence, but I consider the question of offense definition apart from actual sentence. In particular, I take no specific account of the death penalty; that is, I assume that the maximum penalty is different only in degree from lesser sanctions. As I argued in the preface, this is *not* true of capital punishment; I do not believe anyone deserves to die as punishment. My concern here is not with punishment but guilt: How should we define the worst form of murder?

Premeditation

For most of this nation's history, premeditated murder has occupied the highest level on the criminal hierarchy of most jurisdictions. In both ordi-nary talk about murder and in the formal rules of law, we find the idea that a cool and preconceived design to kill is the hallmark of the worst form of homicide. In this section I argue that the moral force of the doctrine comes from the way that premeditation often serves as a proxy for the worst mo-tives to kill, and that culpability analysis should focus on those motives, not the coolness or calculation of the decision to do wrong.

Premeditation doctrine has several historical antecedents. Although Eng-lish law has never formally included a rule of premeditation, early English murder definitions contained similar ideas.[3] In pre-Norman times "murth" or "murther" meant a secret killing.[4] Secrecy implied (although it did not re-quire) planning, an activity suggestive of reflection and cool emotion at the time of killing. English common law later emphasized *malice prepense*, also called malice aforethought, as the defining element of murder. In its original usage, malice aforethought emphasized planning. The term may have come from the Old Testament admonition that, "if a man shall kill his neighbor deliberately and by lying in wait, thou shalt take him from mine altar that he may die."[5] By contrast, English law deemed a purposeful killing to be manslaughter when it was committed in the heat of passion. As we will see in the next chapter, English law declared voluntary manslaughter a less serious offense than murder because, although purposeful, it was committed upon "chance-medley," that is, in the heat of a physical altercation,[6] or upon stark and immediate provocation, such as a husband's discovery of his wife in the act of adultery.[7]

The American doctrine of premeditation dates back to the late eighteenth century. Following the American Revolution, the new states embarked on a program of criminal justice reforms, hoping to rid their laws of the "sanguinary" punishments of "despotic" England. Leading the way was Pennsylvania, which in 1794 reduced the number of capital offenses and separated murder into two degrees.[8] Declaring that "the several offenses, which are included under the general denomination of murder, differ so greatly from each other in the degree of their atrociousness that it is unjust to involve them in the same punishment,"[9] the Pennsylvania legislature limited capital punishment to certain felony murders and "all murder perpetrated by poison or by lying in wait, or by any kind of wilful, premeditated and deliberate killing."[10] All other murders were designated murders of the second degree to be punished by imprisonment at hard labor. Many other states followed suit, and by the early twentieth century most American jurisdictions recognized some form of premeditation doctrine.[11]

Premeditation has long proved an interpretive challenge to the courts. Because premeditation represented the main distinction between those purposeful killings that were second-degree murder and those that were first-degree, ordinary principles of statutory interpretation suggested that premeditation should mean something more than purpose to kill. On the other hand, following this interpretation might mean relegating some heinous offenses to second-degree status, thus risking the public's wrath. Finally, the concept itself was not exactly self-defining. The jurisprudence of premeditation has reflected all of these tensions.

In the mid-nineteenth century the Pennsylvania Supreme Court quoted with approval the observation of an earlier state jurist that "*no* time is too short for a wicked man to frame in his mind his scheme of murder, and to contrive the means of accomplishing it," thus coining a phrase never far from the lips of prosecutors in a premeditated murder case.[12] The court continued, however: "But this expression must be qualified, lest it mislead. It is true that such is the swiftness of human thought, that no time is so short in which a wicked man may not form a design to kill, and frame the means of executing his purpose; yet this suddenness is opposed to premeditation, and a jury must be well convinced upon the evidence that there was time to deliberate and premeditate. The law regards, and the jury must find ... the fully formed purpose to kill, with so much time for deliberation and premeditation, as to convince them that this purpose is not the immediate offspring of rashness and impetuous temper, and that the mind has become fully conscious of its own design."[13] On another occasion the same court observed that even with time for reflection "causes may affect [the offender's] intellect, preventing reflection, and hurrying onward his unhinged mind to rash and inconsiderate resolutions, incompatible with the deliberation and premeditation defining murder in the first degree."[14]

In these words we find the rationalist argument for premeditation—that the more carefully considered the decision to do wrong, the more the person commits to wrongdoing and the more the wrongdoing reveals the person's essential nature. In just the same way that we may dismiss another's angry retort in a heated verbal argument as the product of passing emotion ("rash and impetuous temper"), but take to heart what the person says in a carefully phrased letter ("a mind fully conscious of its own design"), so we may see the premeditated deed as a clearer revelation of the person. The person who premeditates has reflected upon his own decision to kill, has engaged in "careful thought and weighing of considerations."[15] In other words, he has had a chance to think better of it, and still proceeds. Under the argument from meaning, premeditation suggests a more considered, more complete commitment to attacking human value, which deserves proportionately more punishment.

Even if theoretically justified, emphasis on premeditation raises significant proof problems of the kind discussed in chapter 6. As described by many authorities, including the Pennsylvania Supreme Court, premeditation describes an internal state of mind rather than a reason for action. It may be exemplified by observable conduct, such as planning activities, facial expressions, and words spoken, but in the final analysis, premeditation describes an internal decision process that strongly privileges the first-person observer. Third-party observers must resort to reading secondary signs, signs which themselves are unreliable. For example, timing would seem to be an important aspect to the idea of premeditation: literally, thinking about before. But we find that timing is not a reliable indicator, because the real test is of mental coolness and calculation, which can only be hinted at through timing considerations. Premeditation can occur quickly if the right mental process occurs—the person actual considers and reconsiders the consequences of his conduct. Nor does the passage of time between initial homicidal impulse and act necessarily indicate premeditation. Only if the time period is used for careful thought about killing does premeditation occur. But how are we as outside observers to know? As noted in chapter 6, emphasis on the quality of choice-making (as opposed to type of choice) puts third-person observers at a serious disadvantage. Decision makers may still feel they can judge premeditation, but there will be few means of reviewing the accuracy or the reliability of their judgments.

The doctrinal history of premeditation only reinforces these concerns. Premeditation has proven to be a classic allusive form of mens rea, one that inspires lawyers to make elaborate jury arguments but gives rise to few legal criteria. By the early twentieth century, one of the nation's great state court judges, Benjamin Cardozo, observed that premeditation was essentially a legal device for the exercise of mercy by the jury.[16] Jurors had to decide premeditation, but with little guidance and virtually no oversight by the courts. This trend has continued into the late twentieth century, with many state courts approving determinations of premeditation based on evidence of a "conscious purpose to bring about death."[17] As a matter of law these courts require only proof that the offender desired the victim's death; no separate consideration of planning or coolness is required.[18]

The vagueness of premeditation doctrine has made it hardy—with such open definitions, who can accuse the law of being soft on crime? But vagueness here is no more commendable than anywhere else in the criminal law: it opens decision makers to the otherness temptation. As discussed in previous chapters, decision makers who must rely essentially on intuition to resolve guilt issues may well be influenced by nonmoral factors such as their personal affinities for the accused or the victim.

Premeditation also implicates the ideas about responsibility for emotion critiqued in chapter 5. Premeditation doctrine seems to build on the idea that passion mitigates responsibility because it represents an external force that interferes with rationality. Yet as we saw in chapter 5, emotion has its own rationality, and intensely personal, and thus expressive of the person. We saw there that emotion should not be considered a monolithic force in responsibility; it must be closely analyzed for moral content. Thus the degree of passion or dispassion does not prove a reliable measure of culpability. This becomes clear when we look at cases where courts have, against the general trend, attempted to give independent and enforceable meaning to premeditation.

In the late sixties, the California Supreme Court, then one of the leading liberal courts in the nation, made coolness and calculation a judicially enforced prerequisite for premeditated murder in the case of *People v. Anderson*.[19] In this case the court resolved that premeditation must have a meaning independent of purpose to kill and rigorously applied that independent meaning to the case before it, revealing in the process some of the conceptual inadequacies of premeditation.

In *Anderson* the California Supreme Court found that the prosecution had failed to prove premeditation in a man's ferocious knife assault on a ten-year-old girl, Victoria Hammond. Anderson, who had been drinking heavily, stabbed Victoria more than sixty times. There was no clear evidence that the crime was planned, the manner of killing was frenzied, and the relationship between victim and defendant—Anderson was the live-in boyfriend of the girl's mother—did not suggest a carefully calculated act.[20] The appellate court found insufficient proof of premeditation and reduced Anderson's capital murder conviction to second-degree murder.[21]

As a matter of statutory interpretation, the *Anderson* decision is defensible. Premeditation does seem to involve coolness and calculation, and proof of these was weak at trial.[22] In its three-factor analysis, the court made a commendable effort to provide relatively objective, third-person criteria for what is otherwise a deeply internal analysis. But for all its legal merits, the decision seems morally lacking. Even if we assume the killing was unplanned and impassioned, there were significant aggravating circumstances. The case involved the slaughter of a child by an adult under circumstances that strongly suggested a sexual motivation. The girl was found nude, her body stuffed under her bed, her blood-stained and shredded dress beside her. Under the bed in the master bedroom was her slip, its shoulder straps torn off; a large blood stain covered the center of the bed indicating she had been placed there at one point. Many of the knife wounds were to the girl's genitals.

The butchering of a child for reasons of sexual frustration and rage represents an extreme challenge to the value of human life. It ranks high on any intuitive scale of wrongdoing, and may explain why many appellate courts have been so reluctant to take premeditation seriously—it leads to decisions like *Anderson*. In particular, the case leads us to doubt whether an impassioned decision to kill is necessarily less culpable than a dispassionate one. In

Anderson the source of the rage represents a major aggravating factor. Nor does lack of planning constitute a reliable sign of lesser culpability. As in *Anderson*, depending on motivation, an unplanned killing may present a more culpable offense than a reflective killing by a brooding, self-doubting, self-reflective offender.[23] *Anderson* suggests that what premeditation misses is the moral importance of the motive for the homicide. A case of mercy killing will make the point even more powerfully.

On December 24, 1985, John Forrest went to visit his terminally ill father in the hospital. In his pocket was a pistol.[24] While Forrest sat with his father he became visibly upset by his father's suffering. The North Carolina Supreme Court described what happened next:

> Alone at his father's bedside, defendant began to cry and to tell his father how much he loved him. His father began to cough, emitting a gurgling and rattling sound. Extremely upset, defendant pulled a small pistol from his pants pocket, put it to his father's temple, and fired. He subsequently fired three more times and walked into the hospital corridor, dropping the gun to the floor just outside his father's room.

Forrest admitted the killing to hospital personnel. He said: "You can't do anything to him now. He's out of his suffering. . . . I promised my dad I wouldn't let him suffer."

Forrest was charged with first-degree murder. At trial the court refused to give an instruction for the lesser offense of manslaughter. Three times the jury asked for further explanations of the legal requirements for murder. Finally, the jury convicted Forrest for first-degree murder. The Supreme Court of North Carolina affirmed, stating that premeditation and deliberation were shown by the defendant's use of the gun and statements he made before and after the killing that suggested a degree of planning.

In reaching its decision, the North Carolina Supreme Court was faithful to the doctrine of premeditation, yet its decision is morally doubtful. The defendant's act was wrong, but his motive made his action morally distinguishable from most criminal homicides. Forrest may have killed because of an appreciation of his father and the value of his father's life. He may have respected and cared for his father as a choosing, moral being, and sought his death only because his suffering made a meaningful existence impossible. At the very least, Forrest's motive should have been a mitigating factor leading to conviction of a lesser offense. As Chief Justice Exum noted in dissent:

> Almost all would agree that someone who kills because of a desire to end a loved one's physical suffering caused by an illness which is both terminal and

incurable should not be deemed in law as culpable and deserving of the same punishment as one who kills because of unmitigated spite, hatred or ill will. Yet the Court's decision in this case essentially says that there is no legal distinction between the two kinds of killing. Our law of homicide should not be so roughly hewn as to be incapable of recognizing the difference.

To sum up, the courts have presented us with a choice of premeditation evils. In order to ensure the highest conviction of the most culpable, that is, to avoid cases like *Anderson*, most courts—including the current California Supreme Court—have left premeditation to jury interpretation.[25] This effectively eliminates judicial review of one of the main distinctions between first- and second-degree murder. The law simply trusts jurors, or in some cases trial judges, to get it right. This violates a basic principle of our criminal law, that liability decisions should be subject to judicial review to minimize errors in the application of rules. On the other hand, some courts have strictly interpreted premeditation, in decisions like *Forrest* and *Anderson*, cases which illuminate the definitional error inherent in the concept. A strict interpretation of premeditation will get many cases morally right, largely because premeditation serves as a proxy for motive analysis, but it will get other cases wrong. As in *Anderson*, a conscientious interpretation of premeditation will result in the morally erroneous downgrading of some homicides, and as in *Forrest*, the wrongful upgrading of others.

Felony Murder

The inadequacies of premeditation as a criterion for aggravated murder have remained hidden for many years not only because judges have given it a broad interpretation, but because of the expansive sweep of another homicide doctrine, the felony murder rule. In its simplest form, the felony murder rule holds that an individual is guilty of murder, regardless of actual attitude or intent toward killing, if in the course of committing a particular felony he causes another's death. To take the most common example, if a robber kills another in the course of a robbery, he will be liable for felony murder even if the killing is entirely accidental. The felony murder doctrine essentially covers for the shortcomings of premeditation by providing for first-degree murder convictions where coolness and calculation may not be present but other aggravating factors are. For example, the only reason the premeditation discussion in *Anderson* was critical was because the court also found insufficient proof of an independent felony—in this case child sexual assault—to support felony murder.[26] Had such a felony been proven, first-degree murder status would have been secure, regardless of Anderson's mens rea toward the death of his victim. As we will see, the felony-murder doctrine allows us to treat killings motivated by an immoral reason—such as the successful commission of crime—as extremely serious. Unfortunately, the felony murder rule extends well beyond such cases, making it grossly over-inclusive.

The history of felony murder, like virtually everything about the doctrine, is controversial. Its first articulations are found in the writings of the early commentators on English law, rather than in reported decisions, leading some to wonder whether the doctrine was not the creation of legal commentators rather than judges or legislators.[27] As originally described, the rule was simply stated: the commission of a felony that led to death amounted to the capital offense of felony murder. The great synthesizer of the common law, Sir Edward Coke explained the doctrine as follows:

> If the act [leading to death] be unlawful it is murder. As if A meaning to steale a deer in the park of B, shooteth at the deer, and by the glance of the arrow killeth a boy that is hidden in a bush; this is murder, for that the act was unlawful, although A had no intent to hurt the boy, nor knew not of him. But if B the owner of the park had shot at his own deer, and without any ill intent had killed the boy by the glance of his arrow, this had been homicide by misadventure and no felony.[28]

In other words, the same entirely accidental killing of a boy by a hunter might be murder (a capital offense) or entirely lawful, depending on whether the hunter had the right to hunt in the forest.

The history of the felony murder doctrine since Coke's time has been filled with the efforts of courts and legislatures to avoid distinctions as arbitrary as his hunter's example. The nineteenth-century English jurist and criminal law scholar Sir James Fitzjames Stephen called the doctrine "astonishing" and found it unsupported by any of the authorities Coke had cited.[29] Stephen instructed a jury that the English law of felony murder required an "act known to be dangerous to life and likely in itself to cause death, done for the purpose of committing a felony which causes death."[30] In 1957 Parliament abolished the doctrine entirely in England.[31]

In the United States the overwhelming majority of jurisdictions retain the felony murder doctrine, subject to a variety of restrictions. Some limit the underlying felonies to a short list specified by statute, others to those offenses inherently dangerous, and still other jurisdictions according to whether the felonies are dangerous in the way they are committed by defendants. A complex special jurisprudence of accomplice liability and liability for third-party killings has also arisen with regard to felony murder.[32]

Although the many American limitations on felony murder have brought the rule closer to general principles of culpability, few are satisfactory. Because the doctrine requires no mens rea as to the death of the victim, the connection between legal responsibility and culpability under defense of value remains haphazard.[33] Some felony murderers attack basic human value in the most egregious fashion; others do not. For example, in California both of the following cases constitute first-degree murder on a felony murder theory: (1) a robber deliberately executes his victim to avoid capture and conviction; and (2) a robber displays a weapon and his victim dies of a heart attack.[34] To borrow the language of due process, the felony murder rule can be arbitrary and capricious.[35]

Given the obvious and long-recognized problems with the doctrine, why has the felony murder rule proven so popular in this country? Despite judicial and scholarly hostility, it enjoys wide public support.[36] The answer is simple: felony murder is emotionally satisfying. In some cases, the felony murder rule feels right because it produces morally justifiable results. It provides severe punishment for some of the most serious offenses. The robber who kills a police officer to make his getaway deserves his first-degree murder status, regardless of premeditation. In other cases, where the doctrine is morally overbroad, its results nevertheless feel right because of a common human failing: we confuse character with conduct. We allow our animosity toward the felon to influence our analysis of the homicide. Having proven himself to be a Criminal by committing a felony, which then causes death, we want to label him a Murderer as well. As the California Supreme Court has explained: "Once a person perpetrates or attempts to perpetrate one of the enumerated felonies [required for felony murder], then in the judgment of the Legislature, he is no longer entitled to such fine judicial calibration, but will be deemed guilty of first-degree murder for any homicide committed in the course thereof."[37] That is, having proven himself criminally culpable to some extent, we can declare him culpable to the maximum extent. This kind of reasoning is reminiscent of the cynical phrase often used by bureaucrats: good enough for government work. We should demand more of our criminal law.

Capital Murder Definitions

There is a third source of worst-offense definitions in American homicide law: the law of capital murder. Although as stated before I am not concerned here with the particulars of capital punishment, we need to look at least briefly at the law of the death penalty, for this is where legislatures have done their most important work on homicide definition in the last thirty years. Here legislatures have devised a number of statutory aggravating circumstances, including victim identity, manner of killing, and motive, which suggest other possibilities for first-degree murder definitions.

Since 1972, when the United States Supreme Court overturned all existing capital punishment schemes, most American jurisdictions have effectively redefined murder for purposes of the death penalty. All capital jurisdictions have established some form of narrowing system that requires decision makers to select capital murder cases from a larger group of criminal homicides, usually first-degree murders. This narrowing process may take place in the murder trial itself, what is called the guilt phase in capital cases, at the sentencing proceeding, called the penalty phase, or, most commonly, at both phases.[38] A few jurisdictions, like South Carolina, have not altered the definition of murder for guilt determinations, but require that specific aggravating factors be found at the penalty phase in order to support the death penalty.[39] Other jurisdictions, like California, require proof at the guilt phase of special circumstances in addition to the traditional first-degree murder requirements in order to make an offender eligible for the death penalty, then the decision maker must consider additional factors at the penalty phase before the death penalty can be imposed.[40]

California's special-circumstances law gives a good example of narrowing by offense definition. A defendant may be convicted of a capital offense (otherwise known as special circumstances first-degree murder) if the jury finds that the defendant intentionally killed, and did so for financial gain, or was previously convicted of murder, used an explosive device, killed a peace officer on duty or in retaliation for official duties; killed a witness to a crime to prevent or retaliate for testimony; killed a prosecutor, judge, or elected official in connection with their official duties; killed the victim "because of race, color, religion, nationality or country of origin"; killed while lying in wait; killed in the perpetration of certain specified felonies; or if the murder manifested "exceptional depravity," meaning that it represented a "scienceless or pitiless crime that is unnecessarily tortuous to the victim."[41]

As with most criminal law schemes, California's capital murder law reflects many influences. It encompasses traditional law in the concept of lying-in-wait and felony murder (though here restricted to purpose-to-kill homicides); addresses particular fears of great harm (explosives); the manner of killing (tortuous death); concerns for particular victims (peace officers, firefighters, prosecutors, witnesses, elected officials, and others); and new moral concerns (the group animus provision). Nevertheless, we can discern a larger theme here, albeit not a universal one: the worst form of murder requires purpose to kill and an especially bad motive. Most of the provisions involve a purposeful killing for a reason that specially attacks our moral values—a killing for money, to thwart the criminal justice process, as part of a sadistic attack, out of group hate. In this respect, the California law seems very much on the right track.

A Proposal for Aggravated Murder: Purpose and Motive

Recall the killings of Ted Bundy described at the beginning of this chapter. What made these such heinous offenses? Bundy premeditated the attacks, but as we have seen, other premeditated killings appear far less serious challenges to basic human value than Bundy's offenses. The killings occurred during the commission of serious felonies, but as we have seen, this also does not supply a reliable measure of the worst crime. So what is the essential evil in these evil deeds? I argue it lies in Bundy's purpose to kill, and in his motive, his reason for wanting to kill. Bundy killed for power, for the sensual and other satisfactions of taking human life. This is what makes his crimes appear so demonic and why they so deeply challenge our basic moral values.

I propose that the most serious form of murder, what I call aggravated murder, should be defined as follows:

> *Aggravated murder is the purposeful killing of another human being for profit, to further a criminal endeavor, to affect public policy or legal processes, because of animosity toward the victim's race, religion, ethnicity, sex or sexual orientation, or to assert cruel power over another.*

The proposal creates a two-pronged mens rea requirement: purpose to kill with a statutorily specified motive. The purpose-to-kill requirement is a familiar one and should not require extended discussion. The motive requirement is new to Anglo-American law, at least in this form, and requires considerable explication and justification.

Although, as we will see in chapter 9, some unintentional killings rank high on our intuitive moral scales, the most serious offense category should be reserved for killings where the offender launched an intentional, fatal attack on his victim. Intentionality here has two forms: an intent to kill or intent to use great violence. By great violence I mean violence likely to cause severe injury or death.

When we determine that the individual has shot or stabbed or beaten another with the conscious objective of causing death, we determine that the person has made a basic, personal commitment to the destruction of a life. The individual has directly chosen to destroy the victim's value, his autonomy. He has made killing a central part of his plans. But what about cases where the person acted with intent to use great violence but not intent to kill? Because such offenders have not clearly decided to end another's life, they seem to present less of a challenge to human value than do intentional killers. But when we look at particular cases that also involve especially bad motives, the distinction between intent to kill and intent to use great violence diminishes substantially.

In some cases a conscientious decision maker may find that the accused unleashed great violence against the victim in an intentional, intensely emotional outburst, but without clear evidence that death was the end sought. For example, in the *Anderson* case, there is language at the close of the majority opinion suggesting that Anderson may have been so frenzied in his violence that he never actually intended to kill Victoria Hammond. As a matter of common sense, this seems bizarre. How could a stabbing attack of this ferocity by an adult against a ten-year-old not demonstrate intent to kill? But if we were to interpret intent to kill as requiring a clear mental decision to end another's life, perhaps the very ferocity of the attack, which continued well after death, indicates a blind rage that never permitted the formation of a clear homicidal intent. The question now becomes, assuming no demonstrated intent to kill, does this amount to mitigation? If coolness and calculation are not critical to culpability, for all the reasons mentioned in the premeditation discussion, why should the failure to confront the most basic consequence of violent action amount to mitigation? We still have the intentional use of deadly violence for an especially bad reason. We still have an extreme attack on human value.

We can imagine other cases where the lack of intent to kill was much clearer but still does not argue for mitigation. Assume a sadist takes another person prisoner and then uses the victim for torture. Because the sadist enjoys the infliction of pain, he wishes the victim to live, not die, but his tortures go too far and he causes death nevertheless. Here the offender did not attack with the purpose of causing death, but for such an evil purpose that the killing is as egregious as if he had intent to kill.

In any event, we should not make too much of the intent-to-kill versus do-great-violence distinction. Decision makers confronted with cases where the accused intentionally used great violence against the victim and so caused the victim's death will almost always find that the accused acted with intent to kill. The real reason for making the distinction explicit is to keep the law's focus on the intentionality of severe violence and the underlying reason for which it was used.

Motive is relevant to culpability in murder because it reveals the depth and nature of the offender's attack on value. The worst motives for killing are those that demonstrate the greatest commitment to individual or community disregard. The worst killings express a philosophy deeply hostile to individual human value and usually to the value of the community. Such a killing expresses the view that human existence has no moral dimension, that life is simply the war of all against all. The hallmarks of such killings are: (1) extreme selfishness, and (2) extreme hostility to the idea of a lawful, moral community.

Selfishness is a trait associated with most immoral actions, but in the worst killings we find an extreme variant. We find persons who place their own concerns so far above the value of others that even the total destruction of another seems (to the killer) justified in order to achieve a personal end. A spouse may be killed to ensure the killer's financial security. The killing may be an integral part of a violent scheme for sexual gratification. Or the killer may find satisfaction in the total domination of another—and there is no domination more total than homicide. These and other killings demonstrate an extreme elevation of self over other.

Some killings display a radical hostility not just to individual value but to the value of our particular human community. In a society committed to the lawful resolution of disputes, attacks on those involved in the legal system represent a fundamental moral challenge. In a society committed to democracy, the use of fatal violence to protest, to threaten, to retaliate against persons because of their association with controversial public policy ideas represents a similar challenge. In a society committed to diversity, the same community hostility is shown by the killer who kills out of group hatred.

If we reserve our most severe punishment for purposeful killings with motives such as these, we proportion punishment to severity of disregard. Killings with other motives remain serious wrongs, but not of the same degree. The distinction should become clearer as we look harder at the different kinds of motives that make up aggravated murder. I will consider these in a rough progression from least to most controversial.

For Profit

Killing for profit has long been the quintessential first-degree murder. The murder of a spouse or relative to collect on an insurance policy, the hit man's assassination for a fee are among the worst killings we can imagine, for they show how little the offender values human life.[42] We call such killings cold-blooded, for in the profit motive we find the coldness of the killer's radical lack of fellow feeling. Such killers do not seem driven by psychic demons or inner turmoil, but are lured to homicide by the crass desire for material wealth. The mundanaeity of such a motivation makes these killings morally terrifying. In the dialogue about the meaning of conduct, one who kills for profit says that life's meaning comes only from money, that the physical pleasures and the power that comes with wealth are all that count.

To Further a Criminal Endeavor

The most common form of aggravated murder may be the killing to further a criminal scheme. Sometimes planned, but often impulsive, homicide here is used to further an immoral, criminal goal. The execution of a witness to prevent testimony at a criminal proceeding, the killing of a police officer to escape the scene of a robbery, the killing of a rape victim to prevent the crime's discovery or prosecution, and the killing of business rivals in the drug trade are among the more common examples.[43] Killings that further the interests of criminal enterprises, such as a drug organization or a criminal gang, would also suffice. All of these killings qualify for aggravated-murder status because we see the defendant's willingness to violate basic community principles. Not only is the individual willing to engage in criminal activity, a violation of a basic community norm, but she is willing to take a human life in order to succeed.

To Affect Public Policy or Legal Processes

Killings to affect public policy or legal processes attack the basic values of American democracy. Killings to affect public policy seem to declare that public authority comes from the barrel of a gun, not the ballot box. Killings to affect legal processes represent similar challenges, in that they seek to use violence to subvert our formal, largely nonviolent means of dispute resolution.

This category of aggravated murder would cover the terrorist who attacks groups or individuals because of a public policy stance with which they are associated. It would cover the radical leftist who attacks the CIA or an abortion opponent who bombs an abortion clinic. The law here must be agnostic toward the policy involved. A fatal attack on the embassy of a repressive regime must be treated the same as the bombing of a church or a Planned Parenthood clinic.

The category would also cover those who kill because of the victim's participation in a legal process, regardless of whether the legal process involves larger public questions. The individual who kills a divorce lawyer or judge because of anger at a marital decree would represent one example of this form of aggravated murder.

Out of Group Animus

Killings motivated by racial hatred and certain other forms of group animus directly challenge the central American ideal that all persons are created equal. Such crimes assert that human value depends on racial and other group identification, not on individual worth. A specific case will help illuminate the special wrongs that such bias crimes involve.

> On October 7, 1989, Todd Mitchell, aged nineteen, was part of a group of young black men and boys hanging out at an apartment complex in Kenosha, Wisconsin. Among the topics of discussion was *Mississippi Burning,* a movie about the civil rights struggle in the South. The group discussed a scene where a white man beat a young black boy who was praying.
>
> Still talking about the movie, some of the group moved outside. Mitchell asked the others: "Do you all feel hyped up to move on some white people?"
>
> A little while later, fourteen-year-old Gregory Reddick walked by the apartment complex on the other side of the street.
>
> As Reddick passed by, Mitchell said to the others in the group: "You all want to fuck somebody up? There goes a white boy; go get him." Mitchell counted to three and pointed the others in Reddick's direction.
>
> The group ran across the street, knocked Reddick down, beat him severely, and stole his sneakers. Gregory Reddick lost consciousness and lapsed into a coma from which he emerged four days later.

Todd Mitchell was convicted of aggravated battery for his part in the attack on Reddick, and because the jury found that Reddick had been selected for attack because of his race, Mitchell was sentenced to seven years in prison. Without the finding of racial bias, the maximum sentence would have been two years.[44]

The *Mitchell* case soon became part of an ongoing legal controversy concerning enactment of what have been called hate or bias crimes: offenses, or penalty enhancements, that focus on criminal acts motivated by a group-based animus, such as racial bigotry. For simplicity's sake, I will refer to all of these enactments as bias offenses.

Most courts and commentators seem to agree that a crime committed out of racial bigotry involves a worse harm, and represents a worse wrong, than one committed for other motives. In a society committed to diversity, persons who attack along the social fault lines of race or other basic group distinctions challenge the ideal of a moral community and inflict a serious harm on society. Thus there seems to be no problem with bias crimes on grounds of deserved punishment.[45]

In addition to general objections to using motive in criminal mens rea—objections addressed later—critics of bias crimes have made two general claims: (1) that the new offenses may increase bigotry rather then reduce it,[46] and (2) that the offenses violate constitutional principles of free speech. While each of these objections raises significant issues, each rests upon a set of concerns well beyond the scope of the current project.

The objection relating to the effect of bias crimes on race relations goes to whether a particular definition of crime fulfills the aims of efficient deterrence. From the outset, I have limited my attention here to the requirements of deserved punishment. My only concern is whether bigoted crimes represent significantly worse wrongs than unbigoted crimes and thus deserve greater punishment.[47]

Similarly, the free speech objections raised implicate issues of First Amendment doctrine and theory that do not significantly overlap with those of criminal responsibility explored here. As a practical matter, the United States Supreme Court has resolved the free speech issue for the foreseeable future by its approval of the Minnesota law used in *Mitchell*. As far as the high court is concerned, there are no fundamental First Amendment obstacles to sentencing enhancements based on racial bias, and the reasoning of the decision suggests no constitutional problems with including group bias in offense definitions.[48] State courts have held similarly.[49]

To Assert Cruel Power over Another

The last of the motive categories—the assertion of cruel power over another—is in a legal sense the least important, for it overlaps significantly with the previously listed motives. Power killings, as I call them, will generally meet the criteria for another form of aggravated murder as well, most commonly furthering a criminal endeavor. The category is worth exploring, however, for some power killings may not involve another especially heinous motive, and, equally important, the category illuminates an aspect of evildoing in homicide that we might otherwise miss. We find here an explanation for what is otherwise inexplicable in the commission of evil.

We commonly call the worst killings senseless.[50] When we hear of the torture-murder of a small child, or a robber who executes a store clerk *after* the clerk has cleared out the cash register, we wonder: Why would anyone do such a thing? The motivation seems beyond human comprehension. Yet the mystery lies more in our own psychology than in the killer's. We need only acknowledge that such killers are in most respects like the rest of us to understand their actions. They have chosen a rational, though extraordinary means to a common human end. In a "senseless" homicide the killer experiences the thrill of ultimate power, the power to take life. By a simple deed he changes the world. He becomes someone important. Killing gives power, and power is one of the most basic motivators of humans.[51] Such a killer challenges, in the most direct and brutal way possible, our commitment to human value and moral community.

But how do we tell which killings are about the "assertion of cruel power"? Read broadly, this phrase could cover all intentional criminal homicides. All intentional homicides involve the assertion of ultimate power over another human being, and if done without justification or excuse, that assertion must be deemed cruel. What distinguishes the power killing is that power is the preeminent motivation for the attack, outweighing all other aspects of the attacker-victim interaction. In a power killing the killer has no personal dispute with the victim. The homicide comes not as the means of settling a personal controversy about money, sex, love, or personal rivalry, but as the end itself. The killer uses the victim's body and life to express personal dominance generally.

The signs of a power killing are varied. Perhaps the most important indication is a negative one—that no other explanation for the killing makes human sense. The ostensible motives of personal disputes or greed do not resonate with what we know of the individuals involved or of human nature generally. Ordinary explanations do not account for the timing, the manner, or the course of the homicide. The case of Robert Alton Harris, detailed later, provides a particularly chilling example.

The affirmative signs of a power killing involve the manner of violence. The use of torture constitutes a telling sign that the killer seeks total, brutal domination of his victim as a motivation for the killing.[52] Here we find a satisfaction in pain indicating that power drives the attack. The intertwining of violence and sexual acts provides another indication. A power killing may come following a sexual attack, as the act of final possession/violation that began with rape or other explicitly sexual violence. Or the killer may use acts of violence to express sexuality directly in stabbing, mutilating, or otherwise attacking the victim's sexual parts.[53]

The serial killer presents the most obvious power killer. Recall Ted Bundy. As the press never failed to note, Bundy had a lot going for him. He was good-looking, charming, intelligent, and had a good education. But he never accomplished much in the law-abiding world. He only truly excelled at assaulting and killing women. His attacks gave him a means of avenging himself for a sense of personal failure.[54] His crimes satisfied a basic need, the need to be someone special, to have power.[55]

Bundy selected his victims according to personal criteria of attractiveness and vulnerability.[56] His criminal enterprise was a kind of hunt in which he experienced "a high degree of anticipation, of excitement, of arousal. It was an *adventuristic* kind of thing."[57] Also a thief, Bundy found basic satisfaction in stealing and illicit possession. In his attacks on women he sought human possession.[58] His attacks normally included a strong sexual element. He raped his victims, often with great violence. Having taken their sexuality, he then he took their lives.[59] He found pleasure in a personal triumph over death. "I want to master life and death," he said.[60] He triumphed over other mortals; he became, for a few moments, God.[61]

Bundy's drive for power is found in the crimes of many other serial killers. English serial killer Dennis Nilson has observed: "My offenses arose from a feeling of inadequacy, not potency. I never had any power in my life." But he did when he killed. Like Bundy, his crimes gave him new companions and new possessions. Nilson referred to the selection of a victim as the recruitment of "a new kind of flat-mate."[62] He enjoyed possessing the corpse. "I remember being thrilled that I had full control and ownership of this beautiful body," he wrote of one killing.[63] The serial killer lusts for the feel of superhuman power, of the immortality that killing can bring. One stated: "What I wanted to see was the *death*, and I wanted to see the *triumph*, the exultation over death. . . . In other words, winning over death. They were dead and I was alive. That was a victory in my case."[64]

As noted before, power killings frequently fall under the furthering a criminal enterprise category of aggravated murder as well. In the case of the power killer, though, the criminal endeavor may be just another indication of the central power motivation. In some instances the crime may be little more than a twisted excuse to cover the attacker's power lust. A widely quoted passage of verse by the philosopher Friedrich Nietzsche explains:

> Thus speaks the red judge, "Why did this criminal murder? He wanted to rob." But I say unto you: his soul wanted blood, not robbery; he thirsted after the bliss of the knife. His poor reason, however, did not comprehend this madness and persuaded him: "What matters blood?" it asked; "don't you want at least to commit a robbery with it?" . . . And he listened to his poor reason: its speech lay upon him like lead; so he robbed when he murdered. He did not want to be ashamed of his madness.[65]

The "bliss of the knife" is the desire to wield the power of death-making. The robbery is a cover for the killer's bloody satisfactions. The murder case of Robert Alton Harris illustrates this dynamic.

> On a summer day in 1978, Robert Harris and his brother Daniel decided to rob a bank. They did not want to use their own car, so they set out to steal another. They were trying to hot-wire a car in the parking lot of a fast food restaurant when Robert noticed another car in which two local teenagers, John Mayeski and Michael Baker, were eating their lunch. Robert put a gun to John Mayeski's head and told him to drive. Daniel Harris followed in the Harris vehicle. The two vehicles proceeded to a remote canyon area, where Robert assured the two boys that they would not be hurt. Meanwhile, Robert yelled to his brother to get the rifle from the back seat of their car. Robert Harris took the boys into the countryside, explaining that they needed the boys' car for a bank robbery. The boys did not resist. Then Robert Harris shot them both. He shot Mayeski in the back and then chased down Baker, finally shooting him four times. When Robert Harris returned to Mayeski, he found that the teenager was still alive. Robert put his handgun to the boy's head and fired one last time.
>
> Daniel Harris described his brother Robert's reaction: "He was swinging the rifle and pistol in the air and laughing. God, that laugh made blood and bone freeze in me."
>
> The Harris brothers drove back to where they were staying. Robert Harris took the bag of the teenagers' unfinished lunch into the house and started in on a hamburger. He offered Daniel an apple turnover, but Daniel was nauseated at the idea. Again Robert laughed.[66]

While furthering a bank robbery was the ostensible motive for the murders of Mayeski and Baker, the circumstances of their homicides suggest that cruel power was the more important motivation for Harris. Robert Harris told his brother they needed a vehicle for the robbery that police could not trace back to him or his brother. Yet he obtained the car in a way that ensured enormous police attention—far more than even a bank robbery would bring. Harris, who had spent much of his life in trouble with the law, must have realized that in killing the boys he had taken an enormous risk for small gain. If his goal was to commit a robbery and evade capture he had gone about it in a stupid, almost irrational way. Of course, if his actual end was raw power over others, then the killings appear in a different light. Then the killings provided more satisfaction than any robbery or its proceeds. Harris delighted in the boys' demise; he laughed wildly about the killings. He relished taking their lives even in the way he consumed their last meal. He relished exerting ultimate power over life.[67]

★

Some may object that power killers as described here do not appear fully responsible. They may be frightening, but they are also deeply disturbed. Under most modern conceptions of mental health, power killers—especially serial killers—are ill and need professional treatment. As a result, some argue that they are not morally responsible, or are less morally responsible than other violent wrongdoers. Here we must distinguish two different kinds of arguments: arguments based on lack of rationality and those based on moral incapacity.

Some serial killers may suffer from such severe rationality problems that they do not deserve punishment. They may be so committed to bizarre fantasies that their horrendous deeds do not challenge our moral values.[68] Their crazy acts are like natural disasters: devastating and requiring forceful response—in this instance civil commitment—but not blame or punishment. Most power killers remain in touch with reality, however. We can understand the ends they seek and the means they use to reach them. They seek power, a central human motivation, and they obtain it through brutal domination, an ugly but time-honored method. Although their approach to life is self-destructive in the long run, in the short run it provides significant rewards that we can all readily understand.[69] For these reasons their actions challenge our moral values.

Most who seek either mitigation or excuse for power killers do so on the ground that, even if rational, such persons lack the capacity for fully responsible choice. They argue that such killers are psychopaths and cannot feel for others.[70] Most have not shown any significant emotional attachment to another human being. Their killings appear compulsive, in the sense that they may occur even while the killer expresses desires to do otherwise ("stop me before I kill again") and in circumstances where the crime is destructive to the killer's own interests. Therefore we may plausibly conclude that such killers could not do otherwise. As argued at length in chapters 2 and 3, I believe moral responsibility does not depend on psychological could-have-done-otherwise. It depends on participation in the ongoing argument about the meaning of human life. Serial killers may present the most dramatic examples of persons shaped by genetics and environment for criminality, but they are not the only ones. In fact, all of us have our moral characters shaped by our genetic and environmental heritages, and to the same extent. Some of us are just more fortunate in our heritages than others. Serial killers remain responsible because their killings express a comprehensible philosophy about human value: that the only person who has value is oneself and that others may be used in whatever way the self desires.

General Objections to Motive: Tradition and Vagueness

The major objections to the proposed redefinition of homicide will come from those who have generally questioned the wisdom of motive analysis in the criminal law. These objections fall under two headings: (1) that use of motive violates the best traditions of Anglo-American criminal law, and (2) that motive analysis makes criminal law vague and so promotes unjust decisions.

An oft-stated maxim of Anglo-American law holds that motive is irrelevant to criminal liability.[71] While this saying contains a kernel of truth, it represents a considerable overstatement. In fact, while most crimes are not defined with reference to motive, motive is an important part of many criminal law doctrines. For example, depending on motive, a purposeful killing may be justified, because committed in self-defense, it may constitute a killing in the heat of passion meriting moderate punishment, or it may qualify for the law's most severe punishment.[72] Motive is critical to a number of defenses, including insanity, duress, and necessity and to the definition of some nonhomicide offenses.[73] Motive distinctions are commonly made in sentencing.[74] Nevertheless, modern criminal schemes rarely employ motive in offense definition.[75] In sum, while motive has played a significant role in some criminal law doctrines and is consistent with many others, it remains an exceptional feature of culpability analysis in Anglo-American criminal law.

Legal traditions will not resolve the question in any event. The real question is whether motive analysis will improve our law of murder. The real question is whether we can rebut the claim that motive analysis makes for vague law. Critics maintain that criminal offenses with motive elements involve vagueness at both the level of definition and application. First, some critics argue that in contrast to traditional criminal intent, motive involves inherently controversial questions of morality. Since we fundamentally disagree about these issues, legal determinations involving motive will be unpredictable and systematically unjust. We cannot, even as a matter of abstract definition, agree on what kinds of motives should suffice. Second, critics maintain that motive analysis will lead to mistakes in rule applications because motive is too hard to ascertain in a criminal trial.[76] Many argue that motive analysis requires psychological information beyond the reach of lawyers and jurors. As one commentator recently put it, motive determination requires "plumbing the murky depths of the springs of human action."[77]

In defining the motive element of aggravated murder, drafters can, as they do with all criminal law, make basic moral and legal policy that decision-makers will apply. A law that requires proof of particular motives, such as a killing for profit or out of group animus, should be distinguished from common law offense definitions that require proof of a general evil motive.[78] As with most criminal offenses, the most controversial moral question—how to define the offense—will have been resolved by the legislature. The determination of particular motives involves essentially the same mix of factual and normative judgment that standard criminal intent does. Careful definition of motive should also alleviate concerns about errors in rule application.

As described in chapter 6, motive analysis simply extends the standard criminal intent inquiry one step further. With regard to a fatal shooting, the basic criminal intent question may be: What was the shooter's purpose in pulling the trigger? We look to see whether the shooter wished to kill, to scare, or whether the gun's firing was accidental. These questions address the most basic kind of why questions—why the shooter acted as he did. Assume that we decide that the shooter meant to kill. Then we might ask a second why question: Why did the person want to kill? Was he angry or scared? Did he want to gain money or power? This is the motive question.

Careful definition will limit the depth of the motive inquiry. In theory, we could push motive beyond the second why question to third- or fourth-level why questions. If we determine that the shooter purposely killed (addressing the first why question) in order to collect on an insurance policy (addressing the second why question), we might then ask, Why does he want the insurance money? (addressing a third why question). If we answer that the shooter has an overwhelming lust for money, we can ask once again: Why? Why does he care so much about money? (fourth why question). Obviously, the deeper we push our motivational investigation, the more data we require, the more variables we must assess, and the less reliable the ultimate verdict becomes. But again: that we could do this does not mean that we should. For purposes of determining criminal culpability the second why question provides the most important moral insights. We need go no further.

These restrictions on motive greatly lessen the force of the objection that determining motive requires special psychological insights, that we would need a jury with the combined talents of Freud and Dostoyevsky to make accurate legal judgments. Like traditional mens rea, motive concerns the defendant's reasons for action. As discussed at length in the previous chapter, we do not need to read the offender's mind, or soul, to ascertain standard mens rea, and the same is true of motive. In all cases we analyze conduct according to our understanding of the situation, the individual, and human nature. We ask, Why would *this* person want to do *that*?[79]

The Real Challenges of Motive Analysis

Even with a limited definition, adding motive to mens rea does make criminal decision making more difficult. Proof of motive requires both more information about, and better understanding of, the offender and his conduct. Motive analysis also introduces a new kind of normative judgment to mens rea: jurors must not only determine whether a particular motive played a role in the conduct, but also how important a role.

Motive analysis does require the decision maker to look further into the background of the defendant's conduct. In most cases, as with standard mens rea, the circumstances of the crime, statements made by the defendant and others, and basic insights into human nature will provide the necessary information. In *Mitchell*, for example, the combination of the racial remarks by Mitchell and the fact of an entirely unprovoked attack by blacks on a white boy provided clear evidence of racial motivation.[80]

As with standard mens rea, the real challenge for jurors will be in interpreting the evidence. Does the fact that the victim was raped and then beaten to death indicate a power killing? Does the fact that the defendant collected on a large life insurance policy on the victim indicate a killing for profit? Was the bombing of the government building motivated by the defendant's anger at losing his job or hostility to government policy? We should not pretend that these will be easy questions to answer. We may well need more facts about the particular offense, and more insight into homicide generally.

Including motive in aggravated murder will require considerable work for all involved in the processing of such cases. To date, motive has not been a central concern of police, lawyers, or anyone else involved in the processing or study of homicide cases.[81] If we change the law, everyone from police officers to defense attorneys will have to think much harder about motive. In the courtroom the heaviest load will fall on prosecutors, who must prove motive beyond a reasonable doubt to obtain an aggravated murder conviction. As has become common in child abuse and rape cases, prosecutors may seek to educate jurors by calling experts to testify concerning common patterns of violent behavior. Despite its prevalence in our entertainment and news cultures, homicide is not an everyday part of life. Those who have the most professional experience with homicide, such as police officers and criminologists, may be called to inform the jury of the different varieties of killings and their characteristics. As with all such witnesses, courts must try to ensure that expert testimony is illuminating but not determinative. Homicide experts may provide important information about relevant patterns of human killings, including patterns relevant to motive, but the ultimate decision on motive must be the jury's.[82]

Among the hardest determinations for juries will be judging the relative importance of different motivations. We commonly act not for one reason but for a combination of overlapping reasons. I suggest that conviction of aggravated murder should require proof that the particular motive was a substantial factor in the homicidal act.[83] In other words, the decision maker must resolve that the bad motive represented an important reason for the killing.[84] To the extent that the prosecution's proof on the importance of motive fails, the result is the same as with the failure of proof of any part of mens rea: acquittal on the particular charge, with the decision maker then to consider any lesser-included charges, in this case other murder or manslaughter offenses.[85]

The real difficulties of motive analysis argue for its use in only limited circumstances. In homicide we should employ motive analysis at either end of the culpability spectrum—for aggravated murder and, as we will see in chapter 8—for manslaughters that involve legally adequate provocation. The great majority of homicide offenses will fall in between these two doctrines and should remain crimes that rely on traditional mens rea forms, without reference to motive.[86]

Conclusion

> If anyone considers me a monster, that's just something they'll have to confront in themselves. For people to want to condemn someone, to dehumanize someone like me is a very popular and effective, understandable way of dealing with a fear and a threat that is incomprehensible."
> —Ted Bundy, interview with the *New York Times,* 1986

Much as we might like to think otherwise, the worst murders are not the work of monsters or demons. Ted Bundy's deeds may repulse us; we may be sickened by the virulence of his attacks on women and girls, but we should not mistake their nature. Too often we have avoided looking hard at the worst crimes, repelled by their evil. As a result, we have been content to condemn such homicides in the broadest terms, leaving the details to intuition. We have been content to make, and apply, bad law.

As we have seen, the doctrines of premeditation and felony murder often produce morally acceptable results, but they suffer from vagueness and overbreadth. Premeditation makes too much of dispassion and not enough of motive. Felony murder recognizes an important connection between other criminality and homicide, but does not make the connection in the right way. In both instances we find a body of law that does not produce reliable judgments of highest culpability.

On looking more closely at those killings which offend us most, we discover the importance of motive and the mundane side of evil. The worst killings are done for common human reasons, made evil by their expression in fatal violence. These are intentional killings for profit, for crime, for the pleasure of hurting others, for bigotry, for power. In defining aggravated murder according to purpose and particularly bad motives, we commit ourselves to recognizing human evil. We acknowledge that deeds of appalling inhumanity have familiar human motives.

8

Crimes of Passion

On the morning of April 2, 1993, Ellie Nesler lost control.

She had gone to court with her young son, who was due to testify at the preliminary hearing of Daniel Driver. Driver stood accused of sexually molesting Nesler's son and three other young boys at a camp several years earlier. Driver had convictions in two previous cases for child molestation. Nesler also had a past involving child molestation—she had been a victim of it as a child.

The preliminary hearing was a traumatic event for Nesler's son. Driver had reportedly threatened to kill the boy and his mother if the boy ever told anyone about the molestation. The boy had vomited repeatedly in anticipation of his courtroom appearance.

According to defense witnesses, as Driver was brought into the courtroom that morning he smirked at Nesler and her son; Nesler lunged at Driver but was held back by relatives. Then another mother told Nesler that the prosecution's evidence had been weak so far and that Driver "was going to walk." On hearing these words Nesler took a small .22-caliber pistol from her sister's purse which was hanging in the court hallway, returned to the courtroom and emptied the gun into the handcuffed Driver, killing him.

Nesler was tried for first-degree murder but was convicted of voluntary manslaughter, the jury determining that she killed in the heat of passion.[1]

Anglo-American criminal law has always had a soft spot for the impassioned homicide. The doctrine of heat of passion, also called provocation, marks the difference between murder and manslaughter, traditionally the difference between a hanging offense and one punished by less severe sanctions. Today the doctrine no longer plays a central role in determining whether a killer will die, but it still makes a major difference in punishment.[2]

The question is why. What is the principle behind the provocation rule? Assuming the jury's decision was correct, did Nesler deserve less punishment because the pressures on her were so great that she lost self-control and so became less responsible? Or was the verdict correct because she had good reason for rage at Daniel Driver, making the killing a less fundamental challenge to human value than most intentional homicides? To put the question in terms we have discussed before, does provocation depend on reduced capacity to choose, or on a distinction in motivation?

Provocation also raises serious questions about equality and our commitment to nonviolence. By providing less punishment for some impassioned killers, does the law partially condone hot-tempered aggression? How much does provocation—a rule with origins in the code of honor of seventeenth-century Englishmen—permit the expression of harmful assumptions about gender roles? What of the possibility of racial and class bias in this doctrine which permits manslaughter to be the most common verdict in homicide cases involving poor and minority victims?

In this chapter I argue for both a return to legal tradition and a sharp break from it. I defend the traditional theory of provocation that provides for mitigation based on moral assessment of the defendant's rage. I argue that we rightly punish certain provoked killings less than other purposeful killings because of differences in motivation. The person who had good reason for extreme anger at the victim, and killed as a result of that anger, does not challenge our moral values as much as other purposeful slayers.[3] I argue for a break from tradition in the paradigmatic cases of provocation. Instead of the gender-biased, traditional examples of discovery of adultery (by the husband) and mutual combat (of two hot-tempered men), we should employ new examples of reaction to serious, wrongful physical assault. Finally, we should revise our view of provocation's timing requirements in order to take into account morally legitimate differences in how persons express their anger.

★

Our consideration of provocation begins with legal history, for many of the rule's current complexities can be traced to its common law origins. After a brief look at the rule's legal and social beginnings, we move to the contemporary debate about its rationale, whether it is a doctrine about motive, as the common law suggested, or whether it depends more on the experience of strong emotion and resulting loss of self-control as the Model Penal Code version holds. Here we find the now-familiar juxtaposition of responsibility theories: reasons for conduct versus capacity to do otherwise. As elsewhere in the book, I argue for the former, then propose a revised rule for provocation based on normative assessment of anger.

The remainder of the chapter addresses a number of recent criticisms of the basic concept of providing less punishment for provoked killings. After rejecting the argument that provocation doctrine is necessarily pro-violence, we move to the argument that provocation encourages, or at least permits, expression of deep-seated gender, race, or class bias. Of these the most serious proves to be gender bias. The newer, psychologically oriented forms of provocation such as that found in the Model Penal Code (MPC) permit mitigation based on men's trauma at losing female intimate partners, thus reinforcing traditional notions of male control of females. Meanwhile, traditional provocation rules express sexist views in the treatment of adultery as provocation and in male-oriented conceptions of quick anger and violence. I argue that the proposed rule should help alleviate, though it will not cure, the problem of gender bias.

We turn next to race and class bias. In its current versions, provocation doctrine may further racial and class-based inequities by turning observations about what persons commonly do into normative judgments about how they should act. By focusing on the psychology of self-control, current doctrine may encourage the view that certain persons, especially minority, underclass men, have less self-control than others. This may permit the justice system to treat as less significant the homicides such men commit, homicides that usually involve victims who are also predominantly minority, underclass men. To the extent that this downgrading occurs because of rule definition, as opposed to other systemic problems associated with race and class, the proposed rule should help alleviate class and race bias.

The chapter closes with an argument for replacing the standard examples of provocation. Instead of using stories of cuckolded husbands and brawling men to illustrate the doctrine, we should employ narratives like that of Ellie Nesler, which involve serious physical assault upon the defendant or a loved one. The new physical assault examples should provide another weapon in the never-ending fight against bias in the doctrine's application.

I must offer one general caveat before plunging into provocation's many controversies. Provocation is, and always has been, a compromise rule. Like a wily politician, the doctrine has survived in many different times and places by promising a little something to everyone. The rule neither entirely condemns nor excuses; it involves analysis of reason and emotion, motive and self-control; it seeks to impose a universal rule, but one that accommodates a host of individual case variations; it sounds in both excuse and justification; its rules are defined in a constant interplay of formal definitions and factual examples, jury decisions, and judicial rulings. The rule's compromise nature makes it both rich in theoretical possibilities and impossible to categorize neatly. Its compromise nature also means that unless we abolish it entirely, any debate about reform is ultimately a debate about the relative emphasis we give to provocation's different component parts. Although often sounding in absolutes, arguments about provocation nearly always reduce to arguments about the proper balance between the elements of the rule. The discussion that follows is no exception. I would emphasize reasons for anger more than the experience of lost control, but both remain important.

A Historical Overview: Common Law Origins

Most legal historians agree that the doctrine of provocation originated in the concept of chance medley, an English corruption of the French term "chaud melee" or hot fight.[4] Chance medley referred to killings that occurred in mutual combat, "upon a sudden falling out."[5] As one English commentator described the law:

> [U]pon words of reproach, or indeed any other sudden provocation, the parties come to blows, and a combat ensues, no undue advantage being taken or sought on either side: if death ensue, this amounts to manslaughter. And here it matters not what the cause be, whether real or imagined, or who draws or strikes first; provided the occasion be sudden, and not urged as a cloak for preexisting malice.[6]

Chance-medley reflected the values of a violent, feudal society where men commonly wore sidearms and norms of honorable combat—a fair fight— were nearly as important as those of refraining from violence.[7] As one historian of the era has noted, in sixteenth- and seventeenth-century English society, "[t]he behavior of the propertied classes, like that of the poor, was characterized by the ferocity, childishness and lack of social control of the Homeric age. . . . Impulsiveness was not reproved, readiness to repay an injury real or imagined a sign of spirit. . . . Moreover, a gentleman carried a weapon at all times, and did not hesitate to use it."[8]

In the sixteenth and seventeenth centuries, chance medley merged into what became known as provocation or heat of passion. Provocation developed two overlapping strands of authority. The first, like chance medley, involved mutual combat, where mitigation depended on the suddenness of the conflict and the honor with which it was conducted. Decision makers looked to whether the killer resorted quickly to violence and whether he gave the victim a fair chance to defend himself.[9] The second strand of cases emphasized the wrongness of the provoking incident. Here courts looked closely at the conduct of the victim to ascertain if his or her actions constituted such a serious insult or threat as to inspire a great and violent passion in the honorable man.[10]

Both forms of provocation were shaped by views of man's "natural honour," about how a gentleman should conduct himself and especially how he should defend his honor.[11] Drawing on the writings of ancient philosophers, especially Aristotle, this conception of honor required the gentleman to respond to insult forcefully, but in careful proportion to the seriousness of the insult. The crime of voluntary manslaughter was committed when a man who was seriously attacked or insulted responded with excessive force and killed the original wrongdoer.

A central example of provocation outside of the mutual combat context was a husband's discovery of his wife's adultery. One of the most cited cases for this form of provocation was the seventeenth-century *Maddy's Case*.[12] Maddy was originally charged with the murder of Franc' Mavers. By a special verdict, the jury determined that "Maddy, coming into his house, found Mavers in the act of adultery with . . . the said Maddy's wife, and he [Maddy] immediately took up a stool and struck Mavers on the head, so that he instantly died." The jury found that Maddy had no "precedent malice" toward the victim. On appeal, the justices of the King's Bench unanimously determined that the killing was manslaughter, "the provocation being exceeding great." The court distinguished the case from an earlier decision upholding a murder conviction in which a husband killed a man in the act of adultery but only after the husband had learned of the adultery from another source and vowed that he would seek revenge.

The English common law as it developed through the eighteenth century has usually been distilled to three elements involving the nature of passion, the adequacy of the provoking act, and the timing of the killing. Under the common law, an intentional killing would be mitigated from murder to manslaughter if: (1) the accused was actually provoked into a great passion by the victim's conduct; (2) the provoking conduct constituted a legally approved category of provocation, usually discovery of adultery, serious battery, or mutual combat; and (3) if the killing occurred before an adequate cooling off period had elapsed.[13] The most important of these elements was, and remains, the adequacy of the provocation.

The Reasonable Man

In the nineteenth century, many American courts exercised tight control over provocation law by restricting the kind of provocation claims that would reach the jury. Unless the defendant offered proof of a provoking incident that fit one of the standard types established in English common law, and only if the homicide occurred fairly swiftly after the provoking incident, within the so-called cooling off period, the jury was not allowed to consider provocation. Beginning with a few isolated cases in the mid-nineteenth century, however, some American and English courts moved away from the common law's preexisting categories approach to a more general rule of "reasonable" provocation. This gave much more decision power to juries who would have to determine reasonableness based on individual case circumstances. The key to this change was the emergence of the "reasonable" man as the standard by which to assess the accused's emotions and self-control.

In the United States, the first appearance of the reasonable man in provocation jurisprudence is usually credited to the case of *Maher v. People* in 1862.[14] In *Maher*, Justice Christiancy of the Michigan Supreme Court described provocation this way:

> [I]f the act of killing, though intentional, be committed under the influence of passion or in heat of blood, produced by an adequate or reasonable provocation, and before a reasonable time has elapsed for the blood to cool and reason to resume its habitual control, and is the result of the temporary excitement, by which the control of reason was disturbed, rather than of any wickedness of heart or cruelty or recklessness of disposition: then the law, out indulgence to the frailty of human nature, or rather, in recognition of the laws upon which human nature is constituted, very properly regards the offense as of a less heinous character than murder, and gives it the designation of manslaughter. [15]

Under this view, heat of passion mitigated due to its interference with the thought processes of a reasonable man. An offense would be manslaughter if the defendant's reason was "disturbed or obscured by passion to an extent which *might render* ordinary men, of fair average disposition, *liable* to act rashly or without due deliberation or reflection, and from passion, rather than judgment."[16] The obscuring of reason by passion was only half the legal equation, though. Jurors also had to judge the defendant's character in order to distinguish those homicides where the law bowed to the "frailty of human nature" from those which reflected a defendant's "wickedness of heart or cruelty of disposition."[17]

The *Maher* court granted the jury new powers to define adequate provocation on the democratic theory that the jurors were better qualified to judge the social expectations that inform reasonableness. Justice Christiancy explained:

[J]urors from the mode of their selection, coming from the various classes and occupations of society, and conversant with the practical affairs of life, are, in my opinion, much better qualified to judge of the sufficiency and tendency of a given provocation and much more likely to fix, with some degree of accuracy, the standard of what constitutes the average of ordinary human nature, than the judge whose habits and course of life give him much less experience of the workings of passion in the actual conflicts of life.[18]

Thus the court ruled that the jury should have heard evidence and received instructions on provocation in a case where the defendant had recently learned that his wife might be committing adultery with the victim, even though, contrary to the rigid categorical rule, the defendant did not actually discover the two in the act of adultery.

The *Maher* case did not immediately change the American law of provocation; rather, it was an early example of an approach that slowly, and rather haphazardly, gathered force over the next one hundred years. Over that time, even within the same jurisdiction, courts gave conflicting signals about what would be reasonable provocation and whether its limits would be set primarily by judges or juries.[19]

The Psychological Approach

During the second half of the twentieth century, a number of Anglo-American jurisdictions were influenced by what may be called the psychological approach to provocation. Instead of emphasizing the nature of the provoking incident and character of the reasonable man, the psychological approach focused more on the intensity of emotion experienced by the accused and its impact on his choice-making abilities.[20] The psychological approach altered the definition or interpretation of each of the three major elements of provocation: the nature of the passion involved, the adequacy of the provoking incident, and the timing of provocation and homicide.

Under the psychological approach, many jurisdictions have expanded the kinds of passion that will suffice for provocation. In California, for example, the offender's passion need not be rage or fear, the two most widely recognized provocation emotions, but any "[v]iolent, intense, high-wrought or enthusiastic emotion."[21] Grief, anxiety, despair are among the new candidates to satisfy the passion element of provocation. Under the psychological approach the new test for passion is not its nature but its intensity; it must be powerful enough to disrupt the person's normal decision-making processes. Under the MPC, which gives fullest expression to the psychological approach, the passion must amount to an "extreme emotional disturbance." This emotion may take any form as long as it is strong enough to overwhelm the individual's ordinary "self-control and reason."[22]

Under the psychological approach, many jurisdictions have greatly increased jury discretion with regard to the adequacy of provocation. Many jurisdictions have essentially eliminated the legal categories of adequate provocation, leaving the question of what is "reasonable" provocation to the trial jury. As a result, jurors may—though they need not—grant mitigation for aggravations or insults that judges would have excluded from jury consideration under the common law.[23]

Again the greatest change may be seen in the MPC. The MPC's version of provocation eliminates the requirement of any particular provoking incident.[24] Instead, the fact finder must determine that there is a "reasonable explanation or excuse" for the accused's extreme emotional disturbance. What counts as a reasonable explanation or excuse is not easily determined, however, for the code drafters deliberately combined psychological and normative analysis of the defendant's emotional state. Under the MPC the decision-maker must start out by viewing the facts of the case through the defendant's eyes. The code states that the "reasonableness of such explanation or excuse shall be determined from the viewpoint of a person in the actor's situation under the circumstances as he believes them to be."[25] As explained by one court, the fact finder should "view . . . the subjective, internal situation in which the defendant found himself and the external circumstances as he perceived them at the time, however inaccurate that perception may have been."[26] Having established the defendant's point of view, the decision maker must then resolve whether the defendant's emotional reaction was reasonable. Reasonableness here may represent a psychological assessment of the normality of the defendant's emotional experience, or it may have moral content, representing a judgment about whether the accused should be blamed for feeling as he did.[27] The code does not specify.

A significant legal problem has emerged along with the development of reasonableness as the central concept in provocation: determining the identity of the reasonable person. To what extent should we invest the reasonable person with the defendant's individual characteristics, and to what extent must we judge the defendant's idiosyncrasies against the more ordinary traits of a "reasonable" person? Since emotions, as we saw in chapter 5, represent quintessentially *personal* reactions to events and situations, knowing the personal characteristics and experiences of the reasonable person will greatly assist in determining the reasonableness of the accused's emotional reactions.

We can easily imagine cases in which the reasonable person must be given some of the defendant's traits in order to make moral sense of the alleged provocation. For example, an accomplished adult athlete will not feel the same hurt at being called a cripple as will a young boy suffering from multiple sclerosis. The emotional impact of a slap may depend on the victim's age and past experience of violence. In both instances the accused's individual characteristics are also relevant to assessing the wrongness of the victim's conduct.

On the other hand, even if we concede that the hot-tempered person becomes more angry at a minor insult than does the even-tempered soul, should we invest the reasonable person with this characteristic? Almost certainly not. Temper seems to be the characteristic we wish to judge in the defendant; we abandon any effort at a universal standard if we use the defendant's temperament as our legal norm. Nevertheless, the drafters of the MPC sought to let jurors decide, on a case by case basis, whether the defendant's particular temperament or character trait should be included within their own formulation of reasonableness.[28]

Where relevant to the claimed provocation, modern courts have often permitted the reasonable person to be individualized with certain obvious physical characteristics of the defendant. Thus courts may instruct jurors to consider whether a reasonable person of the same age, sex, race, or physical disability as the defendant would have been as affected emotionally by the situation.[29] In some cases, certain aspects of the psychological condition of the defendant may also be attributed to the reasonable person, but all jurisdictions hold that a violent temperament should not be included within reasonableness analysis.[30]

Perhaps the most common approach to the individualization problem, however, is to leave it to jury determination. Aside from general remarks about reasonable temperament, jurors are left to figure out for themselves whether a particular trait that seems important to the defendant's emotional reaction is one that the reasonable person would share.

Another result of the expansion of reasonableness analysis under the psychological approach has been the removal of traditional timing restrictions on the doctrine. Instead of requiring a relatively rapid sequence of provoking incident and responsive homicide, some jurisdictions now permit jurors to consider the cumulative effect of a series of aggravations over an extended time period. Under new reasonableness interpretations, juries may resolve that the defendant's extended brooding on an earlier injury may increase rather than diminish its emotional impact and thus reduce his level of responsibility for the ultimate homicide.[31]

Summing Up: New Rules and New Stories

The effect of the psychological approach to provocation on American law depends largely on jurisdiction. Some states have embraced the psychological approach by adopting the provocation provisions of the MPC. Another set of jurisdictions, probably the plurality, employ some version of the *Maher* reasonable person approach, giving juries broad power over provocation and allowing a mix of both psychological and motive analysis to determine the reasonableness of provocation. Finally, some American jurisdictions adhere to a law of provocation that looks much as it did a century earlier, with relatively rigid categories defining the nature of provoking incident and timing of reaction set out by appellate decisions.[32]

Along with changes in doctrine have come changes in the kinds of cases associated with provocation. Most provocation claims still involve claims of injury to male integrity, but under the new rules we see new fact patterns, especially in homicides involving intimate partners. Among male defendants, the new provocation claims involve the torments of romance. In such cases men kill as the result of their partners' infidelity, their partners' accusations of male sexual inadequacies, repeated enticements and rejections, and a host of other romantic wrongs.[33] Most of the victims are women who are either in the process of breaking their relationship with the man, or who have already separated from him.[34] In addition to the usual doctrinal issues involved in provocation, these cases raise questions about social norms governing sexual relationships in contemporary society, including marriage, and responsibility for emotional control in intimate affairs.

Another new set of provocation cases involve women defendants. Provocation claims have increasingly been made by women who kill husbands or lovers in response to male physical abuse.[35] These cases raise a number of important issues, especially involving provocation's timing element. How recent must the abuse be for an abused partner to claim that the deadly retaliation was legally provoked?

The Responsibility Debate: Reasons versus Capacity

The contemporary debate about the law of provocation can be seen as part of a larger debate about responsibility for emotion and chosen action. On the question of responsibility for emotion, proponents of the psychological approach presume that all strong emotion undercuts rationality and thus responsibility. The discussion of emotion in chapter 5 should demonstrate that this view of emotion is dangerously simplistic. Emotion has its own complex rationality, requiring careful analysis to determine its moral content. No general judgments about the moral worth of emotion can be made on the basis of either general emotion type or intensity. Instead, we must examine the moral basis for the particular emotion, regardless of its psychological force. In provocation this means analyzing the reasons for the particular passion.[36]

On the question of responsibility for chosen action, the psychological approach to provocation depends heavily on the kind of capacity analysis discussed in chapter 3. According to this view, if the person was compelled by strong emotion to act in a certain way, that compulsion should lead to mitigation of responsibility.[37] Earlier, especially in chapter 3, we saw major problems with psychological capacity as the key to individual responsibility.

But all this is to anticipate. In order to join the contemporary debate about provocation, we need to see provocation in action, to see how it may apply to flesh-and-blood humans. With this in mind, consider the cases of John Gounagias and Calvin Ott.

Gounagias

John Gounagias was a Greek immigrant to this country who, along with a number of other Greek expatriates, worked in a paper mill at Camas, Washington.[38] On April 19, 1914, Gounagias drank beer with another resident of the house where he lived, Dionisios Grounas, also known as Dan George. During the course of the evening, Gounagias became "helpless and almost unconscious" as a result of either the beer or a drug put in the beer. The Oregon Supreme Court stated that, "after making many insulting remarks concerning the appellant and his wife, who lived in the old country," George set upon the helpless Gounagias and "committed upon him the unmentionable crime, and went away, leaving the appellant in a state of unconsciousness." The "unmentionable crime" was a commonly used euphemism for sodomy.[39] In plain language, George raped Gounagias.

The next day Gounagias protested to George about what George had done, but George laughed it off saying, "You're all right, it did not hurt you."

Gounagias asked George not to tell anyone in the Greek community what had happened, but Gounagias soon discovered the incident was widely known. The court recounted: "Wherever [Gounagias] went, he could hear remarks and see signs made by his countrymen indicating that George had circulated the story, so that the appellant was continually ridiculed and subjected to insulting remarks and gestures on the part of his fellow countrymen." Gounagias suffered severe headaches as a result.

On May 6, nearly three weeks after the attack, Gounagias's headache was so bad he missed work. Feeling depressed, he contemplated killing himself. At 11 o'clock that night he entered a coffeehouse, where he received his final humiliation. On entering, about ten men made "laughing remarks and suggestive gestures" toward Gounagias. Enraged, he rushed to his house. There he

> made a necessary trip to the toilet, went to his mattress, took out the revolver and loaded it, went rapidly up the hill to the house where George lived, entered the house, and by the light of a match found George asleep in his bed, did not awaken him, but immediately shot him through the head, firing five shots, all that he had in his revolver . . . he then returned to his own house, removing the empty shells on the way, put the revolver back in the slit in the mattress, and went to bed, where he was shortly afterward arrested.

At trial, Gounagias tried to claim provocation, but the court ruled that too much time had elapsed between the provoking act and Gounagias's response to constitute the sudden passion necessary for the doctrine. The jury convicted Gounagias of first-degree murder. The Washington Supreme Court affirmed the conviction.

The holding of the *Gounagias* case was, for its time, unremarkable. The nearly three-week delay between assault and retaliation did not fit the common law model of a killing committed in a sudden heat of passion. Yet the decision has since proven controversial, providing fodder for many who see it as illustrative of the psychological blindness of the common law.[40] Certainly the case seems to reveal serious problems with traditional doctrine.

In its provocation rule, the common law envisioned a man courageous enough to confront his enemies directly and decisively. The provoked man's only mistake was to respond too fiercely to injury, killing when lesser retaliation was appropriate. This was not Gounagias. After being raped, Gounagias relied on words for redress; they proved ineffective. His original injury was compounded when George made Gounagias an object of vicious ridicule in a small, insular community. But instead of lashing back as the law's model man would have, Gounagias internalized his hurt. He developed sick headaches, became depressed. Finally, in desperation and despair, he killed the sleeping George. From beginning to end, Gounagias never displayed the boldness and courage the traditional approach required.

Today we view Gounagias's conduct more sympathetically because today we put less stock in open confrontation and more in finding nonviolent solutions to human conflicts. After suffering an unprovoked and devastating sexual attack, Gounagias tried to resolve his problem with George peacefully. When that failed, he was left without any good options. He had reached a psychological dead end. He could not make George apologize and he could not face the constant social humiliation; the final attack was as much an act of desperation as the suicide Gounagias had previously considered.[41]

This reinterpretation of the case offers something for both reason and capacity theories of responsibility. The capacity proponent may argue that the generally nonviolent Gounagias deserved less punishment because George's actions caused Gounagias to lose capacity for rational self-direction, that is, self-control. Along these lines the defense at trial had sought to call an alienist, as psychiatrists were then called, to bolster a claim of lost control. Based on his examination of the defendant, the alienist would have testified that Gounagias "acted under an uncontrollable impulse produced by bringing back to his mind the outrage with such vividness and force that it was as real to him on the night of the killing as at the time when the outrage was committed, and even more so, because of his weakened condition." However the trial court barred this testimony, holding that the three-week lapse between rape and responsive killing was long enough for a reasonable man to cool off.[42] For the same reason, the court did not allow the jury to consider provocation in its verdict.

The reason-for-passion proponent would argue for mitigation based on the wrong done to Gounagias by George. George raped Gounagias, a terrible violation of his physical person.[43] He also ruined Gounagias's social identity, taking away his basic dignity by making him the object of lewd jokes. In this sense George's wrong was a continuing one; it represented a cumulative poison that gathered strength over time unless counteracted. Under this theory, Gounagias had good reason to be outraged at George even three weeks after the attack, and this justified passion provides mitigation for Gounagias's loss of self-control and his resort to ultimate violence.

Ott

State v. Ott presents another view of the contemporary debate about provocation.[44]

To understate the matter considerably, Calvin Ott and Stephanie Brinkley had a stormy relationship. They married three weeks after they met and soon embarked on a series of fights, separations, and reunions. After an initial separation and reunion, Calvin left Stephanie so that her welfare assistance would not be terminated. He returned later and learned that his wife had taken a lover. Calvin tried to fight his rival but Stephanie sent the man away and promised Calvin that she would be faithful to him. This pattern of separation and reunion, with violence and threats of violence over Stephanie's alleged infidelity, was repeated again and again. As the Oregon Supreme Court reported:

There were other separations, and the defendant, upon his return from each separation and his learning of more infidelities, became progressively more upset. This was especially so after the birth of their first child.

At one point, upon Stephanie's invitation to resume living together, the defendant returned home to find his wife engaged in sex with another man. A fight ensued. The police were called, and the defendant was arrested for the crime of menacing. Upon arraignment, the court in that case observed that the defendant appeared to be emotionally disturbed.[45]

The defendant received a probationary sentence in the criminal case, which included mental health counseling.

Stephanie obtained a restraining order against Calvin, but they continued to talk on the phone and occasionally see each other. They had long arguments over their divorce and child custody arrangements. These arguments finally led to Calvin's arrest for harassment. When Stephanie began to see another man, Calvin threatened to kill her. Later Stephanie's son (Calvin's stepson) broke his arm and was taken to the hospital for medical treatment. Calvin and Stephanie saw each other at the hospital on two different occasions. They agreed to meet there a third time.

It was arranged that on the third occasion the defendant was to drive Stephanie home after hospital visiting hours were over. Defendant had the impression from their first two meetings at the hospital that the relationship was improving. He was thus angered and disappointed when his wife's new lover appeared at the hospital on their third meeting to take her home. Defendant left the hospital in a state of agitation. He retrieved a .22 rifle that he had stored at the home of a friend, caught up with his wife and her lover, ran their truck off the road and shot his wife three times.[46]

Calvin Ott was tried and convicted of the murder of Stephanie, despite his claim of provocation. The conviction was reversed on appeal because of faulty jury instructions, however.

At least initially, Ott presents a less sympathetic figure than Gounagias. Where Gounagias killed in retaliation for a rape, Ott killed out of jealousy. Even Ott's grounds for jealousy were weak as Stephanie was no longer his wife or lover. They had met a few times at a neutral location; no resumption of romance had occurred, even if it was in some subtle way promised. The immediate trigger for Ott's rage was trivial, a matter of who would drive Stephanie home. Worse, his rage might be judged immoral; it came from his desire to possess Stephanie, to control her autonomy. His killing of Stephanie seemed to say: If I can't have you, then no one can.[47] If provocation depends on moral assessment of the reasons for extreme passion, these reasons may distinguish *Ott* and *Gounagias*.[48]

If we take the capacity approach to responsibility, however, Ott has at least as strong and perhaps a stronger claim to mitigation than Gounagias. Ott's argument that he killed while in the grip of an overwhelming passion is at least as credible as Gounagias's. While Gounagias had been physically violated and humiliated, Ott had suffered the tortures of an on-again, off-again love. Ott's prior history and the growing intensity of his jealous explosions suggest that he experienced the appearance of his wife's lover at the hospital as a brutal rejection of his own worth. His past history indicated a quick and often violent reaction to romantic insult, suggesting little impulse control with regard to romantic relationships. He had a documented need for mental health treatment. He was emotionally unstable. In sum, Ott was a man who lost self-control due to strong emotions. In a psychological sense, he displayed little, if any, capacity to control his emotions or refrain from violence. The legal question is, Does this matter?

Responsibility for Emotion and Self-Control

All versions of provocation depend to some extent on a determination that strong emotion caused loss of self-control. But what do we mean when we say that an impassioned individual loses control? We can begin with what we do *not* mean. We do not mean that the individual becomes irrational. When Nesler, Gounagias, and Ott killed, they killed for rational reasons.[49] Their reasoning may have been shortsighted, but it made human sense. Each took revenge on the person who caused them great pain.

Nor does the concept of loss of control refer to the physical causes of emotion. In all cases, emotions can be traced to personality type, which has a strong genetic element, and upbringing. In this respect, emotions are no different than any other aspect of rational choice. As we saw in chapters 2 and 3, all rational choices can be traced to genetic and environmental causes, which means that such causes either eliminate all human responsibility or are irrelevant to it. In any case, physical causation plays no special role in determining responsibility for strong emotion.[50]

Instead, when we say that a person lost control due to strong emotion, we mean that she experienced such strong urges to action that ordinary inhibitions were overwhelmed. Strong emotions usually involve strong urges to action. A person passionately in love feels driven to take great risks or do great works to express that love. A person in the throes of rage feels compelled to retaliate. Strong passion rises like a river in flood to overwhelm the usual limits on its flow. Strong passion changes the individual's decision process. The individual does not carefully consider the consequences before acting. Previously effective personal or social inhibitions against violent action now prove insufficient.[51]

In the context of provocation, when we say that a person loses self-control, we mean that she experiences a loss of moral inhibition and impaired moral judgment. She loses *moral* control. She acts in contradiction of those moral beliefs that in calmer moments would guide her conduct. The normative question is, Should we grant mitigation for this reduction in moral control? My response is the same as that offered in chapter 3 when we considered the moral capacity approach to responsibility, and in chapter 5 when we considered responsibility for the passions of punishment. Individual responsibility should track reasons for conduct and emotions, not capacity for doing or feeling.

As we have seen before, the capacity approach to responsibility tends to blur "is" and "ought." Applied to provocation, the capacity approach favors the most violent, because these individuals have repeatedly demonstrated the greatest incapacity to choose otherwise. Compare, for example, Gounagias and Ott. Based on what we know of their prior behavior, we would have to assume that Gounagias had more capacity to control his feelings and conduct than did Ott; Ott frequently resorted to violence in conflict situations where Gounagias did only once. Indeed, Ott fits the profile of what psychologists call the undercontrolled person, one who resorts to violence on minimal provocation.[52] But in fashioning law we must move from what is to what should be. The criminal law must defend the community against the inclination to attack at the least "provocation."[53] As one English court put it:

"[T]hough the law condescends to human frailty, it will not indulge human ferocity. It considers man to be a rational being and requires that he should exercise a reasonable control over his passions."[54] Or, as an American court observed: "The law regards with some tolerance an unlawful act impelled by a justifiably passionate heart, but has no tolerance whatever for an unlawful act impelled by a malicious heart."[55]

What should count most in provocation is the moral justification for the defendant's passion. Only the offender with good reason for extreme passion deserves mitigation.[56] This emphasis on motive does raise an important question, though. If we care so much about the offender's perception of wrong, the perception that justifies resulting passion, why do we also require the passion? Perhaps we should extend mitigation to cases where the killer had good reason to be furious but in fact acted calmly. Perhaps we should not worry about the lapse of time between provoking incident and fatal retaliation.

We grant mitigation when a person has been provoked because of two related determinations: (1) that the person had good reason for strong anger, and (2) that in experiencing such anger, the person's moral restraints were temporarily strained to the breaking point. If the justly enraged individual gives way to the temptation of violence, we read this violence as less of an attack on human value, as less of an act of moral disregard than it would be otherwise because of its origin in a morally based passion. In this sense the provoking situation is like a natural emergency, when the emotions are so powerfully and justifiably engaged that standards of responsibility must be somewhat relaxed. In provocation it is because the temptations to violence were exceptionally strong *and* because they stemmed from a justified sense of injury that the violence appears less blameworthy than it would otherwise. By contrast, where the defendant was wronged but did not react emotionally, or where we judge that his anger was not justified at the time of action, we lack one of the two essential elements of mitigation.

Finally, we need to recall why punishment is deserved even if the killing was provoked. Voluntary manslaughter still remains a crime, after all. Provoked killings deserve punishment because even though the defendant's passion was justified, his action was not. Having cause for rage and cause to kill remain fundamentally different judgments. We blame the provoked killer because private homicide is never a justified response to past wrongdoing.

Crafting a New Rule: From Reasonableness to Good Reasons for Anger

Having established the basic rationale of provocation we are ready to construct a new rule. I propose the following.

> A killing that would otherwise be murder is voluntary manslaughter if the defendant had good reason to believe that the victim committed a serious wrong against the defendant or a loved one, and if this provoked in the defendant at the time of the homicide a great and justifiable anger at the victim.

In this proposal I make two basic changes in the definition of provocation from both traditional rules and rules under the psychological approach: (1) the new rule would restrict the passion of provocation to anger, and (2) it requires that anger be based on a well-founded belief in serious wrong done by the victim.[57]

The Restriction to Anger

If provocation is about killings driven by justified emotion, then its emotional reach should be limited. Simply put, provocation should require justified anger. The modern decision to expand the scope of provocation's emotional range has undercut the normative basis for the doctrine by permitting mitigation for emotions that may be justified but do not justify hostility to the victim.

A person may have good reason to grieve or feel anxious without having any moral cause for hostility toward another. For example, a father who grieves at the death of a child may, as a result of his grief, experience fits of aggression in which minor or even imaginary wrongs by others suddenly grow to enormous proportions. Grief may explain his rage and violence in this situation, but it provides no moral justification for either.[58]

We may well sympathize with the grief-stricken, and our sympathy might even translate into considerations of mercy at sentencing, but such considerations should not change the categorization of what the defendant did to the homicide victim. Like many other defendants, the grief-stricken can say that circumstances not chosen by him caused him to suffer overwhelming emotion and lose self-control. Once more, I argue, reasons for emotion and conduct should be paramount, not psychological capacity.[59]

Besides anger, the only other emotion that presents a strong moral argument for mitigation is fear.[60] Fear can be as powerful an emotion as anger and often has greater moral content. All humans have a right to self-defense, a right based on apprehension of risk. Fear represents the emotion of risk apprehension, thus fear is often relevant to criminal responsibility for violence. Still, there remain sound legal reasons to keep fear-inspired homicides distinct from those inspired by anger. As long as culpability depends on reasons for emotion and for conduct, fear and anger-inspired actions present quite different moral profiles. These differences should be recognized in law by a continued distinction between self-defense and provocation doctrines.

In many homicide cases, defendants claim both self-defense and provocation. The defendant may first claim that the homicide was justified due to an honest and reasonable belief in the necessity of using deadly force, that is, self-defense. If that claim fails, the defendant may assert that the killing was provoked by the victim, and thus that the killing was at worst voluntary manslaughter. Or, where allowed by the jurisdiction, the defendant may claim imperfect self-defense, that he honestly but unreasonably believed in the necessity of using deadly force. If accepted by the decision maker, this claim will also result in a voluntary manslaughter conviction.

Distinguishing provocation and self-defense becomes most important in cases where the defendant feared nondeadly force from the victim or where she feared deadly force at some indefinite time in the future. Picture a husband and wife with a volatile relationship who fall into a bitter argument in their kitchen one night. Infuriated by his wife's comments, the husband slaps and pushes her, knocking her against the sink. The wife grabs a butcher knife from the counter top, lunges for her husband, and kills him. Assuming that the wife did not reasonably fear for her life (as full self-defense requires), at a later trial the wife must assert that she deserves punishment only for manslaughter because of her fear of her husband, her anger at him, or a combination of the two emotions. This raises the legal question of whether we should permit at least some fear-based claims to be handled under provocation instead of self-defense.

One argument for including fear as a provocation passion is the difficulty of distinguishing it from anger. A reaction that begins as fear frequently turns to anger. Different emotions can be hard to distinguish, even for the person experiencing them. This is doubly true in high-stress situations. But note that provocation as we have come to understand it focuses less on the sensation of emotion than on the defendant's *reasons* for hostility. In contrast, the parallel doctrine of imperfect self-defense turns on the *sensation* or *experience* of fear, regardless of its justification. This doctrinal difference mirrors our different moral views of defensive and aggressive force. Self-defense represents a core moral right of human beings while aggressive force represents one of the basic wrongs addressed by the criminal law. This suggests a strong normative basis for distinguishing anger and fear-based mitigation claims.

But what if the wife in the earlier case acted from a *combination* of fear and anger, neither of which would be sufficient to support either imperfect self-defense or provocation when considered alone? Perhaps in this case two halves should be combined to make a whole—fear and anger added together should constitute sufficient provocation. To take this approach, though, would be to value intensity of emotion over its moral basis. It would mean creating an emotional stew pot, in which a dab of fear and a sprinkling of rage might combine to constitute adequate passion when there was no good reason for either great anger or fear. It would, in other words, replicate the psychological approach to provocation.

Keeping fear and anger claims separate does not necessarily doom the wife's provocation claim in the kitchen homicide, however. She can still argue that her husband's violence gave her good reason for great anger. Deliberately threatening another's physical safety, especially in conjunction with a prior infliction of significant injury, constitutes a wrong for which persons may legitimately become angry and may in some cases support provocation. Thus fear can play a role in provocation, but only indirectly. The final judgment about provocation must concern reasons for anger.

From Reasonable Persons to Reasons for Anger

The proposed rule changes the basis mens rea terminology of provocation by substituting reasons for anger for reasonable person analysis. This change will certainly not eliminate the hard issues of provocation—issues about the morality of an individual's emotional reaction to a particular situation—but it should assist decision makers in keeping their moral focus. It should help jurors concentrate on the justification for passion rather than the justification for killing and should ground decision making in the specifics of the incident as opposed to abstract constructs of reasonable persons.

In most American jurisdictions, provocation is defined by what would make the reasonable person lose control. This often leads to a confusion about whether decision makers should analyze the reasonableness of killing (which follows loss of control), or the reasonableness of the passion (which precedes the loss of control). Thus courts and legislatures often speak as if a provoked killing is a reasonable one.[61] Yet by definition a reasonable act is morally and legally appropriate, not a serious criminal offense like voluntary manslaughter.[62] As many have pointed out, the remedy for this confusion is simple. The decision maker should look for anger which would *tempt* a reasonable person to kill rather than on passions which would *make* the reasonable person kill. This makes clear why even the provoked killer deserves punishment.

The more significant problem with reasonableness analysis is that it makes the hard normative questions of provocation even harder by requiring decision makers to decide who the reasonable person is before judging the conduct of the accused. The judge or jury must decide which traits of the defendant are "his problem" and thus should be excluded from the reasonable person's makeup, and which individual traits are part of the "situation" and thus should be included in the reasonable person's identity. For example, we have seen that a person's temper is usually her own responsibility, meaning that the reasonable person will be deemed one with a "reasonable" temper, not the defendant's temper, whatever it happens to be. By contrast, race and age are traits that are often seen as beyond the individual's responsibility, and, if relevant to the provocation, may be included in the reasonable person's identity. Thus the defendant's emotional reaction may be compared with that of a reasonable person of the same age or race. Unfortunately, issues about the identity of the reasonable person normally cannot be resolved on a general, trait by trait, basis. We cannot decide who the reasonable person is without looking at the individual circumstances of the case.[63]

Recall our case of the kitchen homicide, where the wife kills a physically abusive husband. Should gender be taken into account here? Does the reasonable person become female, like the accused? I would argue yes in this situation, because gender may represent an important part of the husband's threat. The threat occurs in a social context in which there are long-standing patterns of violence by men against women. But compare this to a case where a man insults another man by impugning the sexual integrity of the other's mother. While I grant that men generally take such insults more seriously than do women, making the reasonable person male here would create a separate "boys will be boys" moral code that cannot withstand moral scrutiny. Why should males be entitled to great rage at verbal insult when females are not? Where is the commitment to universal moral standards here, or the commitment to nonviolent dispute resolution?[64] This suggests that in most male versus male conflicts, the reasonable person should have no specified gender.

The new rule will not eliminate the moral complexities of such issues, but it should help decision makers recognize the moral issues involved. Under the new rule we see that the question is whether the anger is justified—thus gender, race, or any other trait, is relevant only if it is relevant to the wrong done by the victim. Under the reasonable person formulation, decision makers may miss the normative issue and focus on general group distinctions. In determining reasonableness, juries may not easily distinguish the argument that "that's the way men are" (i.e., boys will be boys) and that "no one should become so upset over a stupid insult" (a universal norm of emotional assessment). Decision makers may readily assume that the reasonable person, like all other persons, has a sex, that the reasonable person's sex is the same as the defendant's, and that social attitudes common to that sex have normative importance.[65] What is becomes what should be. By contrast, the new rule, with its insistence on anger justification, makes the normativity of the provocation question clearer.

Arguments for Abolition

So far I have argued that provocation, properly conceived, is morally sound and has a proper place in our law of homicide. A number of recent critics, however, have sought to abolish provocation entirely, on the grounds that either the concept of mitigation for provoking circumstances is fundamentally flawed, or that the doctrine is inextricably intertwined with sexist notions about human behavior.[66] To these criticisms should be added the possibility that provocation decisions necessarily express racial and class bias. The proposed rule must meet all of these objections to win approval.

Provocation as Pro-Violence

Several commentators have recently argued that provocation should be abolished because it weakens the law's commitment to nonviolence.[67] Stephen Morse has argued that because it is not *that* hard to refrain from killing even when impassioned, by partially condoning intentional, unjustified killing provocation undercuts the law's commitment to nonviolence.[68] To the extent that provocation is morally relevant, it should be considered only at sentencing. Certainly Morse is correct that most persons have little trouble refraining from killing even when greatly aggravated, suggesting that even provoked killings deserve significant punishment. The real question is, if provoked by a great wrong, should this change the level of offense? Or, to put it another way, does provocation represent the kind of category distinction that jurors rather than judges should make? I would argue that the provocation distinction is a vital and intensely factual one, and therefore most appropriate to jury decision making, subject to the procedural safeguards of a trial rather than the more discretionary decision making of judges at sentencing.

Another abolitionist, Jeremy Horder, asserts that provocation is conceptually unsound because the emotions it judges worthy have no moral value. He notes that the doctrine bases mitigation on a desire for aggressive retaliation and questions why the law should condone, even partially, the aggressive urge to hurt another. He suggests that the emotionally justified response is righteous indignation: a desire to demonstrate the wrongness of the act to the wrongdoer rather than a desire to attack him.[69] While I agree that righteous indignation represents a worthier response than the desire for retaliation, this distinction does not eliminate the moral basis of provocation. Here again we confront the compromise nature of the doctrine. Provocation deals with moral gray, not black or white. It represents a concession to human shortcomings, not only in self-control but also in emotion. We human beings are not saints; if pricked we not only bleed, we rage. While we must urge victims like Nesler and Gounagias to avoid the personal anger that inspires hate and retaliatory violence, while we urge them through law to find nonviolent means of redress and punish them if they do not, we should recognize how their victimization affects the *degree* of their wrongdoing. Although they broke the fundamental rule of nonviolence, their homicides make different moral statements than do murders. The proposed rule expresses this difficult but important distinction and requires that it be made in the most formal and public fashion possible, as part of the jury's verdict.

Provocation, Sexism, and Gender Difference

Feminist critics of provocation have leveled three major criticisms against current provocation law: (1) that under the psychological approach, modern rules permit the expression of sexist assumptions about gender roles; (2) that traditional provocation doctrine directly promotes patriarchal values, especially in its treatment of adultery; and (3) that the traditional timing restrictions of the doctrine unfairly penalize women who seek to make provocation claims. In my view, each of these criticisms has substantial merit; the proposed rule aims to reduce these forms of gender bias.

Provocation and the Psychology of Love

Earlier we noted the emergence of a new fact pattern in provocation cases under the psychological approach: the claim of the distraught male lover that romantic trauma caused him to lose self-control. While these cases also frequently involve allegations of infidelity and insult, critical to the claim of overwhelming passion is the trauma of a romance gone bad. In a recent study of homicide trials involving provocation claims, Victoria Nourse has shown that in jurisdictions influenced by the psychological approach, a large percentage of trials in which provocation claims were presented to the jury involved either the decision of a female partner to leave the relationship or her longer-standing separation from the male defendant.[70] While juries usually reject provocation claims in such cases, that outcome is by no means certain. Thus a man who kills a former intimate and claims provocation based on the emotional trauma associated with romantic rejection may obtain mitigation either by jury verdict or by pretrial plea bargain.[71]

Who can doubt that romantic trauma exists, or that it has a powerful effect on human emotions? We know as a matter of basic human experience that the end of an intimate relationship often causes great emotional turmoil. Separation from a spouse or lover frequently inspires fierce, painful, and volatile feelings. We know that such emotions regularly cause persons to lose their ordinary self-control in a variety of ways. People say and do crazy things because of love. This means that if provocation depends on the psychological reasonableness—the normality—of the accused's emotional reaction, then many claims of provocation stemming from intimate rejection may be accepted. But this only illustrates the moral emptiness of psychological assessment. That the loss of a romantic connection does cause emotional trauma does not mean that all emotions stemming from the loss are justified.

As Nourse notes, the psychological approach to provocation, because of its emphasis on the intensity of emotion, opens the law to sexist decision making. Its rules permit assumptions—or observations—about how men experience rage as a result of romantic loss to become partial excuses for violence in response to women's efforts at romantic separation. Permitting men mitigation for fatal violence due to romantic rejection reinforces the idea that women are more responsible than men for making intimate relationships work. Such mitigation claims symbolically penalize women for asserting their independence; it is this independence, after all, that causes the man's trauma.[72] Manslaughter verdicts in these cases treat more leniently homicide due to loss of self-control, even when the killing represents a last-ditch effort to control over another. It permits mitigation for what may be an act of desperate patriarchy.

Adultery and Patriarchy

As flawed as the psychological approach to provocation is, the traditional rules of provocation may be even worse in terms of gender bias. The most obvious example of gender bias is in perhaps the most-cited example of provocation: discovery of adultery.[73] At common law, this referred to a husband's discovery of a wife's adultery. As the English Lord Chief Justice John Holt explained in 1707: "[W]hen a man is taken in adultery with another man's wife, if the husband shall stab the adulterer, or knock out his brains, this is bare manslaughter: for jealousy is the rage of a man, and adultery is the highest invasion of property."[74] According to Holt, "a man cannot receive a higher provocation."[75]

Originally this form of provocation was explicitly limited to men, for adultery was deemed an invasion of the man's right of sexual possession of his wife. Today such a claim may be made by a woman as well, but in fact the overwhelming majority of defendants claiming provocation on this ground are men.[76] Statistics on killing reflect a similar pattern: jealousy in one form or another is the most common motivation of men who kill their partners, while women kill their partners most often do so in response to male violence.[77]

The traditional rationale for provocation based on discovery of adultery must be rejected. Marriage should be a partnership between fully responsible, independent adults; no one surrenders autonomy on taking marriage vows and the value of marriage cannot rest on one partner's "ownership" of another. Nor should we accept the traditional double standard, that a man's place in the community depends on the sexual virtue of his woman but is essentially unaffected by his own adventures in extramarital intimacy.

Modern law should also take account of many social changes involving marriage and extramarital relations. The liberalization of divorce and the acceptance of what has been called serial monogamy means that marital relationships are long-term but not life-long arrangements for many Americans. Attitudes about extramarital sex have also changed substantially. While adultery remains generally disapproved conduct, it may be more common and certainly has less legal significance than before. Equally important, most

Americans no longer live in small communities where reputation for up-standing sexual conduct is critical to social acceptance.

As always, the question for criminal law is how we judge these social changes. That people do act this way does not mean that the law should condone their conduct. I would certainly celebrate the demise of marriage-as-possession, but, like most Americans, I have serious reservations about changes involving sexual fidelity in marriage. Even if we grant adults greater sexual autonomy, adultery still represents a serious wrong, the betrayal of a basic trust. This means that the discovering partner may have justification for anger, even great anger in some situations.

The challenge for modern provocation law is to distinguish between at least two different kinds of provocation-for-infidelity claims—those based on betrayal of a particular, personal trust, and those based on patriarchal rage-at-dispossession. Again the distinction comes not in the sensation of anger, but in the reasons for it. Imagine a case in which the married partners have made a particularly strong commitment to sexual fidelity. Perhaps one partner has suffered in the past from a lover's infidelity and made fidelity a special requirement of the current relationship. In this case discovery of adultery may support great rage. But in other cases we may read rage at infidelity less as an expression of moral betrayal and more as an assertion of a man's (or in some instances a woman's) need to possess and control a partner. We need to look at the whole context of the relationship and especially the state of the relationship prior to the infidelity. Did the infidelity violate a fundamental norm of the partners at the time, or was it just one in a series of mutually hurtful actions in a troubled relationship? Did it occur during a separation period or when the bonds of loyalty and partnership were still in full force?[78] These are the questions that should predominate under the proposed new rule.

More important than any change in the analysis of infidelity cases, though, would be eliminating adultery as a basic example of provocation. Judges, lawyers, and legal commentators must stop using discovery of adultery as a prime example of a legally provoking incident. The moral force of such cases comes from the confluence of norms we accept (sexual fidelity in marriage) and norms we should reject (male possession and control of female sexuality). Instead of providing the strongest imaginable argument for provocation, discovery of adultery should be considered a conceivable, though problematic basis for mitigation, one highly dependent on the particular facts of the case. On our list of exemplary cases, it should come last, if it comes at all.

Abuse of Intimates and Gender Differences in Aggression

Now we come to the most complex, and perhaps most important issue involving gender—how provocation should apply to the killing of intimate partners by those they have abused. For the most part, we are concerned here with women killing the men who batter them, often wives who kill their husbands. Here we must deal with the problem of gender difference with regard to aggression. We must confront traditional images of women as nonviolent and responsible for family harmony. We must also consider sociological evidence of gender-related differences in aggression.

Sociologists report that men tend to view aggression more positively, and resort to it more quickly, than women, who tend to view it as disgraceful and employ it only as a last resort. If reliable, this observation raises a question about provocation's timing requirement. Traditional doctrine holds that a provoked killing must occur shortly after the provoking incident, a requirement that seems to fit the standard pattern of male aggression. But what of those persons, often female, who use violence only with great reluctance, and who therefore kill only well after the original provocation? Perhaps provocation's rule needs to be modified to fit nonmale patterns of aggression.

We begin with an empirical inquiry. Are there really gender differences with respect to aggression? Answering this question requires us to engage in a dangerous business, to make generalizations about men and women. It is a dangerous business because we can easily fall into stereotyping—assuming that statistical trends determine the nature of individuals. Yet the general differences between men and women with regard to aggression are too important to ignore in fashioning general rules for homicide.

Recent work in sociology points to a significant gender distinction in understanding and use of aggression and violence. Sociologist Anne Campbell has argued that men often see aggressive acts, including violence, as appropriate ways to assert control over others.[79] The man who pushes back when pushed gains the respect of other men, and often of women as well. This has been called the instrumental model of violence.

Campbell argues that women, by contrast, tend to shun overt aggression and violence. They see aggressive, violent acts as shameful because they represent failures of the central female norm of cooperative interaction. As a result, women are far less likely than men (and girls less than boys) to engage in openly aggressive acts, including violence. Women experience the same levels of frustration and anger as do men, but they try harder to repress these feelings.[80] If their rage and frustration grow too great, however, women also resort to violence. In contrast to men, such violence is designed to vent women's pent-up frustrations rather than to control the victim. Thus it may be called the explosive model of violence.[81]

Before we consider the normative implications of these models, I must add one more caution about gender generalization. Although a variety of data suggest that most who employ the instrumental model of violence are male and most who employ the explosive model are female, we can find striking counterexamples. Some girls and women use violence to assert control over others.[82] Female violence in schools is on the rise as girls come to see violence as a legitimate means to establish and defend social status.[83] Likewise, we have already seen a case—*Gounagias*—in which a man's reaction to wrongdoing fits the explosive model of aggression. This reminds us that even if the models generally track sex differences, sex does not determine the individual's approach to violence. Individual cases must be resolved on individual facts, not gender generalizations.

Now we move from the empirical to the normative, from description to prescription. Are killings that fit the instrumental model worse than those that fit the explosive model? Accounts of explosive violence often suggest that the individual suffered diminished responsibility. For example, Campbell gives the following first-person account of Caroline, a woman who was furious with her husband for walking out on a heated argument to take a shower.

> I just sort of whirled around and I tried to pick up the phone. I don't know if I wanted to throw it, but I knew it wasn't going to go far enough. So I picked up this frying pan that was right there and I tossed it right through the [shower] curtain. I didn't even think about it and then he came out dripping, holding the frying pan. And he said, "You could have killed me! You could have killed me, do you know that?" I still didn't realize I could have killed him because I didn't feel like I wanted to kill him. I mean, it wasn't even in my head at the time that I was throwing it. I could have flung it against the wall. I just threw it at him. I really have a very blind rage sometimes when I seem to get really crazy.[84]

Caroline's language is full of excuse arguments. She says she experienced a "blind rage" when she became "really crazy," suggesting a form of insanity. She says she did not mean to hurt him, let alone try and kill him. Yet Caroline made a series of rational, intentional choices that belie her excuse suggestions. Angry at her husband, she contemplated throwing the phone but realized it would not go far enough. She then selected the frying pan, obviously realizing that it would make a more effective missile. As she notes, she could have thrown the pan against the wall, but instead she threw it straight at the target of her rage, her husband. She acted out her anger in perfectly logical fashion.

In the end, Caroline gives a generic account of rage. A man who attacked his wife in the heat of a domestic argument might describe his "blind rage" in the same words.[85] This reinforces the basic point that responsibility for emotion must track the reasons for feeling and not simply intensity. Thus the explosive model of violence has legal significance only if it sheds new light on why the person acted as she did, when she did. In order to determine this, we need to return to provocation and its traditional timing requirement.

The common law's requirement that provoked killings occur within a fairly short time of the provoking incident had two rationales: (1) a judgment that the courageous, self-respecting man immediately and openly confronts one who injures or insults; and (2) an assumption that sudden passions have a more devastating impact on self-control than other kinds of emotion. Both rationales raise the specter of gender bias. Under the explosive model of aggression and violence, individuals value cooperative methods of dispute resolution over courageous confrontation and self-assertion. Faced with a wrong done by another, the person who values cooperation over conflict will initially suppress the instinct to rage and channel emotions toward a peaceful resolution of the conflict. We should applaud this effort. But we must recognize its cost—if the wrongdoer denies the wrong and spurns reconciliation, the injured person will be emotionally blocked. The hurt experienced will find no legitimate outlet. This means that later reminders or aggravations of the original wrong may constitute the emotional breaking point for the one wronged. It means, in other words, that sudden loss of self-control from great passion may occur much later than it would in a person who fits the instrumental model of violence. All this provides a different perspective on cases where battered women who kill their abusers, particularly those involving so-called nonconfrontational homicides.

Women who kill their domestic partners in response to physical abuse sometimes act at a moment of relative calm in the relationship. The woman kills at a time when she faces either a nondeadly threat from her partner, or no immediate threat at all.[86] This makes self-defense claims problematic. Traditional provocation law fits these cases poorly as well, for women often attack well after the most significant act of provocation, thus violating the strictures of the cooling off period. As a result, such defendants are often convicted of murder. If this result seems unjust, we should consider how the law might be changed.

Many have tried to revise self-defense law to accommodate nonconfrontational homicides, arguing for the admission of new evidence, especially concerning psychological syndromes, new interpretations of the requirements of reasonable apprehension and immediacy of threat, and rewording of the basic self-defense rule, among other changes.[87] Considering the worthiness of these reforms lies beyond the scope of the current project, however. Our concern remains provocation. To what extent should provocation law accommodate these cases? Do these cases better fit under provocation analysis rather than self-defense?

In answering these questions, we might begin with our moral intuitions. Do we sympathize with battered women defendants in nonconfrontational homicides because we perceive they acted to save lives, or because they were motivated by justified rage? At least some nonconfrontational homicides by victims of abuse seem to involve retaliation rather than defense. The pattern of events suggests that the defendant did not kill to remove an immediate threat but rather to rid herself of a tormenter in the only manner she could imagine. The defendants fit the model of explosive violence in just the way that Gounagias did, their sudden and unexpected resort to violence occurring in reaction to a cumulation of wrongs.[88]

Under our new conception of provocation, the timing of the homicide should not prove an insuperable barrier for the defendant. The question is whether the accused had reason for great anger at the victim at the time of the offense. If we determine that the victim had seriously hurt the defendant in the past, and that the defendant made sincere efforts to achieve a nonviolent resolution of their problems, we may judge a killing in eventual reaction to the victim's wrongs was legally provoked.[89]

The new approach to provocation accommodates both cases of quick violence in response to a single wrong, and those where a series of aggravations following an original wrong push a nonconfrontational individual over the edge. In all cases, timing remains an important factor, but one that must be evaluated in light of the individual wrong done to defendant and the defendant's efforts to seek peaceful resolution of the dispute. For example, the person who suffers an original harm, and then, without suffering any significant aggravation of that hurt, works himself up into a killing fury, deserves full blame for his rage. In this situation the killer demonstrates neither the aggressive defense of personal integrity which traditional doctrine presumed, nor the commitment to peaceful reconciliation which some delayed-retaliation cases present.

Although the new perspective on timing is related to gender differences, the provocation rule should be stated in gender-neutral terms. As the case of John Gounagias reminds us, culpability tracks individual conduct, not gender generalization. Gounagias tried to achieve a peaceful resolution of his conflict with George; he tried to suppress his emotional reactions, but after a series of aggravations finally gave way to homicidal rage. As with the immediate-but-excessive-retaliation homicide of the traditional model, here we find a person who has been seriously wronged, had reason for great anger, but failed to maintain self-control. We find a person who should be able to argue for mitigation via the provocation doctrine.

Class and Race Bias

Provocation as currently constituted may be sexist, but the bias indictment may not end there; the doctrine may also either encourage or permit race or class bias. These forms of discrimination have received little attention from legal scholars, which means that the discussion that follows must remain tentative and suggestive. We simply do not know enough about the interaction of the doctrine with race and class differences to make reliable judgments. There is ample reason for concern, though. We will look at three particular bias issues: (1) whether class differences in style of homicide—either deliberative or spontaneous—should have the legal significance that current homicide law gives it; (2) whether cultural differences associated with class and race should have legal significance in determining adequate provocation; and (3) whether the law has sufficient safeguards against discrimination based on low social status of the victim. Interestingly, all of these problems involve discrimination not against defendants, but against victims. Because homicide tends to be an intragroup offense—members of one racial/ethnic/social group tend to kill members of the same group—how defendants of a particular group are treated cannot be considered separately from how victims of that group are treated. The issues often represent two sides of the same legal coin. We need to be sure that if the homicides committed by certain group members are generally treated more leniently than other homicides, that the different treatment comes because of moral differences in the homicides and not a devaluing of the group's homicide victims.

As we have seen, provocation provides mitigation for some cases of essentially spontaneous homicide. The most common perpetrators and victims of such homicides are lower middle class, working class, and poor young men. When wealthier Americans kill, even in domestic situations, they are more likely to do so with deliberation and be convicted of murder.[90] In this country the perpetrators and victims of unplanned homicides are also disproportionately members of racial minority groups, especially young African American men.[91]

If we agree that deliberation necessarily makes a harmful act worse, then the current structure of murder law in most jurisdictions is sound; premeditation represents an aggravating factor, and killing on a "sudden falling out" represents a mitigating factor. But if, as I have argued here and in the previous chapter, planning and timing considerations do not reliably track culpability, then we need new criteria for distinguishing between greater and lesser homicides.

One possibility for reform would be to explicitly take into account factors associated with class and race, specifically cultural differences. In this heterogeneous society, we frequently celebrate cultural difference, recognizing that diverse cultures cannot and should not be melted into a single dominant American culture. Perhaps the law should seek to accommodate different cultural views of emotion and violence.

The past gives us many instances of cultures with different norms of emotion and violence than those of middle class America today. Provocation doctrine originated in an English culture that valued male aggression and, to a lesser extent, male violence.[92] Similar, perhaps even more extreme norms of honorable violence thrived in white male society in the American South during the nineteenth century, especially before the Civil War.[93] Modern criminologists have observed that many instances of spontaneous violence can be traced to subcultures of violence: groups that view violence in a relatively positive fashion and employ it more frequently than others in the society. In 1958 Marvin Wolfgang, in connection with perhaps the most famous study of homicide, observed cultural differences according to race and sex:

> The significance of a jostle, a slightly derogatory remark, or the appearance of a weapon in the hands of an adversary are stimuli differentially perceived and interpreted by Negroes and whites, males and females. Social expectations of response in particular types of social interaction result in differential "definitions of the situation." A male is usually expected to defend the name or honor of his mother, the virtue of womanhood . . . and to accept no derogation about

his race (even from a member of his own race), his age, or his masculinity. Quick resort to physical combat as a measure of daring, courage, or defense of status appears to be a cultural expression, especially for lower socio-economic class males of both races.[94]

This brings us back to a question first raised in chapter 1: Should the criminal law be pluralist and permit different standards for different cultures within the society, or should we strive for a single standard that governs all?

In favor of a variable standard, we should recognize that subcultures of violence arise in reaction to oppressive conditions set by the more powerful in society. Such subcultures represent the desperate efforts of otherwise devalued young men to establish norms of honor and dignity for themselves.[95] How many of us have the strength of character to reject the predominant norms of our peers? How many of us had that strength of character when we were young?[96]

Yet the arguments against value pluralism in criminal law are even weightier. I have argued throughout that the criminal law not only defends our moral community; it helps create it. Especially in the context of homicide, the law's prohibitions define the kind of society we have. If we give up the ideal of a single criminal law, especially with regard to a harm as fundamental as homicide, we also give up the idea of a single community in which all individuals have moral obligations to others. In so doing we would lose one of our most powerful moral tools for making ourselves and our society better. Even as we valued human diversity in our criminal law we would diminish the value of individuals. We would win the battle at the cost of the war.

Yet all this says much less than it seems to. Few—if any—argue that the law should have separate standards according to race and class. The hard issues involve not our commitment to a universal standard of self-restraint and nonaggression, but how to judge variations in culpability in a wide variety of conflict situations. They involve the always hard task of distinguishing between those cultural differences that have normative significance and those that do not. For example, a man supporting a family on minimum wage work, whose week's earnings are stolen, suffers a different injury than a middle-class professional who loses a week's salary, even though the latter may lose a much greater sum. Similarly, race membership of the victim and defendant can change the harm—the wrong—of racial insult. Racial insults between members of the same race group lack the sting of those between different groups; particular histories of racial antagonisms between particular groups may also change the wrong of the particular cross-group insult. As we saw with gender difference though, group membership has no universal moral worth. The law should give no sanction to those groups who hold that aggression is the best proof of manhood, that minor insults require physical retaliation, that wives should never disobey husbands. Nor should decision makers ever resolve that because violence is more common among certain groups, that members of that group have less self-control and thus are less responsible than others.

The proposed rule for provocation should assist in the assessment of cultural differences by keeping decision makers focused on the normative judgment of emotion rather than on assessment of psychological capacity. As was true with gender, the psychological approach to provocation presents the greatest opportunity for biased decision making because it blurs observations about the way people feel and act with moral judgments about how they should feel and act. A decision maker may translate an observation of class and race differences in aggression into a legal judgment that members of that class and race have less capacity for emotional restraint.

While I think that the proposed reform would make class and race bias somewhat less likely than many current rules, I want to be cautious about promising major improvement. First, I do not know the extent of current discrimination, and second, assuming that such discrimination occurs in a significant number of cases, I do not know how much it stems from legal definition. I will simply lay out some suggestive evidence.

In chapter 7 we saw that in capital punishment the most serious racial discrimination is that based on the identity of the victim, not the accused.[97] Unfortunately, we can only guess at the existence or nature of similar discrimination in the processing of noncapital cases. In contrast to capital punishment, where a number of sophisticated studies have been done, the evidence of race-of-victim discrimination in provocation is largely anecdotal. It is disturbing nonetheless.

In cities with large minority populations, a high percentage of homicide offenses, sometimes even a majority, are disposed of by pleas to manslaughter, this despite the law's presumption that manslaughter represents the exceptional rather than the average purposeful killing.[98] A colleague who was for many years a public defender in Los Angeles reports that many defense attorneys, in arguing for lenient treatment of a black man charged with a homicide case, would term the killing a "150th Avenue misdemeanor." The street reference was to the heart of the black community in South Central Los Angeles. The phrase was meant to convey the speaker's perception that the killing was just part of the ordinary pattern of life in the area—a dispute about gambling, women, or drugs or the like that led to violence. It signified that the killing was no big deal. The phrase was the lawyer's equivalent of the Los Angeles Police Department slang for crimes involving disfavored victims: NHI, which stood for No Human Involved.[99] The danger is that a criminal justice system run by white middle-class decision makers devalues the lives of poor and minority victims by routinely classifying their killings as manslaughter, not murder.

In a society fundamentally shaped by group differences, legal decisions will inevitably be affected by group differences, sometimes in legitimate and sometimes in illegitimate ways. The best that we can hope for our law of provocation is that it will point decision makers to the need to judge the moral source of emotion, taking into account morally relevant individual circumstances. A law that explicitly directs decision makers to judge justification for emotion will perform that task better than one that emphasizes psychological capacity, intensity of feeling, and general reasonableness.

Changing Stories: Making Physical Assault the New Classic of Provocation

No reform of provocation's rule will be effective without an accompanying reform of its classic stories.[100] Stories have always been central to the doctrine. For example, in describing what constitutes adequate provocation, one nineteenth-century commentator wrote: "It is best that we begin with illustrations, and derive the rule, if any can be found, as we proceed."[101] As befits a compromise doctrine, provocation's rule has always been understood at least as much by its stories, its classic examples, as by formal statements of its rule. Anglo-American lawyers have long told stories of cuckolded husbands bursting in on adulterous wives and their lovers, of men in taverns falling to deadly blows in order to explain the concept of provocation. These stories are as much the source of provocation's current ills as any particular rule formulation.

Today the paradigm case of voluntary manslaughter should be neither discovery of adultery nor mutual combat, but a killing provoked by serious physical assault. This assault may be sexual, as in the Nesler and Gounagias cases. Sexual attacks represent serious violations of personal integrity that warrant great anger.[102] Or the assault may involve straight violence: a husband who batters his wife; a young man who, without any necessity, delivers a vicious blow to another.[103] Such cases also illustrate justified outrage in reaction to serious attacks on human value.

By comparing claimed instances of provocation to these new examples of serious physical attack, we can limit the tendency of provocation to reflect class, gender, and race biases, because we should agree that wrongs as severe as these assaults transcend any group differences. If the new paradigms take hold in our legal culture, they should push to the fringes of provocation doctrine the old examples of adultery and mutual combat. As we have seen, some cases involving infidelity may support provocation, but only under special circumstances. Similarly, homicides following mutual combat might still fall under provocation's rule, but only when the killer suffered a serious and unwarranted physical assault by the victim prior to the homicide. A verbal insult to male honor should not suffice, nor should the fact that a combat was spontaneous and fairly fought.[104]

Conclusion

For the scholar of criminal law, studying provocation proves both an inspiring and a humbling experience: inspiring because the doctrine provides raw material for nearly every imaginable kind of responsibility theory—and humbling for the same reason. It contains the raw material to argue against virtually any theory. Indeed, the doctrine defeats all theory in the end. As a compromise rule, a fact-sensitive doctrine that seeks to encompass rather than reduce the complexity of human interaction, the rule resists any permanent categorization.

Determining provocation in particular cases proves an especially messy business. Like an elected official who must take tenuous, compromise positions to retain public support, the doctrine requires drawing lines between is and ought, between blame and reprieve that constantly threaten to collapse into unprincipled power preferences. Contemporary critics have shown that provocation has often partially condoned the moral shortcomings of certain groups in society, namely hot-tempered, patriarchal, heterosexual men, at the significant expense of other groups. Indeed, the argument against provocation today is so strong that it admits of only two viable responses: abolition or reform. Because I believe that a reconceptualized provocation expresses such an important moral judgment that it should be part of the decision making of trial juries, I favor reform.

9

Crimes of Indifference

"I'm not a racist. I don't hate anybody."

"He's not a bad person. He didn't mean to hurt anyone."

"The worst you can say of her is that she was a little careless. She did not realize what would happen."

Each of these speakers makes a common assumption about evildoing. Each assumes that to do evil a person must act with hostile intent or at least with the awareness that harm to another is likely to result. Each assumes that without intent or awareness, the actor is blameless. I disagree. The failure to look out for and prevent doing harm to others may be culpable, even without actual awareness of risk. It represents one of the most common forms of evil, which deserves more attention in both law and everyday morals.

In this chapter we move from intentional to unintentional criminal homicide. Specifically, we take up the mens rea rules for depraved heart murder and involuntary manslaughter.[1] I argue that the modern trend to require that the defendant have actual awareness of fatal risks for serious criminal punishment is a mistake, based on a misconception of responsible choice. When a person acts in a way that involves obvious and unjustified risks to human life and causes death, punishment may be deserved even if the actor never realized the risks of her behavior, as long as the person's conduct demonstrates an attitude of indifference to the welfare of others.

We begin the consideration of the two rival approaches to culpability—what I call the awareness and the indifference approaches—with a review of the basic law of murder and manslaughter as applied to unintentional homicides. We then move to an overview of the basic arguments in favor of awareness of risk as the key to culpability. We find that at the center of the dispute between indifference and awareness approaches is a disagreement about responsible choice—about what kinds of mental activities count as choices. Awareness advocates see choice as what occurs following perception of certain morally critical facts; indifference advocates urge that the perceptive process be considered part of choice, so that the failure to perceive certain facts may sometimes be attributed to a blameworthy choice. This focus on choice leads to a brief digression into new work in cognitive science, which inspires new ways of understanding the interaction between perception and decision making. The argument then returns to familiar ground—an application of the responsibility theory set out in part 1 to a number of particular cases. The chapter closes with a proposed redefinition of murder and manslaughter offenses based on the indifference approach to culpability.

An Introduction to Depraved Heart Murder and Involuntary Manslaughter

Anglo-American criminal law divides unintentional criminal homicides into two basic categories: depraved heart murder and involuntary manslaughter. Excluding felony murder, which also covers fatal carelessness, depraved heart murder represents the most serious form of unintentional homicide in Anglo-American law. Its hallmark is extremely dangerous conduct for which there is no justification. In the eighteenth century William Blackstone described it by reference to a workman who throws a heavy object, such as a large stone or timber, from a rooftop into the street below, killing a pedestrian.[2] He noted this would not constitute a crime if the workman shouted a warning first and if the incident occurred in a country village with few passersby. If the workman threw the stone or timber, after a warning, from a roof in London, or other populous town, where people are continually passing, "the fatal action would constitute the lesser crime of manslaughter," Blackstone wrote, "[b]ut if the workman knows that people are passing below and throws the stone or timber without warning, then he commits murder, for then it is malice against all mankind."[3]

As they did with other common law offenses, early English and American courts defined depraved heart murder in terms of moral character. Instead of focusing on a particular state of mind of the offender, courts condemned the moral traits revealed by the offender's action.[4] An early Pennsylvania court described depraved heart murder as a killing that demonstrates "wickedness of disposition, hardness of heart, cruelty, recklessness of consequences, and a mind regardless of social duty."[5] Courts have typically labeled such conduct as "wanton," "wicked," and "vicious," all demonstrating an "abandoned and malignant heart."[6]

★

The modern law of depraved heart murder bears a close resemblance to its common law ancestors. The factors Blackstone identified as critical in the eighteenth century remain important today in resolving the legal status of homicidal acts, but the law's articulation of the required mens rea has changed.[7] Today the Anglo-American law of murder relies primarily on assessment of the accused's awareness and notice of risk. Under English law, depraved heart murder is encompassed within a general mens rea of intent to kill or intent to do great bodily harm, though this latter phrase is given a broad interpretation.[8] American law generally permits a murder conviction based on extreme recklessness that demonstrates great moral callousness. To oversimplify somewhat, United States jurisdictions take two different views of the recklessness required for murder. Many jurisdictions take the awareness approach to culpability and require proof that the defendant was aware of a great, unjustified risk to life. The rules of these jurisdictions will be the main focus of the chapter. In a second group of jurisdictions, greater emphasis is placed on the obviousness of risk, its severity and lack of justification than on awareness of risk. These latter jurisdictions have essentially adopted the indifference approach, although not in the explicit terms that are proposed later in this chapter.[9]

The Model Penal Code's definition of reckless murder provides a good example of the view that full awareness of risk is critical to criminal responsibility. The MPC divides the mens rea for reckless murder into four parts: that the offender have (1) consciously disregarded, (2) a substantial, and (3) unjustifiable risk to human life, (4) under circumstances manifesting extreme indifference to the value of human life.[10] I will refer to these components as the awareness, danger, necessity, and indifference elements. The danger and necessity elements require proof that the defendant's conduct created a significant risk to human life for no good reason. The risk must be so substantial and unnecessary that "its disregard involves a gross deviation from the standard of conduct that a law-abiding person would observe in the actor's situation."[11] The standard permits risk taking where there is an overriding necessity. Thus, surgeons and police officers may knowingly risk others' lives as long as they have an overriding medical or legal reason for their conduct. The awareness element requires that the defendant realize: (1) the great dangers of his conduct, and (2) its lack of justification. In most cases the key question will be whether the defendant realized the dangers involved.[12] The last requirement, that the circumstances demonstrate extreme indifference to the value of human life, calls for a qualitative judgment of the moral attitude demonstrated by the risk taker.

The lesser offense of involuntary manslaughter has traditionally lain in the shadow of murder, defined largely by reference to the greater offense. If not murder, a culpable, careless act that causes the death of another must be manslaughter.[13] Involuntary manslaughter normally covers less risky behavior than that of depraved heart murder: conduct that is less obviously dangerous and, perhaps, more justifiable.[14] Most importantly, involuntary manslaughter usually involves a different mens rea: negligence rather than recklessness.[15] In most states, involuntary manslaughter requires proof of grossly negligent conduct causing death: that the offender should have realized his conduct represented a substantial and unjustifiable risk to human life.[16] Here the individual need not have been aware of the risk; it is enough that a reasonable person in his situation would have been.[17]

As noted in chapter 6, the reasonable person standard represents a modern form of allusive mens rea, in which the decision maker must compare the conduct of the accused with that of a person possessed of ordinary prudence and self-control. The breadth of reasonableness analysis may be illustrated by the MPC's definition of criminal negligence. The MPC provides that a person acts negligently if "considering the nature and purpose of his conduct and the circumstances known to him," the individual's conduct "involves a gross deviation from the standard of care that a reasonable person would observe in the actor's situation."[18] As the Commentary notes, there is "inevitable ambiguity" in determining what the phrase "actor's situation" should cover.[19] After setting out a few illustrations of what should and should not be included, the drafters left further articulation to the courts.

Awareness versus Indifference: Arguments about Choice

For the last thirty years or more, criminal law scholars have debated whether awareness of risk should be a prerequisite for criminal culpability for careless harmdoing. One group of scholars has argued that without awareness, we cannot say the person chose to put another at risk, and so the person does not deserve criminal liability.[20] Others have contended that notice of risk is the key: if a person acted in disregard for obvious and unjustifiable dangers to others we may judge her guilty of indifference to the value of others. Indifference proponents contend that moral and legal responsibility includes the obligation to look out for harms to others when one acts.[21] In doctrinal terms the debate has concerned the difference between recklessness, which normally requires actual awareness of risk, and negligence, which rests on a judgment that under the circumstances the offender should have been aware of risk, though he was not.

To paraphrase Justice Jackson's famous dictum about mens rea, the notion that culpability depends on awareness of risk is no passing fancy of morality.[22] Responsibility arguments of many kinds turn on the assumption that the individual's awareness of certain facts determines his responsibility. It is built into much of our moral discourse. The assertion that the person understood the likelihood of hurting another before acting almost always counts as an aggravating factor; the assertion that the person did not understand usually counts as a mitigating factor, and often a complete excuse.

The law's paradigm examples of depraved heart murder—fatalities caused by wanton shots fired into occupied structures, games of Russian roulette, and racing cars careening down streets crowded with cars and pedestrians— also suggest a central place for awareness of risk in the legal scheme of culpability.[23] These cases seem to exemplify conscious risk taking. How could anyone engage in such activities without understanding the risks involved? Indeed, why would anyone act so dangerously, for so little justification, if danger was not in some sense the point? In such cases we are struck by the underlying hostility of the actor. Even if the offender did not intend to kill a particular person, he acted with evil intent toward people in general. This reading of the paradigm cases brings us back to the model of intentional wrongdoing with which the chapter opened. In this sense, cases of culpable but unintentional killing merely represent a subset of the larger category of intentional wrongs.

But are we always sure that persons who endanger others in obvious ways are actually aware of those dangers? And are we confident that persons who are not aware of the dangers of their conduct are therefore excused from the most serious kinds of blame? Can we ever blame for failing to *consider* the risks involved? In England, appellate courts have gradually moved away from a strict awareness-of-risk conception of mens rea toward one where notice of risk plays a critical role. In that nation an offender may be found criminally reckless not only if he was actually aware of a significant and unjustified risk, but also where he "fail[ed] to give any thought to whether or not there is any such risk in circumstances where, if any thought were given to the matter, it would be obvious there was."[24] Here the key to culpability is the failure to exercise the mental faculties needed to realize the risk.

Many commentators on English law have criticized this change, arguing that awareness of risk must be a precondition to culpability. In essence, critics contend that seriously blameworthy choices involve what a person decides to do *after* perceiving a risk. If the person sees the risk and ignores it, he chooses to endanger others and may be punished. If the person does not see the risk, then he does not, in a sense, make a choice about endangering others. At least for purposes of criminal law, the argument is that perception of risk occurs (or does not) prior to responsible choice.[25] By contrast, indifference advocates argue that at least in some cases, a person may be responsible for choosing not to perceive. The failure to look out for others may in itself be a blameworthy choice. This allows us to see that the dispute between approaches is fundamentally a dispute about choice. What kinds of mental activities, or inactivities, should we hold ourselves responsible for? Or to put it another way, what kinds of choices are associated with unintentional wrongdoing?

Choice and Perception: From Internal Choosers to Neural Networks

The puzzle of choice in the context of unintentional conduct may be introduced by a personal story. My older daughter has always held her parents to the highest standards of family care. My wife and I try hard, but alas, we sometimes fall short. For example, when she was a toddler, we would often set out on trips without some vital item—toy, blanket, food—that we had planned to bring, and that she was counting on. I would tell Leah: "I'm really sorry. I just forgot." In response, Leah would ask: "Why did you forget?"

Ever the teacher, I was always sorely tempted to educate my daughter on the concept of a category mistake. I wanted to tell her that she had asked a why question, appropriate to ascertain the intent of an intentional action, but inappropriate when addressed to an unintentional action. Forgetting, after all, involves a mental stumble, an instance when intents do not match up with actions. By definition, forgetting describes the absence of a critical choice. It makes no sense to ask about the reason for a choice when there was no choice in the first place.

But the more I thought about Leah's question, the more it struck me as an important one. Forgetting does not occur randomly. It often can be traced to choices for which we are responsible. For example, deciding to pack the morning of departure instead of the night before greatly increases the chance of forgetting. In moral terms, we often blame for carelessness, even when the harm done was unintended and unanticipated. Leah's question suggested the need to think harder about the kind of choice involved in unintentional wrongdoing.

Returning now to unintentional homicide and the awareness approach, we must judge failures of perception rather than failures of memory. We ask: Does it make sense to blame persons for failing to perceive risk? Awareness advocates urge a negative answer, arguing that failures of perception are not chosen. And oftentimes, the awareness position will prove correct; culpability does stand or fall on extent of actual perception of the risk. But with the help of recent work in cognitive science, I will argue that the awareness approach in criminal law often goes too far; failures of perception sometimes should be attributed to blameworthy choices.

As the discussion so far should illustrate, assumptions about the intentionality of choice play a large role in our assumptions about responsibility. The way we talk about chosen action often emphasizes the importance of awareness. Asked to recount a choice, we normally speak in terms of what we had in mind at the time. Consider an automobile accident in which a driver swerves to avoid one vehicle, then strikes another. Asked to explain her decision to swerve, the driver will likely say something like: "I figured it was my only chance to avoid a collision," an answer indicating that she deliberatively weighed various options before swerving. Or the driver may say: "It all happened so fast I had no time to think. I just reacted instinctively." This suggests a belief that instinctive action differs from chosen action, perhaps because instinct is not self-aware.

Such introspective accounts of choice (introspective because they are produced by the person's own thinking about choice) usually take a narrative form; they tell a story with a beginning, middle, and end. The beginning is perception, the middle is organization and preliminary evaluation of information perceived; the end is the decision reached. Asked to recount what happened, the driver in the accident will likely tell what she perceived (I saw the truck cut in front of me), how she evaluated that perception (I could tell I did not have enough room to stop), and what she decided (so I swerved right to try to avoid the truck). Such narratives suggest a basic and normative distinction between perception and decision making. Perception involves the passive gathering of relevant information; choice occurs only when this information has been sorted and presented to the self-conscious mind. In the narrative of rationality, choice represents the last act, the climax of the narrative. Introspection about choice suggests that if the narrative stops short of self-conscious decision making, we do not choose.

This picture of choice should sound familiar; it accords with the internal chooser metaphor reviewed and critiqued in the previous chapter. Again we see the seductive power of the metaphor. We know that good decision making requires good information. We need efficient sense organs: sensitive ears to hear and sharp eyes to see. We need a clear head (i.e., well-organized, powerful brain) to assemble relevant information in an orderly fashion to understand our options. The metaphor suggests that if the internal chooser is blessed with skilled information gatherers and collators, the dangers of a particular activity will be dramatically presented before a decision is made. Cognitive bells will ring and lights flash, warning the internal chooser prior to decision making. A less fortunate internal chooser, who works with blurry vision, muddled hearing, or incompetent information collators, may receive such poor information that he may entirely miss the dangers involved. We naturally conclude that failures to perceive should be treated like mechanical malfunctions; cause for dismay and remedial efforts, but not blame.

The common view of perception assumes that it is a passive, mechanical process that happens to the real person. In fact, the gathering and selecting of relevant information represents an affirmative mental activity of the individual. Information processing is something we do, not something that is done to us.[26] We speak of *paying* attention as opposed to *falling* asleep. Like talking or eating, perception requires affirmative effort by the individual even if it does not demand a great deal of conscious direction.[27] Nor is perception mechanical in the sense that it is hard-wired in the brain. While some basic perceptive abilities may be genetically encoded, the great majority must be learned. An infant will instinctively duck to avoid an object overhead, but she must literally learn to see. Genetic patterns may provide the structure to learn perception, but not the details of its functioning.[28]

But none of this changes the basic fact of humanity that our perceptive abilities have severe limitations. We cannot process all the information available to our senses. For example, although the brain can simultaneously process different kinds of information for different purposes, we recognize that human abilities in this regard are limited.[29] When my children ask me something while I am on the telephone, I often lose track of both their question and my phone conversation. Realizing this, I try to limit the information I have to handle at one time. I tell my daughter, I'm sorry, I can't talk to you when I'm on the phone. Or, if I am driving in the car, trying to negotiate a contested L.A. intersection, I may ask others in the car to be quiet for a moment. These relatively conscious decisions about information intake mirror less conscious decisions we make about what we will attend to and what we will ignore. Which brings us to the central responsibility problem: recognizing that our perceptive resources are limited, do we use them in a morally acceptable fashion?[30]

Our perceptions of the world depend largely on preestablished attention hierarchies.[31] For example, I read the sports page every day but I read much more about basketball and soccer than baseball or football. At parties I attend to conversations about relationships, politics, and the movies but tune out talk of restaurants and real estate. In short, I attend most to those matters which engage me most—in which I am most interested.[32] The same kinds of attention hierarchies affect more morally significant activities, such as how we wield power at work, how we interact with friends and partners. They affect what we hear and thus what we understand about the needs of those with whom we deal.

The awareness advocate may interject at this point: your description is fine, but what about prescription? If you want to hold a person responsible for his attention agendas, you must show that the person chose that agenda. Unless the person rationally and without coercion decided at some point to become disinterested in a particular set of risks, how can he be blamed for not looking out for those risks? Herein lies a problem. No one seems to deliberately choose his or her attention agendas. Most attention agendas seem to be the product of unconscious mental processes—they simply develop without our own understanding—and once formed, prove quite resistant to conscious efforts to change. This hardly looks like a choice for which we should be held responsible.

I agree that most of our attention agendas do not stem from highly self-aware decision making and in this sense they are not the products of conscious choice. But the line between conscious and unconscious decision making here proves more tenuous, and less significant than it first appears. There is no clear boundary between conscious and unconscious thought that can distinguish responsible from nonresponsible mental activity.

Recent work in cognitive science emphasizes the similarities between what are commonly called unconscious and conscious thought processes. Many scientists assert that, contrary to common belief, conscious and unconscious thought do not involve fundamentally different kinds of mental activity.[33] Instead, many researchers view consciousness as an emergent property, a state or function that arises out of nonconscious mental activity rather than a separate brain function that supervenes on nonconscious information processing.[34] We become more self-aware as the brain performs more levels of data processing, not because data is processed in a different way or in a different place. The line between aware and unaware mental activity appears very much a matter of degree.

Cognitive scientists report a complex interaction between conscious and nonconscious processes. Deliberative processes affect nonconscious thought processes and vice versa. One way of understanding the interaction is through the distinction that cognitive scientists make between automatic and controlled mental processes.[35] A controlled mental process involves full self-conscious awareness. My writing this chapter represents a controlled process because I self-consciously decide what words to put on the page. An automatic process is one directed by preestablished patterns, without conscious direction. Most daily activities depend on automatic processes. Once we learn to walk, run or drive a car, these activities require little conscious awareness to perform. Notice that most automatic processes begin as controlled processes—we had to learn to walk, drive, and speak. Moreover, even after the processes become automatic, they remain subject to conscious control. We still can—and often do—make self-aware decisions about walking, driving, and speaking.

Attention depends on a similar interaction between aware and unaware processes. Whether we notice a particular fact about the world usually depends on automatic processes, on preset attention agendas and patterns of recognition. But the automatic processes of perception are subject to conscious direction at all times, albeit to different degrees. At some point in the past we made decisions about perception priorities, priorities we can change if we wish.

All of which brings us to the bottom line: What does cognitive science tell us about choice in unintentional harmdoing? Do our new understandings of the brain favor the awareness or the indifference approach? The answer is that cognitive science is agnostic on the responsibility question that concerns us here. Sound moral arguments can be made for either indifference or awareness based on what we have recently learned about human information processing. My aim in taking this brief excursion into cognitive science has not been to find the extramoral or extralegal data that will settle the question, but only to open up the reader's mind to another view of choice. My main target remains the venerable internal chooser and the metaphor's assumption that perception is necessarily divorced from choice. Developments in cognitive science demonstrate how we *might* hold persons responsible for failure to perceive. We may focus our judgments on the person's perceptive priorities. Science will not tell us whether we should do so, however. That argument must be played out in the moral and legal arenas, with the traditional tools of moral and legal reasoning.

Responsibility for Indifference: A Preliminary Account

According to the basic theory of responsibility developed in part 1, we should blame persons for unintentional harms when their risky conduct demonstrates culpable indifference to the value of others. Just as intentional wrongdoing toward another merits blame because the wrongdoer has demonstrated a disregard for others that challenges our community's fundamental values, so there are cases where a failure to look out for another may demonstrate a callousness that challenges the principle of universal human worth on which a moral society must stand.

In most instances of culpable indifference, we judge that the wrongdoer was actually aware of the danger his conduct posed to others. Our judgment of culpability rests on the determination of the actor's decision to proceed, regardless of his own high degree of consciousness of the harms he might do. But in some cases we may judge that the individual was only dimly aware of the risk, or perhaps was not conscious of it at all, yet still acted with culpable indifference. Culpability here rests on a judgment that the failure to perceive risks stems from bad perception priorities. In such a case we judge the person guilty of choosing to assign too low a priority to the value of other human beings.

Where the accused did not perceive the risks involved at the time of his conduct, culpability rests on a judgment about why the person failed to perceive. Did the failure stem from a culpable lack of concern for the victim, or should we attribute it to other factors for which the individual should not be blamed? In illustration, consider two cases in which a driver runs a red light and fatally injures a pedestrian in the cross-walk. In both cases the driver saw neither the red light nor the pedestrian prior to the collision. One case involves a father rushing his severely injured child to the hospital. Another involves a teenager showing off for his friends. Immediately we see the moral significance of the reasons for perceptive failure. Indeed, the reasons for perceptive failure in these cases prove far more significant than the fact of that failure. The father's lack of perception may be attributed to his overriding and morally worthy desire to help his child. The teenager's failure to perceive may be attributed to morally blameworthy priorities. The teenager placed a higher value on winning the admiration of friends than on attending to the risks of fast driving. The teenager's conduct demonstrates an attitude of indifference toward others, a morally culpable state to which society should forcefully respond by conviction and punishment. The father's conduct demonstrates a tragic conflict between valuing his child and valuing others. If he is deemed guilty of indifference to the lives of others—and he may be—his indifference will be of a lesser order than that of the teenage driver.

In unintentional homicide, a determination of culpable indifference depends on three factors: (1) notice of danger, (2) extent of danger, and (3) the defendant's reasons for acting in a dangerous fashion. The more notice of danger, the more likely it is that the person was actually aware, and, even if not aware, the more likely that the person should be blamed for bad perception priorities. The extent of danger goes to our expectations for looking out for others. The greater the potential danger involved in an activity, the higher the moral obligation to consider and minimize those dangers, and the more we blame for failure to consider the dangers. Finally, we must examine the defendant's reasons for acting dangerously—was there an overriding moral justification, or were there constraining circumstances for which the individual should not be blamed? Or was the conduct the result of misplaced priorities?

Indifference in Current Law: Medical Risks and Intoxication

Having laid out the basics of indifference analysis, we now return to the doctrinal arena to see how it works in particular cases. We will see that indifference analysis does not change the outcome of many cases but does promise the significant benefit of better explaining and justifying the outcomes of certain cases than the awareness approach.

We begin with a case involving risky medical conduct that on its surface seems to present a classic instance of wrongdoing according to the awareness approach, but that on closer inspection provides an even better example of the power of indifference analysis. We then take up the law's treatment of intoxication in unintentional wrongdoing and find another kind of support for indifference.

Medical Risks

In 1974, Tony Protopappas, a licensed dentist and oral surgeon, opened a dental clinic in Costa Mesa, California. By September 1982 the clinic employed five dentists and two office managers along with a number of dental assistants. Protopappas established many standard procedures to foster efficient medical processing. These included standardized "setups" of anesthetic injections to anesthetize surgery patients and standardized instructions for his staff dentists on how to maintain patients under anesthesia. Although Dr. Protopappas was the only one at the clinic licensed to administer general anesthetics, much of the actual responsibility for administering and overseeing anesthesia fell to other staff.

On September 28, 1982, Protopappas operated on Kim Andreassen to do a root canal, three fillings, and a crown. Protopappas recognized that the eighty-five-pound, twenty-four-year-old woman was in frail health. Andreassen had told the doctor that she suffered from lupus, total kidney failure, high blood pressure, a heart murmur, and chronic seizure disorder. After contacting Andreassen's general physician, the office manager told Protopappas that Andreassen should not to be put under general anesthesia. Protopappas administered anesthetic drugs by his standardized method, putting Andreassen to sleep.[36] Although Protopappas later denied it, a nurse said that he administered a general anesthetic.

During the procedure Andreassen showed signs of toxicity from the anesthetic drugs and severe respiratory problems. When an assistant brought the respiratory problems to Protopappas's attention, he said, "Maybe that's normal for her because she is so ill." He completed the procedure. By the time he finished she was breathing normally again.

Shortly after finishing, however, Andreassen showed signs of respiratory collapse. After another dentist's efforts did not produce any improvement in the woman's condition, Protopappas administered oxygen by a disposable mask. Such masks provide oxygen for persons who can breathe unassisted; more elaborate positive pressure oxygen equipment is required for a person whose lungs are not functioning on their own. The clinic did not have such equipment. After brief treatment with the disposable mask, Protopappas called paramedics. Andreassen was clinically dead by the time they transported her to the hospital.

Medical experts later said that Andreassen died of a drug overdose. One oral surgeon declared that the drugs given would be massive for anyone "let alone a sickly 88 pound girl," and that their combination was "crazy" because the mix made it impossible to determine their impact on the patient.

Two other patients of Protopappas died in February 1983, also as a result of respiratory failure due to overdose of anesthetic drugs. Medical experts testified at trial that Protopappas demonstrated extreme recklessness in his administration of anesthetics, in his supervision of staff, and in his overall treatment of these patients. A jury found Protopappas guilty of three counts of depraved heart murder.

As the California Court of Appeal noted in its lengthy review of the case, Tony Protopappas did not wish to harm any of his patients: "Dying patients would be bad for business; and nothing shines through this record quite as brightly as Protopappas's enthusiasm for making money—lots of it."[37] Under California law, Protopappas's guilt depended on proof of recklessness—the extent to which he was aware of substantial and unjustifiable risks of death to his patients. At trial and on appeal, Protopappas argued that the prosecution had not proven he was aware of such risks. The jury and Court of Appeal disagreed. Citing numerous instances where the doctor received warnings or made comments indicating his awareness of a hazard, the appellate court held that the prosecution had produced ample evidence to support a determination of recklessness.[38]

As a matter of deference to the original fact finder, the appellate court's decision seems correct. Protopappas was clearly informed of the risks involved, and from this a jury might find that he was actually aware of the risks. Yet if we take the awareness approach seriously, we should not dismiss the doctor's claim too quickly. If we were to require reliable proof that the doctor truly realized—brought into a high level of consciousness—the great and unnecessary risks of his own conduct, then the defense may have had the stronger argument.

We begin with the assumption that the doctor bore no ill will toward his patients and desired a successful practice. Is it likely that such a doctor would consciously disregard serious and unjustified risks to his patients' lives? To put it another way, do we truly believe that Dr. Protopappas realized that his actions were likely to kill Kim Andreassen but proceeded regardless? Although there was evidence to support such conscious disregard, it is not the best explanation for the doctor's behavior. Much more likely, Protopappas evaluated the risks involved and decided they were minimal. In other words, he evaluated the risks badly. Given the warnings he received, Protopappas should have realized that he was taking enormous and unjustified risks. When he made his critical medical decisions, however, he probably did not actually realize the dangers involved.

My guess is that Protopappas never allowed himself to recognize the real risks of his medical techniques. The doctor's primary concern was with efficient, lucrative medical procedures. He used standardized anesthetics and worked on several patients at the same time to maximize profitability. A decision not to operate, or to use individualized anesthesia, or to stop an operation in the middle, would interfere with his overriding goal of efficient patient processing. This predisposed him to use standardized anesthesia and to finish whatever medical procedures he started.

Ego may also have played a role in the doctor's assessment of risk. Protopappas was a highly educated, highly motivated person with a high-prestige job. Most people with these attributes also have big egos. They have a tremendous financial and psychological investment in their own talents and find it hard to admit a mistake or recognize their own limitations. Perhaps the reason that Protopappas discounted the risks was his ego-based disposition to believe in his own techniques. He was so heavily invested in his own expertise that he could not afford self-doubt.

This interpretation of the case raises several legal and moral problems. First, if proof of actual awareness of substantial risk fails here, despite the repeated warnings given the doctor, then depraved heart murder will effectively be restricted to cases of either overt hostility, or those where the defendant confesses to awareness of risk. Such a constriction of murder would conflict with widely held intuitions about culpability. In order to avoid this result, courts and juries in awareness jurisdictions often interpret the awareness requirement in a rough-hewn, commonsense fashion. Courts focus less on whether the defendant *was* aware than whether, given the obvious dangers involved, he *must have been* aware.[39] This leaves the law open to the criticisms that it does not mean what it says, or that its meaning is unclear.[40] But notice what happens when we employ indifference analysis.

Assuming that the doctor never realized that he was needlessly endangering his patients, we ask: Why? Was this a situation where we could not, in a moral sense, expect him to do better? For example, if these events occurred in an emergency room where time pressures were enormous and not of the doctor's creation, this might rebut the presumption of indifference. But the reasons discussed above—ego and money—are selfish reasons that support a judgment of indifference. The doctor put a higher priority on ego, money, or both, than on the safety of his patients. Regardless of whether he had a high level of awareness of the risks he undertook, Dr. Protopappas was properly judged culpable for the murder of his patients.

Intoxication

Another example of the power of indifference analysis to explain current criminal law is the law's treatment of persons charged with recklessness while intoxicated. Here we find that even those jurisdictions which generally require awareness of risk for criminal conviction make an exception for when the offender was intoxicated. The exceptional treatment of intoxication is usually explained in terms of sober-minded decisions to give up full control, but indifference analysis provides a more complete justification. As always, a particular case will make the point best.

> On the evening of August 2, 1987, thirty-six-year-old Deborah Moquin drove her car southbound on State Route 85 in upstate New York. She had been drinking. She had previously been convicted of two offenses involving drinking and driving: in February of 1983 she had been convicted of driving while her ability was impaired, and in June 1984 of driving while intoxicated.
>
> Moquin drove erratically, changing speeds and lanes. In passing another car, Moquin's speed was estimated at 70 miles an hour. When the road narrowed from four lanes to two, Moquin's southbound car crossed into the lane for northbound traffic. Witnesses said she did not put on her brakes or attempt to return to the southbound lane, even when a station wagon approached from the opposite direction. The two vehicles crashed head-on. The station wagon flipped over on impact and came to rest upside down against a guard rail. Mr. and Mrs. Quinn, who sat in the front of the car, were severely injured. Their fifteen-year-old daughter Kathleen, who sat in the back, was killed.
>
> Police at the scene reported that Moquin's breath smelled strongly of alcohol. They found four empty and one half-empty bottles of beer in her car. A blood test revealed Moquin's blood alcohol level was .24 percent, indicating extreme intoxication.[41] Moquin was charged with murder and was eventually convicted of manslaughter.[42]

Moquin's driving was outrageously dangerous. If she drove this way while sober all would agree that she deserved serious punishment, for we could say with confidence that she knowingly put others on the road at great risk. But she was heavily intoxicated. Some argue that such intoxication changes moral responsibility because it diminishes, or in some cases eliminates, the person's awareness of risk. To evaluate this claim we must take a closer look at intoxication's effect on individual behavior.

Drinking can change basic personality. Intoxicated individuals frequently gain self-confidence and lose inhibitions. Alcohol inspires many to express sexual or aggressive desires they would otherwise repress. Consumption of alcohol also predisposes the individual to focus on short-term pleasures rather than long-term consequences.[43] The drinker cares about having fun now, and pushes aside considerations of harm to others or to herself. Thus Moquin might be a cautious person while sober, but when drunk she might disregard or even pursue great risks to herself and others.

English and American courts have uniformly rejected the idea that intoxication should excuse because of its effect on personality. Indeed, few commentators have supported such an excuse, except in very limited situations involving inexperienced drinkers. Such an excuse would contradict the basic presumption that the physical person determines the self that is held responsible. As we saw in chapter 3, individual responsibility requires a strong presumption that a continuously existing physical person is a single chooser. All of us have many different sides to who we are; we act differently when angry or sad, when drunk or sober; nevertheless we presume that we remain the same person for purposes of basic responsibility. Who else would it be that is angry, sad, or drunk if not the person whose body is engaged in the conduct? Reinforcing the general presumption of identity in voluntary intoxication is the fact that the intoxication is chosen. Assuming an informed choice to drink, the drinker decides to risk change of personality and so should be held responsible for the consequences.[44]

Most who argue for an intoxication excuse do so on the narrower ground that intoxication negates awareness of risk. Alcohol intoxication commonly impairs perception. A drunk driver may be less able to see objects and to judge speed and distance than when sober.[45] Thus Moquin may not have realized how fast she was going, how close other cars were, or even that she was on the wrong side of the road.

Some awareness advocates have argued that persons like Moquin may be justly punished for recklessness because they knew the risks when they began to drink. The argument is that all drinkers know the dangers of intoxication—from impeded motor skills to impaired judgment—and this general awareness of risk may substitute for awareness of the particular hazards taken while intoxicated.[46] Thus we could say that Moquin, like virtually every adult in modern America, knew that drinking and driving is dangerous, and therefore that her drinking and later driving posed a serious risk to others' lives. The problem with this argument is that it conflates two quite different kinds of awareness. Realizing that driving while intoxicated statistically increases the risks of an accident is quite different from realizing that you are driving over the speed limit on the wrong side of the highway. The former supports a conviction for driving under the influence; the latter is what the awareness approach seems to require for murder in the Moquin case.

The strictest proponents of the awareness approach argue that intoxicated harm-doers deserve punishment only for taking risks they realized when sober. They advocate the creation of a new offense of dangerous drinking: drinking where the individual knows that intoxication may lead to dangerous conduct. Under this approach we might punish Moquin for drinking under circumstances where she knew she was likely to drive while drunk and where, because of her previous convictions, she had been specially warned of the legal and moral wrongs of drunk driving.[47] Liability must rest on sober awareness, though. Once intoxicated, the individual loses sight of the hazards of her conduct and so becomes nonresponsible criminally.

Here, as elsewhere, the strict awareness approach founders in its sharp separation of perception from choice. Advocates argue that we should distinguish between choices to disregard risks of which a person is aware and failures to recognize those risks in the first place. But often the failure to perceive stems from a choice or series of choices that express the person's attitude toward the value of self and others. In deciding to drink heavily, Moquin disregarded a number of risks, including that she would make bad judgments when drunk. In deciding to drive while intoxicated, Moquin disregarded further risks. In speeding down the wrong side of the road Moquin chose an action that heightened risks to others. At each step along the way, Moquin may not have consciously considered the dangers involved. Like Protopappas, her brain may not have fully processed the warning information available to her. As with Protopappas though, that failure to process should not be attributed to a mechanical glitch. The failure to process stemmed from putting a higher priority on other concerns. Like Protopappas, Moquin made a series of choices, motivated by selfish concerns, to commit certain acts and in effect ignore the dangers involved. In Moquin's case, her need to drink motivated the disregard of otherwise obvious, lethal hazards to human life. Looking at her whole course of conduct, we see a person acting according to a philosophy that devalues human life.

By contrast with the liability theory supplied by the indifference approach, consider the awkward moves required to accommodate intoxication in an awareness jurisdiction. For example, the Model Penal Code, which generally takes an awareness approach to culpability, creates an entirely new form of recklessness to apply in cases of voluntary intoxication. When an accused charged with recklessness was intoxicated at the time of the harm doing, the code instructs the decision maker to determine, not whether the intoxicated person was aware of the risk, but whether the person *would have been aware* of the risk if sober.[48] Not only does this seem to contradict the responsibility theory behind the awareness approach, but it requires the decision maker to engage in difficult hypothetical reasoning, imagining what the sober accused would have seen in a situation perhaps critically different (by virtue of intoxication) from the one that actually occurred.

Instead of treating intoxication as an exception to the awareness-culpability principle, we should view it as proof of the indifference-culpability principle. Awareness of risk does yeoman service as a culpability test in most cases, because awareness usually serves as a proxy for indifference. In the usual case, facts that indicate awareness of risk also indicate indifference, while facts that negate awareness tend to negate indifference. Intoxication presents the unusual situation where the same facts that negate awareness (the defendant's intoxication) actually support a finding of indifference. Here the law must choose between the two approaches. We should not be surprised that the law plumps for indifference, for indifference should be the moral principle underlying all punishment of careless conduct causing death.[49]

Indifference and Capacity

One last major objection to the indifference approach remains: that some persons lack the capacity to perceive the risk involved, and so do not deserve punishment. English criminal law theorist Glanville Williams objected to criminal liability for negligent conduct on just such grounds: "Some people are born feckless, clumsy, thoughtless, inattentive, irresponsible, with a bad memory and a slow 'reaction time.' With the best will in the world, we all of us at some times in our lives make negligent mistakes. It is hard to see how justice (as distinct from some utilitarian reason) requires mistakes to be punished."[50] In other words, if the person did not have the capacity to perceive better, he should not be blamed for failing to do better.

The most sophisticated version of a capacity argument in the context of unintentional criminality was that offered by English lawyer and philosopher H. L. A. Hart. Hart contended that persons who acted dangerously despite notice of the risks involved deserved punishment only if their capacity to perceive risk were established. According to Hart, culpability for unintentional harms depends on proof that: (1) a reasonable person would have realized the risk, and (2) the individual had the capacity to comprehend the risk.[51]

Only some instances of unintentional wrongdoing raise capacity concerns. For example, Protopappas had the medical training necessary to understand the medical risks of his conduct. When sober, Moquin could perceive the risks in speeding down a state highway in the wrong lane, and since her loss of capacity when drunk is attributable to voluntary drinking, she might be blamed for its loss. But what about other cases, where the accused, through no fault of her own, seems to lack the capacity to comprehend the risk? Does indifference analysis apply to such cases?

Throughout this book, and especially in chapter 3, I have criticized efforts to ground responsibility on judgments of psychological capacity. I extend that criticism here. Admittedly, the capacity argument has special appeal with respect to perception. Surely we do not wish to punish a person for being nearsighted or hard of hearing or of low intelligence. But as we will see, the perceptive failures that homicide law normally addresses rarely involve these kinds of disabilities. Nevertheless, there may be some cases where persons should be excused for dangerous conduct because they lacked the physical abilities, intelligence, or training necessary to perceive the risks involved. Isn't a capacity excuse necessary to handle these?

I argue that defining liability according to a person's capacity to perceive confuses the responsibility issue. Here, as elsewhere, capacity analysis creates the danger that decision makers will confuse character flaws with excuses. To the extent that capacity analysis involves legitimate moral considerations, it phrases the moral inquiry in a particularly difficult way that requires decision makers to engage in hypothetical reasoning instead of simply judging the reasons for perceptive failures.

As we saw in chapter 3, individual responsibility builds on moral motivation. We blame or excuse according to actions motivated by the person's moral or immoral desires. We do not excuse for the lack of moral motivation; we blame for it. In accord with this baseline principle, motivations to perceive or not perceive should be considered part of the individual's core responsibility. Like urges to hurt or to help, perception priorities help define the person. A kindly, sensitive person is kindly and sensitive because she places a high priority on addressing the needs of others. She is highly motivated to look out for the welfare of fellow humans. A callous person sets a low priority on others' needs, explaining why he may consciously disregard the harmful consequences of his actions, or fail to recognize those consequences in the first place. Like other aspects of character, perception priorities may be neither consciously nor freely chosen. Genetics may influence perception priorities; unchosen environment in the form of a young person's parents and community role models certainly does. But regardless of their source, perceptive motivations are part of what we judge when we judge responsibility. Talk about capacity tends to blur the difference between motivation to perceive and ability to perceive.

Equally important, capacity analysis turns attention away from an important culpability concern, the assessment of reasons for nonperception. While we will find relatively few cases in which the reason for nonperception was inability to perceive, we will find a number of cases—like Protopappas—where the need to attend to other concerns explains the nonperception. In such cases the critical question is the moral status of the other concerns. In Protopappas, concerns with ego and money caused the nonperception, thus supporting a judgment of indifference. The following case represents another side of the same issue. It also presents an excellent vehicle for exploring the difference between capacity and indifference analysis.

The Williams Case

Walter and Bernice Williams were loving parents to seventeen-month-old William Joseph Tabafunda.[52] Walter Williams was twenty-four years of age and worked as a laborer. He was a full-blooded Sheshont Indian and had a sixth-grade education. Bernice was twenty years old, had an eleventh-grade education, and was part Indian. In early September of 1968 little William fell sick. The trial court found:

> The defendants were ignorant. They did not realize how sick the baby was. They thought that the baby had a toothache and no layman regards a toothache as dangerous to life. They loved the baby and gave it aspirin in hopes of improving its condition. They did not take the baby to a doctor because of fear that the Welfare Department would take the baby away from them. They knew that medical help was available because of previous experience. They had no excuse that the law will recognize for not taking the baby to a doctor.[53]

The baby died because he had an abscessed tooth that, left untreated, led to infection and gangrene. These conditions caused malnutrition and a fatal case of pneumonia. During the time when medical care would have saved the child, the baby was fussy, could not keep food down, and had a cheek that swelled and turned bluish. An expert testified that at some point during this period the infection in the baby's mouth may have created the characteristic smell of gangrene: the smell of rotting flesh.

Mr. and Mrs. Williams were convicted of involuntary manslaughter, the trial court finding that they were negligent in failing to contact a physician about their child's illness. The Washington Court of Appeals affirmed the conviction.

Washington law at the time defined involuntary manslaughter as a killing caused by negligence. Unlike most jurisdictions, state law made no distinction between civil and criminal negligence.[54] In *Williams* the court explained that the law requires "the kind of caution that a man of reasonable prudence would exercise under the same or similar conditions. If, therefore, the conduct of a defendant, regardless of his ignorance, good intentions, and good faith, fails to measure up to the conduct required of a man of reasonable prudence," then he is legally negligent.[55] Under this standard, the liability question in *Williams* becomes: Would a reasonably prudent person believe that a small child, who has a tooth problem, becomes fussy, and will not eat over a period of days, then develops a swollen, bluish cheek that emits a terrible smell, should be taken to the doctor? The answer is clearly yes. But if we want to judge culpable indifference, this analysis seems inadequate. Although an unreasonable medical decision concerning the child may be an important factor in assessing indifference to the child, bad diagnosis does not equal indifference.

The *Williams* case appears in the casebook I use in teaching criminal law, and students normally have strong though conflicting reactions to it. Students generally agree with the judgment that persons of ordinary prudence would have taken the baby to a doctor before the final illness set in. They disagree on whether the couple's misunderstanding of the child's medical condition or their fear of the Welfare Department should constitute an excuse, however. Some see the couple as blameless victims of ignorance or of racial discrimination; others blame them for putting their desire to keep the baby ahead of the child's health.

I use the case in class to test H. L. A. Hart's proposed capacity test, mentioned at the top of this section. Because the trial court had described the defendants as "ignorant" and emphasized their relative lack of education, perhaps this is a case where the defendants lacked the capacity to understand the dangers of their conduct. Under Hart's test we ask whether husband and wife had "the normal capacities, physical and mental, for doing what the law requires and abstaining from what it forbids, and a fair opportunity to exercise those capacities."[56] This sounds like a test of intelligence and experience: Were the Williamses smart enough and experienced enough to recognize the risk of treating their child at home, given the signs of serious illness? The answer seems to be yes. Putting aside the racist argument that they were congenitally ignorant because they were Native Americans, we are left with their relative youth and modest education—

hardly exceptional qualities for parents. Both husband and wife were smart enough and experienced enough with children and modern medicine to see that their child suffered a serious medical problem that warranted professional attention.

In fact, the *Williams* case is not about incapacity at all. The key to understanding the Williamses' behavior is their fear of the welfare authorities. Had the Williamses trusted the medical and social work authorities, they likely would have taken their son for early medical treatment. The appellate court noted in three different places that the parents dearly loved their child.[57] The parents knew that medical care was available. Only their fear of what the authorities would do when they saw the child seems to have stopped them. The question is what moral role the parents' fear of authorities should have in resolving the case. Under Hart's capacity test, their fear plays no role. That changes under indifference analysis.

Under an indifference standard, the Williamses could point to their love of their child and active concern for its health as evidence that might rebut the suggestion of indifference raised by their medical misjudgment. Their love would not provide a blanket excuse, though. We might decide that the couple cared more for their own enjoyment of the child than for the child's welfare. This returns us to what should be the central issue in the case: the couple's fear of child welfare authorities.

The Williamses' fear of the authorities likely impeded their diagnosis of little William. Hoping to avoid a trip to the doctor and a confrontation with child welfare authorities, they resisted the idea that he was seriously ill. As Native Americans, a people with a history of governmental discrimination, including the forcible removal of children from Indian families by white authorities, the Williamses had reasons for fearing the authorities that many others would not.[58] The couple should have had the chance to argue that their failure to seek medical attention stemmed from their legitimate fear of the wrongful loss of their child and not from callousness toward the child's welfare.

It's worth noting how different the case would be if the parents had a different explanation for their perceptive failure. For example, if the couple's reason for not considering seriously the need for medical attention was due to their fear that child welfare authorities would discover actual incidents of child abuse or neglect by the parents, or their own drug addiction, or any other misconduct on their part, we would have little trouble condemning the Williamses' inaction. In such a case the parents might still lack actual awareness of risk; their diagnostic skills would be no different, but the case would have an entirely different moral tone because of our judgment that their perceptive failure was due to selfish and immoral priorities.

Reform Proposals

Finally, we are ready for rule drafting. Based on the arguments already made, the offenses of depraved heart murder and involuntary manslaughter should be based on the indifference approach to culpability, with decision makers asked to assess the degree of risk involved, the degree of notice of risk to the accused, and the degree of indifference demonstrated by the accused's conduct.

Depraved heart murder should be defined as follows:

A person is guilty of murder who causes the death of a human being by the disregard of an obvious, extreme and unjustifiable risk of death, thus demonstrating extreme indifference to the value of human life.

Involuntary manslaughter should be defined as follows:

A person is guilty of involuntary manslaughter who causes the death of another by the disregard of a substantial, unjustified, and reasonably apparent risk to human life, under circumstances that demonstrate a basic lack of concern for the welfare of others.

These offenses would require the prosecution to prove beyond a reasonable doubt that the defendant disregarded major, unjustifiable risks for culpable reasons. By making culpable reasons for disregard an element of the offenses of murder and manslaughter, these statutory definitions would permit some new mens rea arguments. As we have seen throughout this chapter, some of these arguments would assist the prosecution. But there are a number of indifference arguments that would present new avenues for the defense in homicide cases.

In some cases individual intelligence and education level may be relevant to determinations of indifference. In all instances the prosecution must prove that the defendant's disregard of risk was the result of culpable, selfish motivations, meaning that it must rebut any indications that disregard of risk was due to low intelligence or lack of education. In cases involving hazards stemming from complex instrumentalities, education and intellect may prove quite significant.[59] As suggested by the discussion of the *Williams* case, though, most careless homicide cases turn on issues of notice of risk and individual value priorities, not intellectual ability.

Youth represents another nonculpable cause of poor reasoning ability, though one rarely weighed independently under current law.[60] The indifference standards created by the new offense definitions would permit direct consideration of youth. A jury might find that a young person had not had enough experience with hazardous situations to merit the judgment that careless action demonstrates criminally culpable indifference. A jury might also rely on youth to guide its decision whether a culpable homicide should be categorized as murder or manslaughter.

The use of indifference would make clear the relevance of provocation to culpability, even in unintentional killings. As we saw in chapter 8, most provoked killings are intentional. Nevertheless, we may imagine situations where provocation leads to a careless killing: an angry person may respond with more force than he intends to employ or may try to attack the provoking party but accidentally kill a third party. In both instances the state might charge the defendant with a reckless (to use current terminology) or indifferent (my terminology) murder. Assuming we follow the definition of provocation established in Chapter 8 as a killing where the defendant had good reason for rage at the offender, provocation should negate the charge of murder based on indifference. However, provocation should only operate as mitigation, not excuse. Regardless of its legitimacy, anger never represents a morally justifiable, or excusable, basis for killing. At the minimum, a provoked killing should be punished as involuntary manslaughter.[61]

Finally, the indifference mens rea's would require the state to establish the basic rationality of the accused killer in those cases where the facts cast doubt on the accused's mental stability. To show that nonperception of risk was due to indifference, the prosecution would have to exclude the possibility of disregard of risk due to mental disease. This change would likely affect only a small number of cases. Most homicides by persons with serious mental problems are intentional killings and so would not fall under the indifference offense definitions. Generally the individual's rationality problem contributes the motive for a purposeful attack, such as a paranoid belief that the victim is plotting against the accused. Nevertheless, there may be instances where a defendant's misperception of the situation or the degree of risk involved may be attributed to mental disease and so be relevant to assessment of an unintentional killing.[62]

A Final Test Case: Religious Belief

The greatest challenge that indifference analysis brings is normative. By requiring consideration of the reasons for disregard of risk, indifference requires decision makers not only to make judgments about degree of danger and notice, degree of perception, and perceptive effort, the decision maker must also consider whether rival claims on a person's interests and sometimes even rival values may preclude a judgment of callousness. We caught a glimpse of the difficulties of this analysis in the *Williams* case, where the jury would have to decide whether the couple's fear of a child abuse claim stemmed from a legitimate fear of the authorities or a selfish concern for parental control. Sometimes the issues will be even harder. For example, consider the death of Shauntay Walker.

> Laurie Grouard Walker was the mother of four-year-old Shauntay. In late February 1984 Shauntay came down with what seemed like the flu. After four days of mild illness the child developed a stiff neck. Consistent with her beliefs as a Christian Scientist, Laurie Walker did not seek medical attention for the child, but treated her by prayer. Walker contacted a church prayer practitioner who prayed for and visited the child, and a Christian Science nurse who attended the child on three separate occasions. The child's illness—later determined to be meningitis—grew progressively worse, however. Shauntay lost weight, became irritable and disoriented. After a seventeen-day illness, Shauntay exhibited heavy and irregular breathing. A short time later she died. The Sacramento district attorney later charged Walker with involuntary manslaughter and felony child endangerment for the death of her daughter.[63]

In a pretrial review of the charge against Walker, the California Supreme Court rejected her proposed defense of good motive. The court held that involuntary manslaughter depends on criminal negligence, to be determined by whether "a reasonable person in defendant's position would have been aware of the risk involved."[64] Ms. Walker's concern and good faith in treating her child therefore would not be an excuse.[65] As in *Williams*, this ruling eliminated the defendant's best argument for acquittal.

To most in contemporary America, Ms. Walker's belief that disease is a manifestation of mental errors to be treated by prayer and not medicine is crazy.[66] The healing power of contemporary medicine is demonstrated daily. If we were to take a utilitarian approach to punishment, the case is a fairly simple one. Parents like Walker may be strongly encouraged to seek medical treatment for children by the threat of punishment. But I remain concerned with deserved punishment for homicide. Did Walker's inaction demonstrate moral indifference to her child?[67]

By her calculated refusal to seek medical assistance, Ms. Walker did flout a basic American value. She rejected the value of medical science. But does this amount to moral indifference? According to the stated facts, Walker cared for her daughter as she thought best. The only way we can charge Walker with moral failure here is if we decide that her own need to believe in Christian Science represented a selfish motivation that should not have interfered with a clear-minded concern for her child's health. This involves one of the hardest legal and moral issues under our constitutional scheme because it requires us to judge the worth of Walker's religious beliefs. While religiously inspired acts may be criminally condemned—we should severely punish human sacrifice or deliberate abuse regardless of religious precepts, for example—we are committed to providing maximum space for religious belief within the bounds of basic human value.

The advantage of indifference analysis here is that it makes the central moral issue in the case the most important legal issue. Unlike negligence, which excludes religious motivation from formal consideration, indifference requires the judge or jury to determine its moral weight in this context. This framing of the issue also reveals the disadvantage of indifference analysis, however, for it puts on a decision maker's shoulders a controversial moral question that we might prefer to consign to the legislature or private choice.

Personally, I am inclined to the defendant's side in the Walker case. Given the course of the illness and Walker's efforts to care for her child, I see this as a case of tragically misguided concern rather than of culpable indifference. But I can envision other cases involving unusual religious beliefs where because of differences in notice of risk and active involvement in risk creation I would urge a different result.[68] The bottom line for our purposes is that hard moral cases remain hard under an indifference standard. The major difference between indifference and traditional mens rea forms, especially negligence, is that under indifference the important moral issues in hard cases cannot be swept under the legal rug.

Conclusion

In F. Scott Fitzgerald's *The Great Gatsby*, the narrator, Nick, saves his harshest judgment for Tom and Daisy, a wealthy and charming couple whose callousness proves devastating to all around them. After Tom's mistress is run over by a car driven by Daisy, Tom and Daisy abruptly depart Long Island, leaving the blame and consequences to others. "It was all very careless and confused," Nick observes. "They were careless creatures, Tom and Daisy— they smashed things and creatures and then retreated back into their money or their vast carelessness, or whatever it was that kept them together, and let other people clean up the mess they had made."[69] With their wealth and charm, Tom and Daisy invited the love of others, but neither fully reciprocated nor considered the consequences. Their desire for a carefree existence inspired them to act carelessly with others.

People like Tom and Daisy do not figure prominently in modern moral and legal culture. We seem more impressed—to the point of obsession—with the purposeful wrongdoer. In our culture of violence, the most celebrated and feared offender is the sadist. When killers appear in fiction, television, or the movies, they invariably commit purposeful homicides and often seem to revel in others' suffering. Our moral discourse reveals the same preoccupation with intentional wrongdoing: we often seem unwilling to condemn harmful conduct absent dramatic evidence of aggressive and deliberate injury to others. Yet the most common cruelties are acts of indifference. In our daily lives we are more likely to confront Tom and Daisy than a serial killer.

Even when we acknowledge the fault of carelessness, we often limit its scope by requiring awareness of risk. We minimize our own obligations to others by denying the duty to look out for risks when we act. We diminish the moral community by divorcing perception from choice. Even in a liberal, capitalist democracy this constitutes too meager a set of moral obligations. Like it or not, we live in close proximity with others and daily employ a host of powerful instruments that may harm them. The modern human community requires more than avoiding deliberate aggression; it requires active concern, at least for the lives of other human beings.

Appendix
Proposed Jury Instructions

Jury instructions occupy a peculiar place in the criminal law. Appellate courts traditionally give jury instructions closer scrutiny than perhaps any other aspect of the trial. Convictions are regularly reversed because of legal misstatements in the instructions or failures to instruct on critical issues. Judicial attention, however, focuses far more on the legal accuracy of instructions—what they mean to the legally trained—than their comprehensibility to laypersons. Courts ask how a reasonable juror would understand the instructions, but as persons deeply familiar with legal terminology and modes of expression, judges are poorly situated to answer the question. When confronted with studies showing poor comprehension of instructions by laypersons, courts often ignore them, preferring to presume that what seems obvious to the court will seem obvious to jurors as well.[1]

Nor have jury instructions received the scholarly attention they merit. Scholarly analysis of mens rea doctrine almost always focuses on the language of statutes or appellate decisions rather than the standard jury instructions used by trial courts. This disregards the enormous problem of translating complex legal principles into comprehensible ordinary language. It is as if a diplomat, called upon to give a speech in a foreign language, endures agonies to find the right words in his native tongue but pays no attention to how those words are translated for his audience. It makes no sense.

What follows is a set of proposed jury instructions corresponding to the main issues addressed in part 2 of the book—definitions of mens rea and the offenses of aggravated murder, voluntary manslaughter, depraved heart murder, and involuntary manslaughter. My aim here is to explain the concepts and rules involved as clearly and efficiently as possible. The instructions should be considered a first-draft effort only. Among other shortcomings, they have not been tested on a lay audience to determine their comprehensibility and reliability. They should give some indication of the possibilities of clear jury instructions, however.

Mens Rea and Its Proof

PROPOSED JURY INSTRUCTION

Once you have resolved that the defendant in this case committed a voluntary act, or a legally sufficient failure to act, you must make a further determination concerning the nature of the defendant's conduct. You must determine what the law calls mens rea.[2] Mens rea is a Latin term that has been translated in many ways, but for purposes of this case refers to the goals, thoughts, and attitudes that informed the defendant's act. Broadly speaking, mens rea provides one of the most important means of separating criminal from noncriminal acts. Mens rea may distinguish between a deliberate criminal harm and an accidental, noncriminal harm. It may also provide a means of determining the relative severity of an offense.

Every offense has its own requirements with regard to mens rea, and you should listen closely to the instructions I give about the offenses charged in this case. Before I give those instructions, however, I want to describe generally the basic forms of mens rea and how they may be proven.

The best way to describe the different forms of mens rea, is by example. I will use as my example a case where a defendant is charged with a criminal killing. Assume that in this case that the jury determines that the defendant's voluntary conduct caused the death of the victim. Then the jury must resolve the issue of mens rea. The jury may be asked to decide whether the defendant meant to kill the victim. This form of mens rea is called purpose. If the defendant had purpose to kill, the jury might be further required to decide why he wanted to kill. This form of mens rea is called motive. If the jury finds that the defendant had no purpose to kill, then it may be asked to determine whether the defendant realized that the victim would almost certainly die as a result of his conduct. This form of mens rea is called knowledge. Finally, if knowledge is not proven, a jury might be asked to determine whether the risk of death was obvious to one in the defendant's situation and whether, in light of all the circumstances, the defendant's conduct demonstrated callousness to the well-being of the victim. This form of mens rea is called indifference.

Issues of criminal mens rea require you to determine, if you can, why the defendant committed the alleged criminal act. In making this determination you should consider the circumstances of the conduct, the conduct itself, and any statements the defendant made before, during, or after the incident which might shed light on his conduct. You need not read the defendant's mind to resolve criminal mens rea; instead, you should focus on the defendant's reasons for action. You should evaluate the defendant's mens rea in light of what you know of human nature generally—indeed, this is one reason you have been chosen as jurors—but you should remember that your responsibility is to determine what the defendant actually did in this case. In other words, you must decide whether there is anything about this defendant or the circumstances of this case so that ordinary expectations concerning the conduct do not apply. Finally, you should remember that the prosecution bears the burden of proving, beyond a reasonable doubt, the defendant's criminal mens rea. If you find that the prosecution has not met its burden as to a particular form of mens rea, then you must acquit on the charge that requires that mens rea.

Aggravated Murder

Statutory Definition

Aggravated murder is the purposeful killing of another human being for profit, to further a criminal endeavor, to affect public policy or legal processes, because of animosity toward the victim's race, religion, ethnicity, sex or sexual orientation, or to assert cruel power over another.

PROPOSED JURY INSTRUCTION

Aggravated murder represents the most heinous form of homicide and is reserved for crimes of exceptional depravity. The state must prove that the defendant acted: (1) with purpose to kill, and (2) and for a statutorily specified motive.

The law designates certain motives that support aggravated murder: a killing for profit, to further a criminal endeavor, to affect public policy or legal processes, out of animosity toward the victim's race, religion, ethnicity, sex or sexual orientation, or to assert cruel power over another. In order to satisfy the motive element of the crime, you must decide that the particular motive provided a substantial reason for the defendant's action. The motive need not have been the only reason for the killing, but it must have been an important force behind it.

A killing for profit is one to gain money or property or to prevent the loss of money or property, for the defendant's own enjoyment.

A killing to further a criminal endeavor is a homicide designed to aid criminal activity. Examples include killing a peace officer to escape capture, or killing witnesses to a crime to prevent their later testimony. Such a killing requires proof of ongoing criminality and that the killing was motivated to further the criminality in some fashion, either by achieving some criminal goal, or preventing discovery, investigation, or prosecution. If the victim was a law enforcement officer, the defendant's awareness of that status may be relevant to this motive. In general, the importance of the victim to the success or failure of the criminal scheme should also be considered.

A killing to affect public policy or legal processes is one motivated by the desire to affect the decisions of matters of public interest committed to democratic processes or the desire to affect the legal decisions of authorized institutions.

A killing based on group animus is one substantially inspired by hostility to the victim's race, religion, ethnicity, or sexual orientation. Here the victim is attacked because of his or her group membership or affiliation.

A killing to assert cruel power over another is a killing undertaken for the satisfaction of exercising ultimate power over another human being—the power to take life. Such killings may be shown by the lack of any other reason for the homicide; by extreme cruelty against the victim, including the use of torture; by acts of domination beyond those inherent in killing; by actions indicating pleasure taken in violence, including sex acts by the offender involving the victim or attacks on the victim's sexual parts.

In considering possible indicators of motive listed here, you should remember these are only possible indicators; your responsibility is to decide the killer's actual motive in this case.

Voluntary Manslaughter

Statutory Definition

A killing that would otherwise be murder is voluntary manslaughter if the defendant had good reason to believe that the victim committed a serious wrong against the defendant or a loved one, and if this provoked in the defendant at the time of the homicide a great and justifiable anger at the victim.

PROPOSED JURY INSTRUCTION

Under the law, a homicide that would otherwise qualify as murder is classified as manslaughter if the victim's seriously wrongful conduct inspired in the defendant a violent rage. The law recognizes that when a person suffers from a substantial wrong done by another, extreme anger at the wrongdoer may be justified, and that anger will make it more difficult for the wronged person to refrain from violence. When the defendant had good reason for extreme anger toward the victim and kills in the heat of that anger, the offense is deemed less serious than murder. You should realize, though, that manslaughter remains a serious offense. Even if the defendant had a legitimate grievance with the victim, the law requires all citizens to refrain from redressing grievances with fatal violence.

To find provocation, you must first determine that the defendant experienced extreme anger. This anger must be so strong that it affected the defendant's judgment, significantly reducing [his][her] ability to consider the consequences of action and to refrain from violence.

Second, you must determine that the accused had a good reason for extreme anger. No person can claim provocation because [he][she] became enraged at a trivial slight or minor threat. Cases where a person's extreme anger might be justified include those where the victim has been responsible for a serious harm such as a sexual or other serious, wrongful assault on the defendant, a relative, or a close friend of the defendant. Significant threats to the safety of the defendant or a loved one may also be cause for such anger.

In determining what constitutes a good reason for extreme anger, you act as conscience for the community. Considering the circumstances of the case, you must resolve whether the defendant faced an unusually aggravating situation such that the defendant's violent response merits less punishment than most criminal homicides.

As part of this determination, you must resolve that the defendant's extreme anger was justified at the time of *the homicide. Even when the victim's conduct represents cause for great anger, the law expects that this anger will diminish with the passage of time. Following a reasonable period, the defendant should regain full control of emotions and actions. The length of time needed to restore basic emotional equilibrium will vary from case to case. In evaluating what is often called the "cooling off period," you should consider the nature of the provocation. The more serious the victim's wrongdoing, the longer the cooling-off period may be. The defendant's efforts to avoid violent confrontation with the victim following an originally provoking event and any subsequent acts of provocation by the victim are also relevant to the justification for anger at the time of the homicide.*

Extreme Indifference Murder

Statutory Definition

A person is guilty of murder who causes the death of a human being by the disregard of an obvious, extreme, and unjustifiable risk of death, thus demonstrating extreme indifference to the value of human life.

PROPOSED JURY INSTRUCTION

Conviction of this offense requires proof that the defendant caused the victim's death by actions or legally sufficient omissions to act in which the defendant disregarded an obvious, extreme, and unjustifiable danger to human life, and proof that defendant's conduct demonstrated an attitude of extreme indifference to the value of human life. I will call these two requirements the disregard requirement and the indifference requirement.

The disregard requirement has three parts: (1) that the defendant's conduct posed a great danger to the life of the victim, (2) that there was no necessity for such a danger at the time, and (3) that the danger and lack of necessity were immediately apparent to one in the defendant's position. For conviction, the degree of danger must be such that death or severe injury of the victim, or a similarly placed person, could be readily expected as a result of the defendant's conduct. The danger must be unnecessary, meaning that there was no overriding justification for it, such as self-defense, defense of another, law enforcement necessity, or medical emergency. Finally, the degree of danger and its lack of necessity must have been obvious to one in the defendant's position. This means that the defendant had enough warning of danger that the defendant, or anyone else with similar physical abilities, training, and knowledge, would have realized the risk involved had they paid minimal attention to the welfare of those endangered. The obviousness of danger may be shown by the nature of the defendant's conduct, by the nature of the situation, by specific warnings given to the defendant, by indications that the defendant was actually aware of the unnecessary danger, or by any combination of these factors.

For a conviction of murder you must also find that the defendant's conduct demonstrated an attitude of extreme indifference to the value of human life. By extreme indifference to human life, the law means a radical lack of concern for the worth of other human beings. Indifferent conduct is that which is cold and callous to others. Persons who are aware of the unjustified and deadly risks of their conduct, and ignore those risks, demonstrate extreme indifference to human life. Persons who are so focused on selfish concerns that they do not consider the obvious, significant, and unjustified risks to others of their conduct also demonstrate indifference to human life.

If you determine that the defendant was not actually aware of the life-threatening nature of his or her conduct, you must determine why the defendant was unaware. You must determine whether lack of awareness was due to a culpable lack of concern for others or whether it may be attributed to other, nonculpable factors. In such cases you should consider any defects in the defendant's reasoning powers caused by mental disease, low intelligence, youth, lack of training, or education. In making this assessment you should remember that all persons are obliged to try to avoid causing lethal harms to others. To the best of their abilities, all persons must look out for serious dangers which their conduct may create for fellow human beings.

[You may also find proof of indifference lacking where the defendant had a legitimate reason for sudden and extreme anger against the victim. Where the defendant

reasonably believed that the victim had committed or was about to commit a serious wrong against the defendant, or a loved one of the defendant, the defendant's failure to heed the dangers of conduct should not be deemed proof of extreme indifference to human life.][3]

Remember, it is the prosecution's responsibility to prove, beyond a reasonable doubt, the requirements of disregard and indifference. If, after considering all the evidence, you have reasonable doubts concerning either requirement, you should acquit the defendant of murder.

Involuntary Manslaughter

Statutory Definition

A person is guilty of involuntary manslaughter who causes the death of another by the disregard of a substantial, unjustified, and reasonably apparent risk to human life, under circumstances that demonstrate a basic lack of concern for the welfare of others.

PROPOSED JURY INSTRUCTION

Involuntary manslaughter requires proof that the defendant caused the victim's death by actions or legally sufficient omissions to act in which defendant: (1) ignored a reasonably apparent, significant, and unnecessary risk to human life, and did so (2) under circumstances that demonstrate a basic lack of concern for the victim's welfare. I will call these two requirements the risk requirement and the lack of concern requirement.

The risk requirement has three parts to it. First, the defendant's conduct must have posed significant risks to the life of the victim. Second, the risks must have been unnecessary, meaning that the defendant had no overriding justification for them, such as self-defense, defense of another, law enforcement necessity, or medical emergency. Third, the nature of the risks must have been so apparent that a person of ordinary prudence in the defendant's situation would have recognized them.

For conviction, the defendant's conduct must also demonstrate a basic lack of concern for the welfare of others. The defendant's conduct must show grave irresponsibility. In this regard, you must decide whether the defendant's failure to recognize and avoid the risks involved was due to a culpable lack of concern for others or should be attributed to other, nonculpable factors. Among nonculpable reasons for failing to perceive risk are low intelligence, lack of training or schooling, or mental disease. The mere presence of these factors is not sufficient to resolve the issue, however. In deciding whether the lack of concern requirement is met, you should remember that all persons are obliged to try to avoid causing lethal harms to others. To the best of their abilities, all persons must look out for serious dangers which their conduct may create for fellow human beings.

Remember as well that it is the prosecution's responsibility to prove, beyond a reasonable doubt, the requirements of risk and lack of concern. If, after considering all the evidence, you have reasonable doubts concerning either requirement, you should acquit the defendant of involuntary manslaughter.

Notes

NOTES TO PREFACE

1. This account is drawn from newspaper stories. For a summary, see Claire Martin, Ernest John Dobbert Jr., Jacksonville Journal, Feb. 2, 1982, at B-1.

2. The reported decisions in the case include: Dobbert v. State, 328 So.2d 433 (Fla. 1976) (affirming conviction); Dobbert v. Florida, 432 US 282 (1977) (same); Dobbert v. State, 375 So.2d 1069 (Fla. 1979) (affirming resentencing).

NOTES TO CHAPTER 1: A QUESTION OF VALUE

1. See Franklin Zimring & Gordon Hawkins, Is American Violence A Crime Problem? 46 Duke L.J. 43 (1996).

While in the last two decades homicide rates around the world have fluctuated, national differences have remained startling. In 1980 the World Health Organization reported that the United States had an annual homicide rate of 10.5 per one hundred thousand persons. This means that for every 100,000 persons, every year more than ten persons would be killed in some form of criminal homicide. The rate for England in 1980 was less than one per 100,000. Bureau of Justice Statistics, *International Crime Rates* (1988). The National Health Center estimated that in 1986–87, for persons aged between fifteen and twenty-four, the homicide rate in the United States was nearly 22 persons for every 100,000 in population. The highest rate for any other industrialized nation for this age group was Scotland, with a rate of 5 per 100,000. Japan had a rate of .3 per 100,000, or not quite one homicide for every 300,000 persons in the same age range. Lois Fingerhut & Joel Kleinman, International and Interstate Comparisons of Homicide Among Young Males, 263 J. Am. Med'l. Assn. (JAMA) 3292 (1990); see also Bureau of Justice Statistics, *International Crime Rates* (1988). While homicide rates have declined significantly in the nineties—compared to earlier U.S. figures—the rates remain far above those of other Western industrialized democracies. For 1995 the U.S. homicide rate was 8 per 100,000 of population. Federal Bureau of Investigation, *Crime in the United States for 1995* (1996).

2. For an excellent introduction to the major punishment theories, see M. M. MacKenzie, *Plato on Punishment* (1981).

3. *An Introduction to the Principles of Morals and Legislation* 170–71 & n. 1 (1823,

1st ed. London 1789). For modern views, see *The Economics of Crime* (R. Andreano & J. Siegfried eds. 1980). For a provocative examination of the possibility of a true utilitarian scheme, see Louis Michael Seidman, Soldiers, Martyrs, and Criminals: Utilitarian Theory and the Problem of Crime Control, 94 Yale L.J. 315 (1984).

4. See Paul H. Robinson, The Criminal-Civil Distinction and the Utility of Desert, 76 Bos. Univ. L. Rev. 210, 212–13 (1996).

5. Controversies in constitutional law often involve disputes about the nature of this value, disputes that mirror in many ways the value versus utility distinction presented here. For example, the Fourth Amendment gives the American people the right to be free from "unreasonable searches and seizures" and states that search warrants must be supported by probable cause, among other requirements. A majority of the justices on the current Supreme Court view the amendment as creating a general reasonableness requirement that requires the Court to balance government needs for information against an individual's interest in being left alone. The Court has used this approach to approve many government searches that take place without probable cause, reasonable suspicion, or a warrant. See, e.g., National Treasury Employees Union v. Von Raab, 489 U.S. 656 (1989); New York v. Burger, 482 U.S. 691 (1987). More liberal justices and many legal commentators view this kind of balancing approach as disregarding the value of privacy enshrined in the Constitution, by determining the worth of privacy according to the countervailing interests of the government in each situation. Instead, they argue, the Court should begin its analysis by recognizing a basic value in privacy enshrined in the Fourth Amendment, one that mandates government use of a warrant and probable cause except in emergency and other carefully restricted situations. For an introduction to the debate, compare the opinions of the majority and dissenters in New Jersey v. T.L.O., 469 U.S. 325 (1985) and Oregon v. Elstad, 470 U.S. 298 (1985). For a similar debate with regard to the Fifth Amendment's self-incrimination clause, compare the opinions of Justices Harlan and Brennan in California v. Byers, 402 U.S. 424 (1971).

For an extended argument using Bentham's writings on utilitarianism to support a set of individual rights of the kind usually associated with deontologic argument, see P. J. Kelly, *Utilitarianism and Distributive Justice* (1990).

6. *The Philosophy of Law* 194–95 (W. Hastie trans. 1887). For other aspects of Kant's writings on punishment and human value, see his *Fundamental Principles of the Metaphysic of Morals* (T. Abbott trans. 1987) and *The Doctrine of Virtue* (M. Gregory trans. 1964), which comprises the second part of *The Metaphysic of Morals*.

7. See Herbert Morris, Persons and Punishment, in *On Guilt and Innocence* 31 (1976); Jeffrie Murphy, Kant's Theory of Criminal Punishment in *Retribution, Justice, and Therapy* 82 (1979).

8. One way of viewing the relationship between value and utility is that value sets limits on what utility would otherwise argue for. See Heidi Hurd, The Deontology of Negligence, 76 Bos. Univ. L. Rev. 249, 253–54 (1996).

9. This is a somewhat flippant way of dealing with a serious matter in moral dis-

cussion—the way in which morals may depend on religious belief. Many people take their moral principles from religion. They believe that God determines what is right and wrong and we learn these principles from God through prayer, clerical guidance, and scriptural authority. In this book I address purely secular arguments about morals and law.

10. For an excellent, more philosophically oriented reply to similar concerns about moral argumentation, see Mary Midgley, *Can't We Make Moral Judgements?* (1991). For a religiously oriented critique of science's domination of public policy discussions, see Anthony E. Cook, The Death of God in American Pragmatism and Realism: Resurrecting the Value of Love in Contemporary Jurisprudence, 82 Geo. L.J. 1431 (1994).

11. This simplistic distinction between science and nonscience does not deal with the significant concerns raised by Thomas Kuhn in his *The Structure of Scientific Revolutions* (1962), that the most important scientific discoveries turn on paradigm shifts that occur outside the standard scientific experimentation model. For a thoughtful critique of Kuhn's argument that science is relativistic and lacks objective standards, see Anthony O'Hear, *An Introduction to the Philosophy of Science* 55–143 (1989). For purposes of my discussion I assume the validity of traditional claims of science to objective verification.

12. But see Richard A. Posner, *Economic Analysis of Law* 67–68 (1972), on the economic efficiency of criminal rules; Richard A. Epstein, The Tort/Crime Distinction: A Generation Later, 76 B.U. L. Rev. 1 (1996), using utilitarian efficiency analysis to critique the scope of current criminal rules.

13. See, e.g., David McCord & Sandra Lyons, Moral Reasoning and the Criminal Law: The Example of Self-Defense, 30 Am. Crim. L. Rev. 97 (1992) (arguing for moral pluralism in criminal law, at least with respect to self-defense claims of battered women).

The question of culture's impact on criminal responsibility emerges most sharply in the issue of whether a cultural defense should ever be recognized as a separate, affirmative excuse or justification. (Cultural beliefs are sometimes relevant under current law to mens rea and some affirmative defenses such as self-defense.) Among the most controversial issues raised by cultural disagreement today is the practice of female circumcision, the removal of the female clitoris and partial closure of the vagina of girls at puberty, a traditional coming-of-age rite practiced in a number of nations, especially in Africa. Some writers have rejected the idea that this, or any other culturally accepted practice should, because of that acceptance, necessarily excuse or mitigate conduct that is otherwise criminal under U.S. law. See Doriane Lambelet Coleman, Individualizing Justice through Multiculturalism: The Liberals' Dilemma, 96 Col. L. Rev. 1093 (1996); Sharon M. Tomao, Note, The Cultural Defense: Traditional or Moral? 10 Geo. Immig. L.J. 241 (1996). See also Holly Maguigan, Cultural Evidence and Male Violence: Are Feminist and Multiculturalist Reforms on a Collision Course in Criminal Courts? 70 N.Y.U. L. Rev. 36 (1995). For views more sympathetic to explicit cultural pluralism in moral and criminal rules, see Leti Volpp, Talking "Culture": Gender, Race, Nation, and the Politics of Multiculturalism, 96 Col. L. Rev. 1573 (1996); Andrew M. Kanter, Note, The Yenaldooshi in Court and the Killing of a Witch: The Case for an Indian Cultural Defense, 4 So. Cal. Interdisc. L.J. 411 (1995).

14. See *Report of the Royal Commission on Capital Punishment, 1949–1953* 432–70 (1953).

15. See sources cited at note 14 *supra*.

16. See, e.g., Brown v. State, 106 N.W. 536 (Wis. 1906). Susan Estrich, *Real Rape* 27–56 (1987).

17. See Estrich, *Real Rape, supra* at 42–56.

18. For an overview of changes in rape law, see Joshua Dressler, *Understanding Criminal Law* 534–56 (2d ed. 1995). On the general pattern of modern reform, see Stephen Schulhofer, Taking Sexual Autonomy Seriously: Rape Law and Beyond, 11 Law and Phil. 35 (1992). Reformers have frequently observed that changes in formal rape law have not cured long-standing problems in the actual investigation and litigation of rape charges. See Estrich, *Real Rape, supra* note 17 at 57–104; Lynne Henderson, Rape and Responsibility, 11 Law and Phil. 127 (1992). For a generally positive view of current legal practices, see Linda Fairstein, *Sexual Violence* (1993). Meanwhile, some others argue that the law and/or social understandings of rape have changed too far in the direction of criminalizing sexual activity. Katie Roiphe, *The Morning After* (1993). The extent to which the law has and has not changed may be revealed in two recent state appellate court decisions: Commonwealth v. Berkowitz, 641 A.2d 1161 (Pa. 1994); State ex rel M.T.S., 609 A.2d 1266 (N.J. 1992).

NOTES TO CHAPTER 2: THE VALUE OF CHOICE

1. See Lloyd L. Weinreb, *Natural Law and Justice* 200–209 (1987). For a discussion of the many senses of desert, see Joel Feinberg, Justice and Personal Desert, in *Doing and Deserving* (1970). For a critical view of retribution, and its notion of deserved punishment, see David Dolinko, Some Thoughts about Retributivism, 101 Ethics 537 (1991).

2. Thus I use physical cause in a quite limited sense to apply only to the genetic and environmental influences on choice. In other legal or moral discussions, cause has a broader meaning, referring to the human and other forces that contribute to a result (see, e.g., H. L. A. Hart & A. M. Honore, *Causation in the Law* (1959)), or to the reasons for which an action is taken. See Donald Davidson, Actions, Reasons and Causes, in *Essays on Actions and Events* 3 (1990).

Another important definitional note: when I refer to science, I mean those sciences that seek to determine the laws of the physical universe, i.e., the rules of gravity, motion, evolution, and the like. Applying this approach to human behavior, the scientist seeks to discover the general laws of behavior that will render it absolutely predictable. Many criminologists take a similar approach. See, e.g., James Q. Wilson & Richard J. Herrnstein, *Crime & Human Nature* 489–507 (1985). This approach must be distinguished from the methodology of many other social scientists who seek to interpret human behavior. See Alexander Rosenberg, *Philosophy of Social Science* 13–17 (1988). Such scientists do not seek to reduce human behavior to its physical causes but try to render it intelligible in human terms. They work within the commonsense structure of reasons, of desire-belief-action analysis, to deepen what we know about the ordinary experience of life. To put this another way, interpretivist scientists try to illuminate and improve on what has been called folk psychology; scientists committed to the physical laws approach generally seek to replace folk psychology with an alternative way of understanding human behavior. For more on reason analysis, folk psychology and the sciences of human behavior, see chapter 6. Since, as we will see, the interpretivist approach essentially parallels the moralistic approach of law, it does not present the challenge of physical science, and is not my subject here.

3. See, e.g., John Hospers, *Human Conduct: An Introduction to the Problem of Ethics* 469–525 (1961); B. F. Skinner, *Beyond Freedom and Dignity* (1971), *Science and Human Behavior* (1953). In criminal law the position was classically presented by Clarence Darrow. See *The Story of My Life* 75–87, 338–49 (1932).

4. For a full statement of the incompatibalist argument in philosophy, see Peter Van Inwagen, *An Essay on Free Will* (1983). Good introductions to the modern free will debate may be found in Ted Honderich, *How Free Are You?* (1993); *Free Will* (G. Watson ed. 1982); and *Freedom and Responsibility* (H. Morris ed. 1961). See also Daniel Dennett, *Elbow Room: The Varieties of Free Will Worth Wanting* (1984); Mark Thornton, *Do We Have Free Will?* (1989); and *Free Will and Determinism* (B. Berofsky ed. 1966).

5. Much of the philosophic debate about free will turns on exactly what the question is. Many philosophers state that free will depends upon an ability to "do otherwise." Thus a person may be held responsible for a choice when he could have chosen otherwise. See, e.g., H. L. A. Hart, Legal Responsibility and Excuses in *Punishment and Responsibility* 28, 30 (1968). The work of several philosophers, especially that of Harry Frankfurt, has indicated that in some situations "could have done otherwise" does not capture the basic moral intuition about chosen action that lies behind the criminal law. See Frankfurt, Alternate Possibilities and Moral Responsibility 66 J. Phil. 829 (1969); M. Klein, *Determinism, Blameworthiness, and Deprivation* 30–48 (1990). My own problems with this formulation are set out in this and the following chapter.

6. See David L. Bazelon, The Morality of the Criminal Law, 49 S. Cal. L. Rev. 385 (1976); Richard Delgado, "Rotten Social Background": Should the Criminal Law Recognize a Defense of Severe Environmental Deprivation? 3 Law and Inequality 9 (1985). For a similar approach resting on utilitarian grounds, see Note,

Freedom, Determinism, and the Externalization of Responsibility in the Law: A Philosophical Analysis, 76 Geo. L.J. 2045, 2067–71 (1988).

7. Some philosophers and legal commentators argue that blame for wrong action stems from the individual's responsibility for having the character trait behind the action. They argue that the person is responsible for the trait either because she initially chose it, or, following the Aristotelian view, was responsible for retaining the trait. E.g., George Fletcher, *Rethinking Criminal Law* 805–6 (1978) (although recognizing problems with responsibility for character). See Audi, Responsible Action and Virtuous Character, 101 Ethics 309 (1991); Aristotle, *Nichomachean Ethics* 1103a–6a. Cf. Peter Arenella, Convicting the Morally Blameless: Reassessing the Relationship between Legal and Moral Accountability, 39 UCLA L. Rev. 1511 (1992) (arguing for character responsibility not based on choice but on the achievement of certain moral capacities). Scientific skeptics simply take the analysis back one more step. At some point, the initial "choice" on character must be traceable to genetics, environment, or chance. And the decision on retaining character seems no more chosen, since it flows from those second-order desires—desires about character—that themselves can be traced to genetics or environment. For critical accounts of responsibility for character from the legal and philosophic perspectives, see Gary Watson, Responsibility and the Limits of Evil: Variations on a Strawsonian Theme, in *Responsibility, Character, and the Emotions*, 256 (F. Schoeman ed. 1987); Joshua Dressler, Reflections on Excusing Wrongdoers: Moral Theory, New Excuses and the Model Penal Code, 19 Rutgers L.J. 671, 695–97 (1988); Weinreb, *Natural Law and Justice, supra* note 1 at 205–14. The concept of second-order desires comes from the work of Harry Frankfurt. See Freedom of the Will and the Concept of a Person, in *Free Will, supra* note 4 at 81–95. For more on character theories of criminal responsibility, see chapter 3.

8. For an introduction to attribution theory, see Marvin E. Shaw & Philip R. Costanzo, *Theories of Social Psychology* 232–58 (2d ed. 1982); *Attribution Theory and Research: Conceptual, Developmental and Social Dimensions* 3–36 (J. Jaspars, F. Fincham, & M. Hewstone eds. 1983).

9. See Wilson & Herrnstein, *Crime and Human Nature, supra* note 2 (reviewing criminologic literature on causes of crime).

10. Michael Moore, Causation and the Excuses, 73 Calif. L. Rev. 1091, 1112–28 (1985); see also Moritz Schlick, When Is A Man Responsible? in *Problems of Ethics* 143–56 (1939).

11. Nevertheless, the suspicion remains that the initial explanation *does* amount to at least a partial excuse. We commonly sense that if we sympathize with Steve because of his situation, we should be more tolerant of his actions. Since we generally consider sympathy and understanding to be good emotional and mental states, because they incline us to lenient treatment, they seem to support at least a partial excuse.

Note that we could build a stable responsibility system if we excused for only one kind of physical causation. For example, consider what would happen if we held persons responsible for actions traceable to genetic influences but not those traced to environment. Under such a regime we might say that Steve's underlying character—his genetic predisposition—is not bad (fundamentally he is a good man), but his original dispositions were distorted by his upbringing. This argument has a Calvinist and premodern feel to it that most Americans would probably reject today, however, for it would represents blaming based on genetic heritage. If, as most Americans believe, we should blame only for chosen actions, then there can be no distinction between environmental and genetic causes of conduct.

12. See Stephen J. Morse, Psychology, Determinism, and Legal Responsibility, 33 *Nebraska Symposium on Motivation* 35 (1986); Michael Moore, Causation and the Excuses, 73 Cal. L. Rev. 1091 (1985); James Fitzjames Stephen, 2 *History of the Criminal Law of England* (1883). See also Robert Nozick, *Philosophical Explanations* 393–96 (1981); Dennett, *Elbow Room, supra* note 4.

13. Some compatibilists go a step farther. They contend that determinism—the idea that human decisions may be predicted given enough information about physical influences on human behavior—may be a necessary condition of responsibility. The only alternative to the idea that our reasons come from genetics or environment is that they were generated in random fashion. But if reasons are randomly generated, this obliterates the idea of responsibility based on an individual's *rational* choices. See, e.g., A. J. Ayer, Freedom and Necessity, in *Free Will, supra* note 4 at 15. One of the central objections to indeterminism is that the only plausible alternative to determinism is chance—that actions cannot be predicted because they occur randomly. Yet random occurrences provide no support for personal responsibility. See George Vuoso, Background, Responsibility, and Excuse, 96 Yale L.J. 1661, 1674–78 (1987).

14. As J. L. Austin put it: "Like 'real,' 'free' is used only to rule out the suggestion of some or all of its recognized antitheses." A Plea for Excuses, in *Law and Philosophy* 318 (J. Feinberg & H. Gross eds. 1975).

15. This stems from the fundamentally different perspectives of the disciplines. By training and practice, scientists are committed to finding the deterministic causes of phenomena, while lawyers concern themselves with human choice. Each ask fundamentally different questions. In fact, the differences between the related disciplines of criminal law, psychology, criminology, and sociology depend upon the different questions each seeks to answer. See Cohen, The Assumption that Crime Is a Product of Environments: Sociological Approaches, in *Theoretical Methods in Criminology* 223 (R. Meier ed. 1985).

16. As with any metaphor, the telephoto picture of reason and cause has its limitations. It suggests that reasons and causes are commensurable, that their only distinction is in their location on the never-ending chain of events that includes a particular human action. Some compatibilists might argue that reasons and causes address different questions and so are incommensurable in a way the telephoto metaphor denies. To save the metaphor we would have to imagine an instrument that

picks up different kinds of rays: the lawyer might examine the scene under natural light, while the scientist would switch to ultraviolet or X-ray vision.

17. *The View from Nowhere* 119 (1986).

18. *Philosophical Explanations* 313 (1981).

19. Much of my argument here is drawn from Anthony O'Hear, Scientific Reductions, in *An Introduction to the Philosophy of Science* 176–201 (1989).

20. See, e.g., John Rawls, *A Theory of Justice* (1971).

21. See, e.g., Thomas Nagel, *The View from Nowhere* (1986); Robert Solomon, *The Passions* 15–19 (1976).

22. Freedom and Resentment, reprinted in *Free Will, supra* note 4 at 59–80.

23. In other words, our reactive attitudes do not change according to what view we hold of determinism and free will. *Id.* at 64–70.

24. *Id.* at 79.

25. See Lloyd Weinreb, What Are *Civil* Rights? 8 Social Phil. & Policy 1, 3–8 (1991). Strawson seems to make a related, but quite different point in his essay. Strawson suggests that our reactive attitudes are fundamental and in fact constitute moral responsibility. That is, he seems to argue that in considering morality, all we can do is examine our own attitudes to determine their efficacy in regulating behavior. There are no independent moral standards by which our attitudes can be judged, because our attitudes *are* our morality. Freedom and Resentment, in *Free Will, supra* note 4 at 80. For an illuminating exploration of this theory, see Watson, Responsibility and the Limits of Evil: Variations on a Strawsonian Theme, in *Responsibility, Character and the Emotions, supra* at 256.

26. Camus, *The Myth of Sisyphus* 3 (J. O'Brien trans. 1955).

27 Note that classical utilitarian theories of punishment do not face this metaphysical problem. A classical utilitarian need only calculate happiness and unhappiness, generally defined in very basic ways; questions of meaning need not be resolved to determine just punishment. Sophisticated utilitarians, on the other hand, face much the same definitional problems as do value adherents. For more on this, see chapter 1.

28. For example, Monty Python's, The Meaning of Life (Celandine Films 1983).

29. See, e.g., A. J. Ayer, *Language, Truth and Logic* 15–16 (1946).

30. See *Philosophical Explanations, supra* note 18 at 594–618; *The Examined Life* (1989).

31. The phrase comes from Lloyd Weinreb, *Natural Law and Justice, supra* at 265.

NOTES TO CHAPTER 3: PUNISHMENT AS DEFENSE OF VALUE

1. This account is drawn from Hal Higdon, *The Crime of the Century* (1975).

2. *On War* (1833).

3. *Moral Education* 176 (1925, 1961). For other accounts of expressive theories of punishment, see R. A. Duff, *Trials and Punishments* (1986); Joel Feinberg, The Ex-

pressive Function of Punishment in *Doing and Deserving* (1970); H. M. Hart, "Criminal Punishment as Public Condemnation" in *Contemporary Punishment* 12 (R. Gerger & P. McAnany eds. 1972); Jean Hampton, The Moral Education Theory of Punishment, 13 Phil. & Pub. Affairs 208 (1984); Benjamin Sendor, Crime as Communication: An Interpretive Theory of the Insanity Defense and the Mental Elements of Crime, 74 Geo. L.J. 1371 (1986). For critiques of expressive theories, see Skillen, How to Say Things with Walls, 55 Phil. 509 (1980); Nigel Walker, Punishing, Denouncing or Reducing Crime? 391–403, in *Reshaping the Criminal Law* (P. Glazebrook ed. 1978); H. L. A. Hart, Punishment and the Elimination of Responsibility, in *Punishment and Responsibility* 170–73 (1968).

4. See Georg Hegel, *Philosophy of Right* 70–71 (T. Knox trans. 1952); Herbert Morris, Persons and Punishment, in *On Guilt and Innocence* (1976). See also Immanuel Kant, *Fundamental Principles of the Metaphysic of Morals* (T. Abbott trans. 1987); R. S. Downie & Elizabeth Telfer, *Respect for Persons* (1970); MacLagan, Respect for Persons as a Moral Principle—I, 35 Phil. 193 (1960).

5. On the move from respect to caring, see Alan Donagan, Morality as a Disposition of Affection and Caring, in *The Theory of Morality* 9–31 (1977); Samuel H. Pillsbury, Emotional Justice: Moralizing the Passions of Criminal Punishment, 74 Cornell L. Rev. 655, 685–89 (1989). The regard principle parallels the obligation of agape, or brotherly love, advocated by many Christian theologians. For an overview, see Gene Outka, *Agape* (1972). Agape is the Greek term used in the New Testament of the Bible to describe man's ideal love for his fellow man and provides an emotive counterpart to the respect principle. Downie & Telfer, *Respect for Persons supra* at 29; MacLagan, Respect for Persons as a Moral Principle, *supra* at 207. Like respect for persons, the obligation of agape is to value all persons, but the valuing is stated in emotive terms. Agape requires not that one respect one's neighbor, but that one "love thy neighbor as thyself." Matthew 22: 37–40. Agape is "the basic 'law of life'" based on man's distinguishing characteristic, his freedom to choose between good and evil. D. B. Robertson, Introduction to *Love and Justice*, Selections from the Shorter Writings of Reinhold Niebuhr 12 (D. Robertson ed. 1957). Agape contrasts with the other Greek word for love, "eros," which refers to passionate, romantic love. See Denis De Rougemont, *Love in the Western World* (trans. M. Belgion 1956). Eros involves a self-interested attachment to another; agape refers to an affection without ego or hope of personal gain.

6. For an interesting treatment of community concerns in the criminal justice context, see Nicola Lacey, *State Punishment: Political Principles and Community Values* (1988). See also John Braithwaite & Philip Pettit, *Not Just Deserts: A Republican Theory of Criminal Justice* (1990).

7. See Lacey, *State Punishment, supra* at 77 (1988); Oldenquist, *An Explanation of Retribution* 85 J. Phil. 464, 467–68 (1988).

8. See W. Moberly, *The Ethics of Punishment* 219 (1968); John Charvet, Criticism and Punishment, 75 Mind 573, 578–79; H. M. Hart, Criminal Punishment as Public

Condemnation, in *Contemporary Punishment* 12 (R. Gerber & P. McAnany eds. 1972). As Nigel Walker noted: "There is nothing like conforming with a rule for inducing a feeling of propriety or even righteousness. An unpunished infraction means two infractions." Punishing, Denouncing or Reducing Crime?, *supra* at 400.

In terms of traditional punishment theory, defense of value is close to retribution but does not meet the classic definition of a justification that focuses entirely on past wrong. Under defense of value, the general justification of punishment depends on the ongoing need to defend value. Nevertheless, this approach differs significantly from the utilitarian because the justification of punishment is not contingent on a calculation of particular consequences and the nature of punishment depends on value-based moral assessment of what the offender did. See R. A. Duff, *Trials and Punishments* 7 (1991).

9. For retributive arguments essentially limiting criminal responsibility to this quartet, see Joshua Dressler, Reflections on Excusing Wrongdoers: Moral Theory, New Excuses and the Model Penal Code, 19 Rutgers L.J. 671 (1988); Michael Moore, Choice, Character, and Excuse, in *Crime, Culpability and Remedy* (1990); Stephen Morse, Culpability and Control, 142 U. Penn. L. Rev. 1587 (1994), and The Twilight of Welfare Criminology: A Reply to Judge Bazelon, 49 S. Cal. L. Rev. 1247 (1976); Hyman Gross, *A Theory of Criminal Justice* 321–28 (1979).

10. See Michael Moore, *Act and Crime* (1993).

11. On this question, see the four volumes of Joel Feinberg's series, The Moral Limits of the Criminal Law: *Harm to Others* (1984); *Offense to Others* (1985); *Harm to Self* (1986); and *Harmless Wrongdoing* (1990).

12. See Elyn R. Saks, *Jekyll on Trial: Multiple Personality Disorder and Criminal Law* (1997); Rebecca Dresser, Personal Identity and Punishment, 70 B.U. L.Rev. 395 (1990). For an introduction to the philosophic literature on identity, see *The Identities of Persons* (A. Rorty ed. 1976).

13. See H. L. A. Hart & A. M. Honoree, *Causation and the Law* 292–322 (1959).

14. See Model Penal Code (hereafter MPC) sec. 2.02.

15. As classically represented in criminal law, the noncoercion requirement explains the defenses of duress and necessity. The noncoercion requirement is often stated in terms of ability to do otherwise. See H. L. A. Hart, Legal Responsibility and Excuses in *Punishment and Responsibility* 28, 30 (1968).

16. See Michael Moore, *Law and Psychiatry* 387–415 (1984). The criminal law's view of rationality is a broad one; desires to harm others, while in some senses self-destructive, are viewed as rational since they provide basic, readily comprehensible, albein short-term satisfactions.

17. For a general introduction to the concept of psychopathy, see Hervey M. Cleckly, *The Mask of Sanity* (1941); Robert D. Hare, *Psychopathy: Theory and Research* (1970); for a highly critical view of the concept of psychopathy, see Hakeem, The Assumption That Crime is a Product of Individual Characteristics: A Prime Example from Psychiatry, in *Theoretical Methods in Criminology* 197 (R. Meier ed. 1985).

Leopold and Loeb were not diagnosed as psychopaths—the category had not yet been invented—but their background included many of the characteristic traits: significant histories of criminality, cruelty to animals, lying, lack of meaningful relationships with others, and no compassion for others.

18. Hal Higdon, *The Crime of the Century* at 126; Leopold claimed he was misquoted here, but the sentiment was one he seems to have repeated in different ways to the doctors who examined him.

19. *Id.* at 155.

20. *Id.* at 216.

21. *Id.* at 217.

22. See Harris v. Pulley, 885 F.2d 1354, 1381–83 (9th Cir. 1988) *as amended on denial of rehearing and rehearing en banc* (1989). See also MPC sec. 4.01(2).

23. See Abraham S. Goldstein, *The Insanity Defense* 49–51 (1967); Wayne R. LaFave & Austin W. Scott 313–14 *Criminal Law* (2d ed. 1986). See also MPC sec. 4.01 (making the requirement one of appreciation) and *The Trial of John W. Hinckley, Jr.*, 47–64 (P. Low, J. Jeffries, & R. Bonnie eds. 1986); Herbert Fingarette, *The Meaning of Insanity* 137–42 (1972); Gregory Zilboorg, Misconceptions of Legal Insanity, 9 Am. J. Orthopsychiatry 540, 552–53 (1939). Broad statements of the insanity rule might be explained by a broad view of rationality that includes the emotions—a sense that persons can have crazy feelings as well as crazy perceptions or ideas. See Morse, Culpability and Control, *supra* note 9.

24. The presumption of incapacity was irrebuttable for those under age seven and rebuttable for those aged seven to fourteen. See LaFave & Scott, *Criminal Law*, *supra* at 398–400. The infancy defense largely disappeared with the advent of the separate juvenile justice system at the turn of this century. See Andrew Walkover, The Infancy Defense in the New Juvenile Court, 31 UCLA L. Rev. 503 (1984).

25. Character, Choice, and Moral Agency, in *Crime, Culpability, and Remedy* (E. Paul, F. Miller, & J. Paul eds. 1990); Convicting the Morally Blameless: Reassessing the Relationship between Legal and Moral Accountability, 39 UCLA L. Rev. 1511 (1992).

26. See Anthony Duff, Psychopathy and Moral Understanding, 14 Am. Phil. Q. 189 (1977); *Trials and Punishments* 262–66 (1986); Michael Bavidge, *Mad or Bad?* (1989); Herbert Fingarette & Ann Fingarette Hasse, *Mental Disabilities and Criminal Responsibility* 218–39 (1979); Herbert Fingarette, *The Meaning of Criminal Insanity* 179–94 (1972); Jeffrie Murphy, Moral Death: A Kantian Essay on Psychopathy, in *Retribution, Justice, and Therapy* 128 (1979); Jeremy Horder, Pleading Involuntary Lack of Capacity, 52 Camb. L.J. 298, 302–4 (1993).

27. *Id.* at 82–83.

28. See Morse, The Twilight of Welfare Criminology, *supra* note 9 at 1255–57; Herbert Morris, Persons and Punishment, in *On Guilt and Innocence* 31 (1976). For a historical perspective, see Allen, Legal Values and the Rehabilitative Ideal, 50 J. Crim. L. & Criminol. 226 (1959); Samuel H. Pillsbury, Understanding Penal Reform: The

Dynamic of Change, 80 J. Crim. L. & Criminol. 726 (1989). On this point, we should remember that even if we are generally committed to deserved punishment, desert may not always represent the overriding moral concern, even within the realm of justice. See Feinberg, *Doing and Deserving, supra* note 3 at 84.

29. On the difficulties of determining capacity in a somewhat different context, that of mens rea, see Stephen Morse, Undiminished Confusion in Diminished Capacity, 75 J. Crim. L. & Criminol. 1, 42–44 (1984).

30. See Harry Frankfurt, Freedom of the Will and the Concept of a Person, in *Free Will* (G. Watson ed. 1982).

31. The Mind of the Rapist, Newsweek, July 23, 1990, at 46, 50–52. In keeping with our general blaming practices, a professional counselor described one rapist who witnessed a brutal assault on his mother by his father and then observed: "That's not an excuse, but it does explain his desensitization to violence." *Id.* at 52.

32. See Stanley Milgram, *Obedience to Authority* (1974).

NOTES TO CHAPTER 4: JUST PUNISHMENT IN AN UNJUST SOCIETY

1. See Allen Beck et al., Bureau of Justice Statistics, *Survey of State Prison Inmates, 1991* 3 (1993).

2. See Sanford H. Kadish & Stephen J. Schulhofer, *Criminal Law and Its Processes* 12 (6th ed. 1995).

3. For a general overview of class and race inequities related to criminal justice, see Jeffrey Reiman, *The Rich Get Richer and the Poor Get Prison* 113–14 (1990). For a study focusing on racial inequities related to drug criminalization, see Michael Tonry, *Malign Neglect: Race, Crime and Punishment in America* (1995). Tonry's work has stimulated provocative critiques of social inequities and criminal justice: Robert J. Cottrol, Book Review, Hard Choices and Shifted Burdens: American Crime and American Justice at the End of the Century, 65 Geo. Wash. L. Rev. 506 (1997); David Cole, Review Essay, What's Criminology Got to Do with It? 48 Stanf. L. Rev. 1605 (1996); Angela J. Davis, Benign Neglect of Racism in the Criminal Justice System, 94 Mich. L. Rev. 1660 (1996).

4. Bureau of Justice Statistics, U.S. Dept. of Justice, *Sourcebook of Criminal Justice Statistics—1995* 562 (1996).

5. *Id.* at 362.

6. *Id.* at 363.

7. For studies that indicate racial discrimination in criminal justice, see Reiman, *The Rich Get Richer, supra* note 3 at 191, n.6. See also Davis, Benign Neglect of Racism, *supra* note 3 at 1675–84 (arguing for need to pay more attention to discrimination in criminal justice decision making). For the view that the racial disparity in punishment comes from disparate rates in offending and not race discrimination by the justice system, see William Wilbanks, *The Myth of a Racist Criminal Justice System* (1987); Joan Petersillia, Racial Disparities in the Criminal Justice System: A

Summary, 31 Crime & Delinq. 15 (1985). See also Michael Tonry, *Malign Neglect* 49–80 (1995) (arguing that with the significant exception of drug crimes, the racial disproportion is largely caused by differential socioeconomic conditions, not discrimination within criminal justice); cf. Randall Kennedy, *Race, Crime and the Law* (1997) (arguing that current practices involve racial discrimination in police investigation but not in drug policies).

8. On the contemporary consensus of criminologists linking social inequity and crime, see David Cole, Review Essay, What's Criminology Got to Do with It? 48 Stanf. L. Rev. 1605 (1996); on eighteenth- and nineteenth-century observations to the same effect, see Samuel H. Pillsbury, Understanding Penal Reform: The Dynamic of Change, 80 J. Crim. L. & Criminol. 726, 734–35, 745–46 (1989).

9. These questions should be distinguished from related arguments about responsible choice. Some argue that the socially oppressed should receive less or no punishment for harmful acts to others because such persons have less ability to choose than others. Given prevailing economic and social conditions, the argument goes, members of the underclass either could not do otherwise, or had a radically reduced ability to do otherwise. This argument essentially repeats the arguments concerning physical cause and moral capacity addressed in chapters 2 and 3. My response—that responsible choice does not require ability to do otherwise—is found there as well. Here I am concerned not with the individual's ability to choose, but with the government's ability to punish.

10. E.g., Richard Dugger, Playing Fair with Punishment, 103 Ethics 473 (1993); Michael Davis, Criminal Desert and Unfair Advantage: What's the Connection? 12 Law & Phil. 133 (1993); Jeffrie Murphy, Marxism and Retribution, in *Retribution, Justice, and Therapy* 93 (1979); Herbert Morris, Persons and Punishment, in *On Guilt and Innocence* 33–36 (1976). See also Willem de Haan, *The Politics of Redress: Crime, Punishment and Penal Abolition* 102–29 (1990); Ralph Ellis & Carol Ellis, *Theories of Criminal Justice: A Critical Reappraisal* 165–83 (1989).

11. George Fletcher argues in addition that social contract theory pushes us to consider the requirements of justice as opposed to the religiously tinged requirements of personal morality. The Meaning of Morality, 64 Notre Dame L. Rev. 805, 815–16 (1989).

12. See Murphy, Marxism and Retribution, *supra* note 10; see also David L. Bazelon, The Morality of the Criminal Law, 49 S. Cal. L. Rev. 385, 386–87 (1976); Richard Delgado, "Rotten Social Background": Should the Criminal Law Recognize a Defense of Severe Environmental Deprivation? 3 Law & Inequality 9, 13–15, 68–70, 77–78 (1985).

13. See Ingo Muller, *Hitler's Justice* (D. Schneider trans. 1991); Mark Tushnet, *The American Law of Slavery* (1981); Symposium on the Law of Slavery, 68 Chicago-Kent L. Rev. 1009 (1993); Kenneth Stampp, *The Peculiar Institution* (1956).

14. See Alfred Blumstein & Daniel Cork, Linking Gun Availability to Youth Gun Violence, 59 Law & Contemp. Probs. 5, 6–8 (1996) (rise in youth homicide rate); see,

generally, Howard N. Snyder & Melissa Sickmund, *Juvenile Offenders and Victims: A National Report* (1995).

15. Federal Bureau of Investigation, *Uniform Crime Reports, 1991* 279–85, 288–89; Althea Knight, Strategies to End the Carnage, Washington Post, Oct. 27, 1993 (increase in juvenile homicides in Washington, D.C.). See also Lois Fingerhut & Joel Kleinman, International and Interstate Comparisons of Homicide among Young Males, 263 JAMA 3292 (1990).

16. Calif. Const., arts. 13A, 13B.

17. For a devastating account of the costs of this triage in an overwhelmed urban criminal justice system, see David Freed, A System in Distress: The Devaluation of Crime in Los Angeles, a series in the Los Angeles Times, p. 1, Dec. 16–22, 1990. For a look at the problems of homicide investigation and prosecution in an overstressed system, see Ted Rohrlich & Fredric N. Tulsky, Not All L.A. Murder Cases Are Equal, Los Angeles Times, Dec. 3, 1996; Ted Rohrlich, Fredric N. Tulsky, & Dan Weikel, In a System Stretched Thin, Wrongful Arrests Happen, Los Angeles Times, Dec. 4, 1996.

18. See Thomas Edsall, Failure to Punish Misdemeanors Fuels Violence, St. Louis Officials Say, Washington Post, April 10, 1994, at A8.

19. Dick Goldberg, Juvenile Court: Is the Concept Too Outdated?, Los Angeles Daily Journal, Aug. 23, 1994, at p. 1.

20. For the link between firearms and juvenile homicide, see Blumstein & Cork, Linking Gun Availability to Youth Violence, *supra* note 14; Lois Fingerhut et al., Nonfirearm Homicide among Persons 15 through 19 Years of Age, 22 JAMA 3048 (1992). For a journalistic account, see David Freed, Guns, Violence Exact a Toll on LA's Youngest Victims, May 21, 1992, at p. 1. Of course many dispute the link between gun control and crime reduction. See, e.g., Gary Kleck, *Point Blank: Guns and Violence in America* (1991).[c]

21. See Brandon Centerwall, Television and Violence, 267 JAMA 3059 (1992); Deborah Prothrow-Stith, *Deadly Consequences* (1991). For a review of studies on media effects of violence concluding that the studies have to date demonstrated only relatively minor effects on behavior, see James Q. Wilson & Richard Herrnstein, *Crime & Human Nature* 337–54 (1985).

NOTES TO CHAPTER 5: MORALIZING THE PASSIONS OF PUNISHMENT

1. The 1992 riots in Los Angeles were triggered by a jury verdict. Los Angeles Times, *Understanding the Riots: Los Angeles before and after the Rodney King Case* (1992). Following the acquittal of John W. Hinckley Jr. for shooting President Reagan and others, on grounds of insanity, the federal government and half of the states made changes in the insanity defense. Peter Low, John Calvin Jeffries Jr., & Richard Bonnie, *The Trial of John W. Hinckley, Jr.* 126–27 (1986). In the 1988 presidential campaign, Republican candidate George Bush gained a significant political edge over his opponent, Michael Dukakis, through campaign television ads that blamed Governor

Dukakis for the release of a murderer (Willie Horton) on a furlough program in Massachusetts. Bush also gained when Dukakis was perceived as being too dispassionate during the second campaign debate when Dukakis was asked about how he would react to the rape and murder of his wife. See Jack Germon & Jules Witcover, *Whose Broad Stripes and Bright Stars* 11–17, 162–65, 410–11, 446–53 (1989); Elizabeth Drew, *Political Journal: Political Events of 1987–88* 266–67, 304–6, 332–33 (1989).

2. For another account of this phenomenon, see Helen Prejean, *Dead Man Walking* (1993), and her account of Vernon and Elizabeth Harvey, parents of a slain young woman whose killer was executed in Louisiana.

3. Henry Weihofen, *The Urge to Punish* 131 (1956). From the late eighteenth century well into the twentieth century, penal reformers and many penal experts held that punishment should be for deterrence and rehabilitation, not retribution; retribution was seen as the hallmark of obsolete, cruel, and revenge-based systems of punishment. See Pillsbury, Understanding Penal Reform: The Dynamic of Change, 80 J. Crim. L. & Criminol. 726 (1989) . A contemporary writer has called this tendency a "revenge taboo"—a tendency to condemn any practice that hints of the emotions of revenge. See Susan Jacoby, *Wild Justice* 1–13 (1983).

4. For a review of traditional arguments of this kind against retribution, see Martin R. Gardner, The Renaissance of Retribution—An Examination of Doing Justice, 1976 Wis. L. Rev. 781, 782; see also David Dolinko, Thoughts about Retribution, 101 Ethics 537, 559 (1991): "Continued adherence to retributionist modes of thought may well encourage even greater vindictiveness and a peculiarly self-righteous and smug indulgence of society's most punitive reflexes."

5. For traditional defenses of the anger of retribution, see Sir James Fitzjames Stephen, 1 *A History of the Criminal Law of England* 478 (1883); *Salmond on Jurisprudence* 120–21 (11th ed. 1957) (quoted in American Friends Service Committee, *Struggle for Justice* 21 (1971). For extended discussions of the relationship between anger and deserved punishment, generally supportive of deserved punishment, see generally Michael Moore, The Moral Worth of Retribution, in *Responsibility, Character and the Emotions* 179 (F. Schoeman ed. 1987); Jeffrie G. Murphy, The Retributive Emotions, Hatred: A Qualified Defense, in Murphy & Jean Hampton, *Forgiveness and Mercy* (1988). See also Aquinas, *Summa Theologiae* (T. O'Brien trans. 1971) vol. 41, 2a2ae, question 108; Robert Nozick, *Philosophical Explanations* 366–67 (1981). For a psychoanalytic approach, see Kent A. Wilson, Vengeance and Mercy: Implications of Psychoanalytic Theory for the Retributive Theory of Punishment, 60 Neb. L. Rev. 276, 287–92 (1981).

In case law, the place of anger has been most prominently discussed in connection with the death penalty. The Supreme Court has justified the death penalty as the community's expression of "moral outrage" at an offense. Gregg v. Georgia, 428 U.S. 153, 183 (1976); Spaziano v. Florida, 468 U.S. 447, 468–69 (Stevens, J., dissenting). The Court has approved a judge's expression of and reliance upon feelings of shock and outrage as a basis for a death sentence. Barclay v. Florida, 463 U.S. 939 (1983). In fact, it is hard to imagine a sentencer finding that an offender deserves a severe punishment without that sentencer experiencing at least an undercurrent of anger at the offender's deed.

6. Roger Wertheimer, Understanding Retribution, 2 Criminal Justice Ethics 19, 34–35 (1983). See also Lester H. Hunt, Punishment, Revenge and the Minimal Functions of the State, in *Understanding Human Emotions* 83–86 (F. Miller & T. Attig eds. 1979). Overall, deserved punishment and revenge bear the same relation to each other as do agape and eros, discussed in note 5, chapter 3. Deserved punishment and agape describe motivations based on publicly declared moral principles. Eros and revenge describe nonmoral personal motivations for action.

7. The Supreme Court has recognized that sympathy may be morally valuable in determining just punishment. Brown v. California, 107 S.Ct. 837, 840 (1987).

8. CALJIC 1.00 (Respective Duties of Judge and Jury); see also Devitt & Blackmar, *Federal Jury Practice and Instructions* (3d ed.) section 11.03 (The law does not permit jurors to be governed by sympathy, prejudice, or public opinion).

Even at sentencing, courts treat sympathy with suspicion. For example, see the prosecutors' arguments in Wilson v. Kemp, 777 F.2d 621, 623 (11th Cir. 1985), cert. denied, 106 S.Ct. 2258 (1986) and Drake v. Kemp, 762 F.2d 1449, 1458 (11th Cir. 1985) (en banc), cert. denied, 106 S.Ct. 3333 (1986) utilizing a nineteenth-century Georgia Supreme Court case where the court denounced "sickly sentimentality" and stated, "If this crime goes unpunished, let our skirts at least be free from the stain of blood guiltiness." In both cases the Eleventh Circuit reversed based on the prosecutors' misleading inference that the sentencing jury could not consider mercy.

For an illuminating, though ambivalent view of "emotion and sympathy" in judicial sentencing, see Marvin Frankel, *Criminal Sentences* 79 (1973).

9. See Bureau of Justice Statistics, U.S. Dept. of Justice, *Sourcebook of Criminal Justice Statistics—1992*, 184–85, table 2.27 (1993) (comparing perceptions of city dangers among urban, suburban, and rural residents); Lucia Zedner, Victims, in *The Oxford Handbook of Criminology* 1206, 1218–20 (1994).

In many cases the two primary emotions of criminal responsibility—fear and anger—are closely linked. Fear and rage are the hallmarks of that paradigm of injustice, the lynch mob. E.g., Furman v. Georgia, 408 U.S. 238, 308 (1972) (Stewart, J. concurring) (need to channel society's "instinct for retribution"); *id.*, 344–45 (Marshall, J., concurring) (Eighth Amendment limits vengeance). See also *id.* at 254 (Douglas, J. concurring) (historical view that Eighth Amendment grounded in need to prevent punishment as political vengeance); *id.* at 304 (Brennan, J. concurring) (suggesting that no state sought "naked vengeance" in punishment); Tison v. Arizona, 107 S.Ct. 1676, 1701–2 (1986) (Brennan, J. dissenting) (decision to execute "appears responsive less to reason than other, more visceral demands.")

General issues of criminal justice policy may also be driven by the twin forces of fear and anger. In California the recent adoption of a harsh "three strikes" bill providing for long imprisonment of repeat felons came as a result of a personal campaign by Mike Reynolds, the father of a murder victim. In the wake of a widely publicized kidnapping and murder of a twelve-year-old girl (Polly Klaas), public anger at and fear of such felons was so strong that even politicians who believed the law was bad policy voted in favor of it. The legislation became law despite the opposition of the California District Attorney's Association and several prominent district attorneys in the state. Proponents strongly argued that the measure was necessary for public safety, although criminologists note that it will focus a large amount of incarceration resources on offenders near the end of their criminal careers. As one columnist described the law: "It's a shot in the dark, motivated by fear and anger and manipulated by politicians who feed on such emotions, just as crooks feed on unlocked doors." Peter H. King, Maybe, Just Maybe, Los Angeles Times, March 9, 1994, at A3. See also Sherry Bebitch Jeffe, In the Face of "Three Strikes," California's Leaders Roll Over, Los Angeles Times, March 13, 1994, at M1. Again we see that deterrent arguments are as susceptible to emotive distortion as are retributive arguments.

10. E.g., Plato, *The Republic*, part 5; Seneca, *De Ira*, in *Moral Essays*, vol. 1 (J. Basore trans. 1928); Rene Descartes, *The Passions of the Soul* in *The Philosophical Writings of Descartes* (J. Cottingham et al., trans. 1985); Immanuel Kant, *Fundamental Principles of the Metaphysics of Morals* 45–46, 72 (T. Abbott trans. 1987). Even within this group, however, careful reading may discern passages compatible with a view of moral value in emotion. See Ronald De Sousa, Self-Deceptive Emotions in *Explaining Emotions* 127 (A. Rorty ed. 1980) (suggesting that Plato saw emotion as compatible with rationality); Kant, The Doctrine of Virtue, in *The Metaphysic of Morals* 115–30 (M. Gregory trans. 1964).

11. For general statements of the traditional view and criticisms of it, see Robert C. Solomon, Emotions and Choice in *Explaining Emotions, supra* at 251; Bernard Williams, Morality and the Emotions in *Problems of the Self* 207 (1973).

12. See Robert C. Solomon, *The Passions* 15–19, 171–250 (1983); Cheshire Calhoun, Cognitive Emotions? in *What Is an Emotion?* 39 (Calhoun & R. Solomon eds. 1984). For the view that emotions provide the key to understanding the self, see David M. Rosenthal, Emotions and the Self, in *Emotion: Philosophical Studies* 169–91 (K. Irani & G. Myers eds. 1983).

13. See Solomon, *The Passions, supra* at xv–xvi; David Viscount, *The Language of Feelings* 11–14, 19 (1976).

14. Ronald De Sousa, *The Rationality of Emotion*, 190–203 (1987).

15. For philosophically oriented views, see R. Gordon, *The Structure of Emotions: Investigations in Cognitive Philosophy* (1987); William Lyons, *Emotion* (1980); De Sousa, *The Rationality of Emotions, supra*; Solomon, *The Passions, supra* note 12; Robert C. Roberts, What an Emotion Is: A Sketch, 97 Philosphical Review 183 (1988). For psychological studies, see N. Frijda, *The Emotions* (1983); see generally, 1 *Emotion: Theory, Research and Experience* (R. Plutchik & H. Kellerman eds. 1980).

16. Lyons, *Emotion, supra* at 53–95; Solomon, *The Passions, supra* note 12 at 171–279.

17. For a full cognitive dissection of anger, see Solomon, *The Passions, supra* note 12 at 283–86.

18. See, generally, Calhoun, Cognitive Emotions? *supra* note 12.

19. See De Sousa, The Rationality of Emotions, *supra* note 14 at 237–64; Solomon, *The Passions, supra* note 12 at 287–88.

20. Ronald De Sousa has suggested that the cognitive assessment of emotion follows a set of internalized paradigm scenarios. See Self-Deceptive Emotions, and The Rationality of Emotions in *Explaining Emotions, supra* note 10. For each emotion we have learned a paradigm scenario. We compare later situations to the paradigm to determine if the emotion is appropriate. Anger involves the imagining of a paradigm of accusation and denunciation, perhaps taken from a scene of parental punishment. A situation that makes us angry is one which fits this model; in recognizing the connection we relive the original scenario, with modifications for the present situation. Robert Solomon argues that we use emotions to develop a constitutive mythology of the world. Solomon, *The Passions, supra* note 12 at 194–238, 276–77. Emotion transforms impersonal reality into personal myth. The experience of anger transforms a perception of wrong into a mythic confrontation between avenging victim and wrongdoer. The angry self becomes the accuser, the adjudicator and punisher; the wrongdoer becomes the accused and the convict awaiting punishment.

21. Empathy thus expresses the active caring of agape, the opposite of which is not hate, but indifference. R. Roberts, *Spirituality and Human Emotion* 109–11 (1982); Joseph Fletcher, *Situation Ethics* 63 (1966).

22. E.g., Lynne Henderson, Legality and Empathy, 85 Mich. L. Rev. 1574, 1584–92 (1987); Sapontzis, A Critique of Personhood, 91 Ethics 607, 613 (1981); Weihofen, *The Urge to Punish, supra* note 3 at 144–45. Commentators have widely recognized this problem in the death penalty context. Margaret Jane Radin, Cruel Punishment and Respect for Persons: Super Due Process for Death, 53 S. Cal. L. Rev. 1143, 1182 n.124; Robert Weisberg, Deregulating Death, 1983 Sup. Ct. Rev. 305, 361, 391.

23. Prosecutors frequently do this explicitly: e.g., Darden v. Wainwright, 477 U.S. 168, 180 nn. 11, 12 (1986) (prosecutor terms defendant an "animal" who "shouldn't be let out of his cell unless he has a leash on him and a prison guard at the other end of that leash"); United States v. Cook, 432 F. 2d 1093, 1106–8 (7th Cir. 1970) (defendant called "subhuman"); see, generally, Arthur N. Bishop, Name-Calling: Defendant Nomenclature in Criminal Trials, 4 Ohio N.U. L. Rev. 38 (1977).

The tendency goes beyond law enforcement, of course. In a recent article about a father, Sam Knott, whose daughter was killed by a California Highway Patrol officer named Craig Preyer, the reporter noted that: "The name Peyer does not pass Sam Knott's lips. Ever. In talking, in testifying—even this day at a San Diego Denny's as he quotes from a legal brief pertaining to his civil suit against the CHP, Sam substitutes 'The Monster' each time he comes across the offending word. He does it matter-of-factly, exactly as if The Monster were Craig Peyer's given name. 'It's part of my therapy,' he explains, but it's more than that: It's an expression of Sam's allegorical world view. There are monsters out there. And one must be ever vigilant, take every precaution and then some, or the monsters will overcome the forces of good." Steve Salerno, A Father's Crusade, Los Angeles Times Magazine, Aug. 21, 1994, at 26, 28.

24. See McClesky v. Kemp, 481 U.S. 279 (1987); Stephen Carter, When Victims Happen to Be Black, 97 Yale L.J. 420 (1988); Dane & Wrightsman, Effects of Defendants' and Victims' Characteristics on Jurors' Verdicts, in *The Psychology of the Courtroom* 104–6 (1982). There is also evidence that American juries generally find black defendants unsympathetic, and that whether or not the defendant appears sympathetic to the jury is an important factor in jury decisions. Harry Kalven & Hans Zeisel, *The American Jury* 194–218 (1966).

25. Duncan v. Louisiana, 391 U.S. 145 (1968); Baldwin v. New York, 399 U.S. 66 (1970).

26. The Supreme Court has held that the federal constitution requires jury unanimity in federal criminal trials for nonpetty offenses, but not in similar trials in state court. Johnson v. Louisiana, 406 U.S. 356 (1972); Apodaca v. Oregon, 406 U.S. 404 (1972). The Court has also approved unanimous juries of six for noncapital cases. Williams v. Florida, 399 U.S. 78 (1970).

27. Carpenters v. United States, 330 U.S. 395, 408 (1947) (no directed verdicts for the prosecution in a criminal case); United States v. Martin Linen Supply Co., 430 U.S. 564, 572–73 (1977) (acquittal by court following hung jury bars retrial).

28. See Glanville Williams, *The Proof of Guilt* 36, 307–8 (3d ed. 1963); Kalven & Zeisel, *The American Jury, supra* note 25 at 418–25, noting the few American jurisdictions that do allow judicial commentary and its effects); Stephen Salzburg, The Unnecessarily Expanding Role of the American Trial Judge, 64 Va. L. Rev. 1, 22–46 (1978).

29. Most continental criminal justice systems rely on verdicts rendered by judges or by tribunals comprised of judges and lay persons. See, e.g., John H. Langbein, *Comparative Criminal Procedure: Germany* 61–63, 80–81 (1977); Williams, *The Proof of Guilt, supra* at 255.

30. See Burks v. United States, 437 U.S. 1, 16 (1978).

31. On appeal the due process standard for sufficiency of the prosecution's evidence at trial is "whether, after viewing the evidence in the light most favorable to the prosecution, *any* rational trier of fact could have found the essential elements of the crime beyond a reasonable doubt." Jackson v. Virginia, 443 U.S. 307, 318–19 (1979).

32. In 1991 of 56,747 defendants charged in federal court, 41,213 pled guilty or no contest; 5,860 had their cases disposed of by jury trial (the remaining cases were dismissed or were resolved by court trial). *Sourcebook—1992, supra* note 9 at 512. In state courts an estimated 8 to 12 percent of cases go to trial. See Stephen Schulhofer,

A Wake-Up Call from the Plea-Bargaining Trenches, 19 Law & Soc. Inq. 135, 140 (1994).

33. The early English criminal trial was a relatively informal process necessarily involving a citizen accuser and the defendant who defended himself or herself without counsel. Jurors could act as both judges and witnesses. See Leonard W. Levy, *Origins of the Fifth Amendment* 19–32 (1968); Stephen, 1 *History of the Criminal Law of England, supra* note 65 at 244–72.

34. The formality of the courtroom setting encourages the expression of public values and discourages the expression of private bias. See Richard Delgado et al., Fairness and Formality: Minimizing the Risk of Prejudice in Alternative Dispute Resolution, 1985 Wisc. L. Rev. 1359, 1387–89.

35. *The City of God* bk. 14 ch. 6 556 (H. Bettenson trans. 1972): "[T]he man who lives by God's standards, and not man's, must needs be a lover of the good, and it follows that he must hate what is evil. Further, since no one is evil by nature, but anyone who is evil is evil because of a perversion of nature, the man who lives by God's standards has a duty of 'perfect hatred' towards those who are evil . . . he should not hate the person because of the fault. . . . He should hate the fault but love the man."

NOTES TO CHAPTER 6: FROM PRINCIPLES TO RULES

1. See Francis Sayre, Mens Rea, 45 Harv. L. Rev. 974 (1932).

2. *The Common Law* 3 (1881).

3. Again I should make clear that a number of important aspects of criminal culpability are *not* covered by this conception of mens rea. Mens rea as I use the term here does not include the requirement of a voluntary act or omission—although as we will see, mens rea and the act requirement are closely related. Mens rea does not include causation, the requirement in homicide that the person's wrongful action was a sufficient cause of the death for liability, nor does it include any of the many affirmative defenses that might be raised, such as duress, self-defense, or insanity.

4. See M.P.C. secs. 210.2, 220.3, 2.02(2).

5. On negligence, see MPC secs. 210.4, 2.02(2)(d).

6. Exodus 20:13 (King James version). Many argue that the commandment should properly be translated as thou shalt not murder, which reveals the legal dimension to the moral command. E.g., Clayton E. Cramer & David B. Kopel, "Shall Issue": The New Wave of Concealed Handgun Permit Laws, 62 Tenn. L. Rev. 679, 724 (1995).

7. Except for death penalty cases, where juries have significant, often primary sentencing authority and those few jurisdictions that still provide for jury sentencing in the general run of criminal cases. See, e.g., Holly Lodge Meyer & Jenifer Sutton, Old Dog, New Tricks: New Sentencing Guidelines, 40 Ark. Lawyer 24 (1996).

8. Most normative assessments present this tension. For example, consider the

problems a college admissions committee faces in developing criteria for admission. It may choose relatively narrow rules based on hard data, such as grades and scores on standardized tests. Such criteria will give applicants the greatest amount of notice and presents the least chance of biased or arbitrary decisionmaking by the committee members. But such criteria are probably insufficient to the larger task of admitting the best possible freshman class—the committee will miss important considerations that make at least some persons with lower numbers better candidates than some with higher numbers. By contrast, the committee could come up with generally worded criteria that relate to academic performance, maturity, discipline, achievement, leadership potential, dedication to the community and so on. This would permit the committee to consider some important criteria missed by the numbers standard, but it would make the possibilities of bias and arbitrariness in decision making by members much greater. Such broad criteria would make it hard for any outside observer to tell whether the committee was applying the criteria fairly, or indeed what the criteria really were.

9. This style might also be called mythic, because such forms of mens rea expressed a central narrative or image of wrongdoing rather than defined by particular forms of belief or acted-upon desire. See Northrop Frye, *The Great Code: The Bible and Literature* (1982) (defining one sense of myth as a special, sacred story used to convey essential truths for a culture).

10. Jones v. Commonwealth, 75 Pa. 403, 407 (1874).

11. *Id.* at 408.

12. See, generally, Paul H. Robinson, A Brief History of Distinctions in Criminal Culpability, 31 Hastings L.J. 815, 837–46 (1980); Richard Singer, The Resurgence of Mens Rea: I—Provocation, Emotional Disturbance, and the Model Penal Code, 27 B.C. L. Rev. 243 (1986).

13. See MPC sec. 2.02.

14. MPC sec. 2.02(2)(c).

15. Sec. 2.02(2)(d).

16. In a number of contexts the MPC employs a particularly broad form of reasonableness. The drafters deliberately left undefined the question of what might be included within "the actor's situation," and with regard to manslaughter provided that reasonableness "shall be determined from the viewpoint of a person in the actor's situation under the circumstances as he believes them to be." Sec. 210.3(1)(b).

17. The clearest example may be California's three strikes law. See Michael Vitiello, "Three Strikes" and the Romero Case: The Supreme Court Restores Democracy, 30 Loy. L. Rev. 1643 (1997); Franklin E. Zimring, Populism, Democratic Government, and the Decline of Expert Authority: Some Reflections on "Three Strikes" in California, 28 Pac. L.J. 243 (1996); Marc Mauer, Politics, Crime Control . . . and Baseball? "Three Strikes and You're Out," 9 Criminal Justice 30 (1994).

18. See Rebecca Dresser, Review Essay, Making Up Our Minds: Can Law Survive Cognitive Science? 10 Criminal Justice Ethics 27, 27 (1991).

19. This picture of brain dynamics is drawn largely from Daniel Dennett, *Consciousness Explained* (1991).

20. See Patricia Churchland, *Neurophilosophy:Toward a Unified Science of the Mind-Brain* (1986); Paul Churchland, *Matter & Consciousness* (1984); Patricia Churchland, Reductionism and Antireductionism in Functionalist Theories of the Mind, in *The Philosophy of Mind* 59–68 (B. Beakley & P. Ludlow eds. 1992); Andrew E. Lelling, Comment, Eliminative Materialism, Neuroscience and the Criminal Law, 141 Penn. L. Rev. 1471 (1993).

21. See Anthony O'Hear, *Introduction to the Philosophy of Science* 223–32 (1989); Thomas Nagel, *The View from Nowhere* (1986). See also chapter 2.

22. State v. Harris, 46 N.C. (1 Jones) 190, 195 (1853).

23. For example, in the most celebrated of the criminal cases to arise from the 1992 riots in Los Angeles, Damian Williams was charged with aggravated mayhem against Reginald Denny. The offense required proof that the person "intentionally causes permanent disability or disfigurement," "under circumstances manifesting extreme indifference to the physical or psychological well-being of another person." One legal commentator told the press that proof of this mens rea would be difficult: "That's the real crusher. How does one ever know what's in somebody's head?" Ashley Dunn, Tough Law, Tough Cases: Courts, Los Angeles Times, Sept. 24, 1993, at B1, B4. In commenting on the jury's verdict in the case, one of the trial prosecutors said that proof of specific intent was difficult because "it's very hard to look into a persons mind." Nevertheless, the prosecutor said intent had been proven by the circumstances. "When you take a brick and hurl it at point-blank range as hard as you can into a helpless man's head, what other logical conclusion is there other than that you are trying to kill him or at least disfigure him?" Edward J. Boyer and John L. Mitchell, Attempted Murder Acquittal, Deadlock Wind Up Denny Trial, Los Angeles Times, Oct. 21, 1993, at A1.

24. I am always reminded of the scene in the original *Terminator* movie where, in the terminator's first appearance, the viewer sees a visual menu of possible verbal responses to a human inquiry; the robot terminator selects the most abusive (Orion Pictures, 1984).

25. See René Descartes, *Meditations on First Philosophy* 50–62 (J. Cottingham trans. 1986).

26. Powerful critiques of the dualist view may be found in Gilbert Ryle, *The Concept of Mind* (1949); Anthony Kenny, *The Metaphysics of Mind* (1989); Daniel Dennett, *Consciousness Explained* (1991).

27. For more on this, see chapter 9.

28. Deavitt & Blackmarr, *Instructions for Federal Criminal Cases* sec. 17.07, at 642 (1988). The dualist assumption in the Sixth Circuit's model instruction is even more obvious: "Ordinarily, there is no way that a defendant's state of mind can be proved directly, because no one can read another person's mind and tell what that person is thinking." Pattern Criminal Jury Instructions of the District Judges Association of the

Sixth Circuit, no. 2.08 (1991). A typical state instruction reads: "It is not always possible to prove a purpose by direct evidence, for purpose and intent are subjective facts. That is, they are within the mind of man." State. v. Huffman, 1 N.E.2d 313 (Oh. 1936). Sometimes the dualist assumption is more subtly stated. In California juries are instructed that guilt requires "a union or joint operation of act or conduct and a certain mental state *in the mind* of the perpetrator." CALJIC 3.31.5 (emphasis added).

29. David Aaronson, *Maryland Criminal Jury Instruction and Commentary* sec. 3.01 (1975).

30. *Id.*

31. In 1979 the Supreme Court held in *Sandstrom v. Montana* that the traditional natural and probable consequences instruction violates the due process requirement that the prosecution prove all the elements of an offense, including mens rea, beyond a reasonable doubt. 442 U.S. 510. See Dresser, Culpability and Other Minds, *supra* note 10 at 56–58. In this and later cases the Court noted that natural and probable consequence instructions, depending on their wording, might either eliminate the jury's responsibility to determine actual mens rea (some instructions suggested that natural consequences determined mens rea) or put the burden of proving lack of mens rea on the defendant. See also Francis v. Franklin, 471 U.S. 307 (1985); United States v. United States Gypsum Co., 438 U.S. 422 (1978).

In response to *Sandstrom*, many courts simply stopped instructing jurors on how mens rea is proven. This avoids the due process problem, and it also avoids lending judicial support to the internal chooser metaphor. The underlying problem of how mens rea should be proven remains, however. Given the prevalence of the internal chooser metaphor in ordinary understandings of responsibility, and in other instructions, silence on proof is unacceptable. Unless they are told otherwise, jurors may well believe that they must read the defendant's mind to determine culpability. Or they may give up on understanding mens rea and decide the case purely on their own intuitions, unguided by law. We have seen the problems with this approach in chapter 5. For a proposed jury instruction on the proof of mens rea, see the appendix.

In text I assume that in serious offenses, mens rea will always be deemed an essential element of the offense. Recent Supreme Court cases on related issues at least raise the possibility that the Court might permit a legislature to eliminate mens rea entirely in serious offenses, or put the burden of its disproof on the defense. In support of my assumption, see Mullaney v. Wilbur, 421 U.S. 684 (1975) (state may not shift burden of proof on provocation, as traditionally defined, to the defense); for cases suggesting more legislative leeway, see Montana v. Egelhoff, 116 S.Ct. 2013 (1996) (no constitutional bar to elimination of intoxication-based mens rea argument); Martin v. Ohio, 480 U.S. 228 (1987) (permissible to put burden of showing self-defense on the defendant); McMillan v. Pennsylvania, 477 U.S. 197 (1986) (permissible to determine punishment in part on sentencing enhancement, proved by lesser standard of proof at sentencing); Patterson v. New York, 432 U.S. 197 (1977) (permissible for state to place burden of showing nontraditional form of provocation on defendant).

1. The facts of the Chi Omega killing are drawn from Bundy v. State, 455 So.2d 330 (Fla. 1984) and Stephen G. Michaud & Hugh Aynesworth, *The Only Living Witness* (1983). On the Kimberly Leach killing, see Bundy v. State, 471 So.2d 9 (Fla. 1985). Book-length accounts include Elizabeth Kendall, *The Phantom Prince: My Life with Ted Bundy* (1981); Richard W. Larsen, *Bundy: The Deliberate Stranger* (1980); Ann Rule, *The Stranger beside Me* (1980); Steven Winn & David Merrill, *Ted Bundy: The Killer Next Door* (1980).

2. E.g., Fla. Stat. Ann. sec. 782.04(1)(a)1,2.

3. The early doctrine of malice aforethought probably involved a notion of prior reflection; see Roy Moreland, *The Law of Homicide* 10 (1952); *Report of the Royal Commission on Capital Punishment, 1949–1953* 75 (1953). As late as the early eighteenth century, Hale wrote that evidence of malice "must arise from external circumstances discovering that inward intention, as lying in wait, menacings antecedent, former grudges, deliberate compassings, and the like." *Id.* at 451. The phrase also had a broader meaning, however, describing a killing without provocation, a felony murder or the killing of a magistrate or officer of the law in the line of duty. Sir James Fitzjames Stephen, 3 *History of the Criminal Law of England* 52–60 (1983) (commenting on Coke's *Third Institute*). Despite a number of reform proposals, English law has never distinguished between different kinds of murder and has never adopted a premeditation formula. See, generally, *Royal Commission, supra*; Andrew Ashworth, Reforming the Law of Murder [1990] Crim. L. Rev. 75 (reviewing report of recent English legislative commission on murder reform).

For other Western nations that used and still use variants of premeditation, see *Royal Commission, supra* at 180, French Penal Code, T.II, sec. 1, par. 1, art. 296–98 (J. Moreau & G. Mueller trans. 1960); Italian Penal Code, T. XII, art. 576 (E. Wise w/ A. Maitlin trans. 1978).

4. *Royal Commission, supra* at 381.

5. Exodus 21:14

6. See Sir Matthew Hale, 1 *The History of the Pleas of the Crown* 453 (1736, 1971); William Blackstone, 4 *Commentaries on the Laws of England* 191–92 (1962).

7. Early murder and manslaughter doctrine did not focus entirely on emotionality, however. As we will see in chapter 8, manslaughter involved motive analysis as well. Informing all aspects of homicide doctrine were prevailing norms concerning physical courage and male honor in the conduct of violence. An assailant who in cowardly fashion laid in wait, attacking his victim when he had no chance for self-defense, was a murderer; one who openly challenged his opponent to a fight and, in a fair fight, slew him was a manslaughterer. See Thomas A. Green, The Jury and the

English Law of Homicide, 1200–1600, 74 Mich. L. Rev. 414 (1976) (tracing the way in which early English approaches to homicide were influenced by the Anglo-Saxon tradition of distinguishing secret from open killings). Early Russian law categorized the worst homicide as that where the victim was killed without drawing his sword; in Sweden the worst killings were of defenseless individuals. Gabriel Tarde, *Penal Philosophy* (R. Howell trans. 1912). Many contemporary European murder statutes contain similar notions. See George Fletcher, *Rethinking Criminal Law* 329 (1978).

8. See Lawrence Friedman, *A History of American Law* 280–99 (2d ed. 1985); Samuel H. Pillsbury, Understanding Penal Reform: The Dynamic of Change, 80 J. Crim. L. & Criminol. 726, 729–38 (1989).

9. 9 Pa. Stat. at Large 600 (quoted in Edwin R. Keedy, History of the Pennsylvania Statute Creating Degrees of Murder, 97 U.Pa. L. Rev. 759, 770–71 (1949).

10. *Id.* The statutory language was taken from the colony's original penal code drafted by founder William Penn in the seventeenth century. *Id.* at 760–61.

11. See Herbert Wechsler & Jerome Michael, A Rationale of the Law of Homicide I, 37 Col. L. Rev. 701, 704–5 (1937).

12. Commonwealth v. Drum, 58 Pa. (Smith) 9, 16 (1868) (quoting from earlier decision in Commonwealth v. Richard Smith).

13. *Id.*

14. Jones v. Commonwealth, 75 Pa. 403, 406 (1874).

15. People v. Caldwell, 43 Cal.2d 864, 869 (1955).

16. Benjamin Cardozo, What Medicine Can Do for Law, in *Law and Literature* 70, 99–100 (1931).

17. Commonwealth v. O'Seara, 352 A.2d 30, 37–38 (Pa. 1976); see also Commonwealth v. Carroll, 194 A.2d 911 (Pa. 1963); Hammil v. People, 361 P.2d 117 (Colo. 1961); State v. Schrader, 302 S.E.2d 70 (W.Va. 1982).

18. Thus at trial the decision maker must resolve whether the killing is premeditated, but the decision maker is not given a clear idea of the difference between premeditation and purpose to kill, assuming there is one, and on appeal any possible distinction between these elements disappears. In effect, appellate courts conclusively presume that all purposeful killings found at trial to be premeditated *were* premeditated.

19. 70 Cal.2d 15, 447 P.2d 942 (1968); see also Moreland, *The Law of Homicide, supra* note 3 at 211–12.

20. 70 Cal.2d at 26–27, 33–34. In this way the *Anderson* decision reflects the importance in rationality analysis of what philosopher Michael Bratman terms "reconsideration." Bratman argues that rationality involves not only the process of making decisions and plans but the process of deciding when and how to reconsider those decisions and plans. *Intention, Plans, and Practical Reason* 60–75 (1987).

21. 70 Cal.2d at 33–34. In so doing the court also changed Anderson's sentence from death to life imprisonment. Four years later, in an unrelated case, the court found the state's death penalty unconstitutional. People v. Anderson, 6 Cal.3d 628

(1972). Other courts concerned with giving meaning to premeditation have concentrated on the timing aspect of killing. E.g., Austin v. United States, 382 F.2d 129 (D.C. Cir. 1967); State v. Bingham, 699 P.2d 262 (Wash. App. 1983), *aff'd*, 719 P.2d 109 (Wash. 1986); People v. Morrin, 187 N.W.2d 434 (Mich. App. 1971).

22. Even so, some might argue that the court overstepped its judicial role in second-guessing the jury's determination of these facts. The *Anderson* court did not hold that the jury was erroneously instructed, but rather that the jury reached the wrong legal conclusion on the facts. Appellate courts normally defer to the trier of fact on factual applications of the law because of the trier's superior access to the facts through live witness testimony.

23. "The suddenness of the killing may simply reveal callousness so complete and depravity so extreme that no hesitation is required," while prior reflection may represent "the uncertainties of a tortured conscience rather than exceptional depravity." MPC sec. 210.6 commentary 127–28 (1980). In criticizing the French doctrine of premeditation, Sir James Fitzjames Stephen cited the following examples: "A., passing along the road, sees a boy sitting on a bridge over a deep river and, out of mere wanton barbarity, pushes him into it and so drowns him. A man makes advances to a girl who repels him. He deliberately but instantly cuts her throat." *Criminal Law of England, supra* note 3 at 94. Stephen's examples strike us as particularly heinous because the killers acted for sadistic or sexually predatory reasons. The examples also illustrate that planning is not a universal proxy for culpability. As courts have frequently noted, a fully culpable decision may be reached quickly, although we generally presume a lack of deliberation from its haste.

24. State v. Forrest, 362 S.E.2 252 (N.C. 1987).

25. See People v. Perez, 2 Cal.4th 1117, 831 P.2 1159 (1992); People v. Jackson 49 Cal.3d 1170, 264 Cal. Rptr. 852 (1989) (first degree murder despite indication of extreme PCP intoxication); People v. Odle, 45 Cal.3d 386, 247 Cal. Rptr. 137 (1988) (first degree murder despite evidence of basic personality change following major brain surgery). See also People v. Waters, 324 N.W.2d 564 (Mich. App. 1982) (premeditation may be found in fatal shooting of woman by defendant at drive-in after victim's husband refused to give defendant's companion a light).

26. In *Anderson* the underlying felony was child sexual abuse.

27. See Stephen, *Criminal Law of England, supra* note 3 at 57–58; People v. Aaron, 299 N.W.2d 304, 307–11 (Mich. 1980).

28. *Third Institutes* 56 (1797).

29. Stephen, *Criminal Law of England, supra* note 3 at 57–58.

30. Regina v. Serne, 16 Cox Crim. Cas. 311, 313 (1887) (punctuation slightly altered from the original reported case).

31. Homicide Act of 1957, 5 & 6 Eliz. 2, ch. 11 sec. 1.

32. For a review of various limits on the felony murder rule, see MPC sec. 210.2, Comment 6, 29–42 (1980); Wayne R. LaFave & Austin W. Scott, *Criminal Law* 622–641 (2d ed. 1986).

33. See George P. Fletcher, Reflections on Felony-Murder, 12 Sw. U. L. Rev. 413 (1981); Nelson E. Roth & Scott E. Sundby, The Felony-Murder Rule: A Doctrine at Constitutional Crossroads, 70 Cornell L. Rev. 446 (1985); Stephen Schulhofer, Harm and Punishment: A Critique of Emphasis on the Results of Conduct in the Criminal Law, 122 U. Pa. L. Rev. 1497 (1974); T. B. Macaulay, *A Penal Code Prepared by the Indian Law Commissioners*, Note M, 64–65 (1837); but see David Crump & Susan Waite Crump, In Defense of the Felony Murder Doctrine, 8 Harv. J. Law & Pub. Pol. 359 (1985). For an empirical study illustrating the culpability problems of the doctrine in practice, see Melanie Myers, Felony Killings and Prosecutions for Murder: Exploring the Tensions between Culpability and Consequences in the Criminal Law, 3 Soc. & Leg. Stud. 149 (1994).

34. See People v. Stamp, 2 Cal. App. 3d 203, 82 Cal. Rptr. 598 (1969) (felony murder where robbery victim who was obese, was generally under stress and had a heart condition, suffered a fatal heart attack in reaction to armed robbery); State v. McKeiver, 213 A.2d 320 (N.J. Super. 1965) (felony murder for heart attack from fright caused by armed robbery where there was no physical contact between robber and victim).

35. For similar criticisms, see Macaulay, *A Penal Code Prepared by the Indian Law Commissioners, supra* note 33; Fletcher, Reflections on Felony-Murder, *supra* note 33.

36. See Crump & Crump, In Defense of the Felony Murder Doctrine, *supra* note 33 at 363–65 (1985) (citing public attitude surveys of crime seriousness and jury studies).

37. People v. Burton, 6 Cal.3d 375, 388, 491 P.2d 793, 801–2 (1971).

38. The United States Supreme Court has struck down death penalty schemes where the fact finder would, by determining offense liability, also determine penalty. See, e.g., Roberts v. Louisiana, 428 U.S. 325 (1976); Woodson v. North Carolina, 428 U.S. 280 (1976); see Hitchcock v. Dugger, 481 U.S. 393 (1987); Skipper v. South Carolina, 476 U.S. 1 (1986).

39. S. Car. Code Ann. sec. 16-3-20.

40. For an overview of the nation's various death penalty schemes, see the following articles by James R. Acker & C. S. Lanier: Capital Murder from Benefit of Clergy to Bifurcated Trials: Narrowing the Class of Offenses Punishable by Death, 29 Crim. L. Bull. 291, 298–302 (1993), "Parsing This Lexicon of Death": Aggravating Factors in Capital Sentencing Statutes, and Aggravated Circumstances and Capital Punishment Law: Rhetoric or Real Reforms? 29 Crim L. Bull. 467 (1993).

41. Cal. Pen. C. sec. 190.2.

42. For examples of spouse killings for insurance proceeds, see People v. Hamilton, 48 Cal.3d 1142, 774 P.2d 730 (1989) (husband kills pregnant wife for insurance proceeds); People v. Hardy, 2 Cal.4th 86, 825 P.2d 781 (1992) (man kills wife and eight-year-old son in order to collect on insurance policy).

43. See Ford v. State, 374 So.2d 496 (Fla. 1979) (killing of police officer); McClesky v. Kemp, 107 S.Ct. 1756 (1987) (same); People v. Weidert, 39 Cal.3d 836, 705

P.2d 380 (1985) (killing of witness); People v. Walker, 47 Cal.3d 605, 765 P.2d 70 (1989) (same); People v. Robertson, 43 Cal.3d 18, 767 P.2d 1109 (1989) (rape-murder).

44. State v. Mitchell, 485 N.W.2d 807, 809 (Wisc. 1992).

45. See James Weinstein, First Amendment Challenges to Hate Crime Legislation: Where's the Speech?, 11 Crim. Just. Ethics 6, 9–13 (1992); Jeffrie G. Murphy, Bias Crimes: What Do Haters Deserve? 11 Crim. Just. Ethics 20 (1992); Frederick M. Lawrence, Resolving the Hate Crimes/Hate Speech Paradox: Punishing Bias Crime and Protecting Racist Speech, 68 Notre Dame L. Rev. 673 (1993); Lawrence Crocker, Hate Crimes Statutes: Just? Constitutional? Wise? 1992/1993 Ann. Surv. Am. L. 485, 492 (emphasizing the historical dimension of the wrong). But see Anthony M. Dillof, Punishing Bias: An Examination of the Theoretical Foundations of Bias Crime Statutes, 91 NW U. L. Rev. 1015 (1997) (arguing that bias does not go to culpability and only sometimes increases the harm done).

46. See Phyllis B. Gerstenfeld, Smile When You Call Me That!: The Problems with Punishing Hate-Motivated Behavior, 10 Behav. Sci. & Law 259 (1992). Others argue that hate crime provisions may have some symbolic value, but will have little actual deterrent effect. See James B. Jacobs, Rethinking the War against Hate Crimes: A New York City Perspective, 11 Criminal Justice Ethics 55 (1992).

47. I recognize that sometimes values other than those of deserved punishment should predominate in structuring criminal law. For example, if it were true that bias crimes inflame racial hostilities and make our society more racially divided, I would consider this a powerful argument against an otherwise warranted bias crime scheme. See Crocker, Hate Crime Statutes, *supra* note 47 at 505–6; Jacobs, Rethinking the War against Hate Crimes, *supra*. I remain skeptical on this point, however.

48. Mitchell v. Wisconsin, 508 U.S. 476 (1993).

49. E.g., in re M.S., 896 P.2d 1365 (Cal. 1995); State v. Mortimer, 641 A.2d 257 (NJ 1994); State v. Plowman, 838 P.2d 558 (Ore. 1992).

One other point concerning free speech issues is worth making here. Bias crimes differ from other crimes *not* because they include communicative aspects in their definition, proof or punishment, and not because they involve a defendant's thoughts, but because the thoughts and communication they involve concern ideas about group discrimination rather than ordinary morals. If we punish a purposeful shooting more severely than a reckless one we distinguish based on the thoughts—the beliefs and desires—of the shooter. In judging motive, just as in judging traditional mens rea, we assess the nature of the accused's conduct—the reasons that inform the action. See Plowman, *supra*, 838 P.2d at 564; in re Joshua H., 13 Cal.App.4th 1734, 1749 (Cal. Ct. App. 1993); Crocker, Hate Crime Statutes, *supra* note 45 at 498. But cf. Gellman, Sticks and Stones Can Put You in Jail, But Can Words Increase Your Sentence? Constitutional and Policy Dilemmas of Ethnic Intimidation Laws, 39 UCLA L. Rev. 331 (1991) and "Brother You Can't Go to Jail for What You're Thinking": Motives, Effects and "Hate Crime" Laws, 11 Criminal Justice Ethics 24 (1992); Martin Redish, Freedom of Thought as Freedom of Expression: Hate Crime Sentencing Enhancement and First Amendment Theory, 11 Criminal Justice Ethics 29 (1992).

As discussed in chapter 3, in committing serious crimes, defendants necessarily express a particular view on a moral issue, an expression that is critical to punishment. While in most instances the defendant's moral expression is unintentional, we can certainly imagine crimes where expression is his preeminent purpose. A youth seeking membership in a gang, who kills in order to prove his criminal mettle, or an organized crime killing designed to frighten business owners into paying protection money—these describe acts whose central purpose is to convey a message to others. Yet no one has suggested that we must treat such violent "message" crimes any differently than other violent crimes because of First Amendment concerns. Finally, the government's enforcement of criminal law is in virtually all cases an intentionally expressive activity. The government intends by its investigation, prosecution, and punishment of crime to express the idea that such conduct will not be tolerated. Prosecutors and other law enforcement officials frequently speak of the need to "send a message" that criminality will be severely punished. Again, no one seems to worry that this violates the First Amendment.

What distinguishes bias offenses from other crimes is that mens rea now extends to beliefs and desires about a matter of public controversy. Like it or not, ours is a nation founded as much on the conquest of native peoples, slavery, and racial segregation as it is on democracy and civil rights. Racial bigotry has become officially unacceptable within the last generation, but its expression remains common and its definition remains hotly debated. Whether discrimination based on sexual orientation should be permitted continues to be a major question of public policy. Thus, unlike most violent offenses, bias crimes implicate matters of current public controversy.

50. See Jack Katz, *Seductions of Crime* 274–76 (1988).

51. See Gwynn Nettler, *Killing One Another* 199–200 (1982).

52. For a classic example of the sexualization of torture and murder, see People v. Bittaker, 48 Cal.3d 1046, 774 P.2d 659 (1989).

53. Thus the *Anderson* case might involve a power killing. For an excellent overview of sexual killings, detailing the intertwining of sexuality and violence, see Carl P. Malmquist, *Homicide: A Psychiatric Perspective* 294–310 (1996).

Sometimes killers experience sensual pleasure in the act of violence. "It felt so good the first time I stabbed her, and when she screamed at me it did something to me, sent a rush through me, and I stabbed her again," Susan Atkins said, describing her killing of Sharon Tate. Vincent Bugliosi with Curt Gentry, *Helter Skelter* 95 (1974) (as reported by a cellmate of Atkins). Atkins described the pleasure of killing as "like a sexual release. It's better than a climax." *Id*. These pleasures may be intertwined with overtly sexual behavior as killers find satisfaction in the sexual and ultimate possession of another. See Elliott Leyton, *Compulsive Killers: The Story of Modern Multiple Murder* 82–108 (1986) on serial killer Ted Bundy. The medieval French killer Gilles de Rais said he killed "solely for the pleasure and delectation of lust; in fact, I found incomparable pleasure in it." Charles Starkweather: "Shooting people was a kind of thrill, it brought out something," quoted in John M. MacDonald, *The Murderer and His Victim* 180–81, 191 (1961). Anne Rice, the modern master of the vampire genre, describes the vampire's urge to kill in strikingly similar terms:

> it was never merely the need for blood ... though the blood is all things sensual that a creature could desire; it's the intimacy of that moment—drinking, killing—the great heart-to-heart dance that takes place as the victim weakens and I feel myself expanding, swallowing the death which, for a split second, blazes as large as the life.

The Queen of the Damned 1–2 (1988). Descriptions such as these are illuminating as a matter of general psychology, but problems of proof mean that, absent an explicit confession, sexual thrills experienced in violence without secondary signs in sexual acts, wounds, or torture will rarely be presented to a fact finder.

54. See Leyton, *Compulsive Killers, supra* at 107–11.

55. See Walter Bromberg, *The Mold of Murder* 8–9 (1961) (noting the creative satisfactions of murder); Deborah Cameron & Elizabeth Frazer, *Lust to Kill: A Feminist Investigation of Sexual Murder* 64 (1987.

56. Bundy described the victims of serial killers as representative of a class of women "that has almost been created through the mythology of women and how they are used as objects." Stephen G. Michaud & Hugh Aynesworth, *Ted Bundy: Conversations with a Killer* 80 (1989). See Deborah Cameron & Elizabeth Frazer, *Lust to Kill: A Feminist Investigation of Sexual Murder* (1987); Jane Caputi, *The Age of Sex Crime* (1987).

57. Michaud & Aynesworth, *Ted Bundy, supra* at 78.

58. See *id.* See also Leyton, *Compulsive Killers, supra* note 53 at 30–33, 110.

59. Bundy observed, "perhaps it came to be seen that the *ultimate* possession was, in fact, the taking of the life." Michaud & Aynesworth, *Ted Bundy, supra* note 56 at 123.

60. Leyton, *Compulsive Killers, supra* note 53 at 107, quoting Kendall, *The Phantom Prince, supra* note 1 at 164. One philosopher has termed this the drive to achieve "significant immortality." Ernest Becker, *Escape from Evil* 37 (1975). Nietzsche described this as the "will to power." *Beyond Good and Evil* (W. Kaufmann trans. 1966). See Caputi, *The Age of Sex Crime, supra* note 56 at 10.

61. See also Bromberg, *The Mold of Murder, supra* note 55 at 50–56 (1961); Cameron & Frazer, *Lust to Kill, supra* note 55 at 60; Philip Lindsay, *The Mainspring of Murder* 33–49 (1958).

62. Brian Masters, Dahmer's Inferno, Vanity Fair, November 1991 at 265.

63. *Id.* at 267.

64. Leyton, *Compulsive Killers, supra* note 53 at 52 (quoting serial killer Edmund Emil Kemper).

65. On the Pale Criminal, from *Thus Spoke Zarathustra* in *The Portable Nietzsche*

150–51 (W. Kaufmann ed. 1968). See also Katz, *Seductions of Crime, supra* note 50 at 274–309.

66. Miles Corwin, Icy Killer's Life Steeped in Violence, Los Angeles Times, May 16, 1982, quoted in Gary Watson, "Responsibility and the Limits of Evil: Variations on a Strawsonian Theme" in *Responsibility, Character and the Emotions* (Ferdinand Schoeman ed. 1987). For a novelistic account of similar robbery killings, see Norman Mailer, *The Executioner's Song* (1979).

67. Note also that the crime that Robert Harris planned to commit, and did— a robbery—is itself a kind of power crime. See Katz, *Seductions of Crime, supra* note 50 at 164–236.

68. See, for example, the account of the case of Richard Trenton Chase, the so-called vampire killer, in Robert K. Ressler & Tom Schachtman, *Whoever Fights Monsters* 1–19 (1992).

69. Criminal responsibility cannot depend on the ability to work for long-term as opposed to short-term ends. The ability to conduct a life for long-term good is one which many people seem to lack, including many we consider fully responsible. Indeed there are few criminal offenders who could pass a test of living for long-term good if that were a responsibility prerequisite. See generally, Michael R. Gottfredson & Travis Hirschi, *A General Theory of Crime* (1990).

70. See sources cited at notes 25 & 26 in chapter 3. For journalistic accounts of the psychopathic coldness of some serial killers, see Masters, Dahmer's Inferno, *supra* note 62 (on Jeffrey Dahmer); Alec Wilkinson, Conversations with a Killer, The New Yorker, April 18, 1994, at 58, 59 (on John Wayne Gacy).

71. E.g., Jerome Hall, *General Principles of Criminal Law* 88–93 (2d ed. 1960) (distinguishing motive from mens rea); Fletcher, *Rethinking Criminal Law, supra* note 7 at 452–63; Glanville Williams, *Criminal Law: The General Part* 49 (2d ed. 1961). In case law, the irrelevance of motive usually refers to the irrelevance of good motive as an excuse. E.g., Regina v. Hicklin, 11 Cox C.C. 19 (1868); United States v. Cullen, 454 F.2d 386, 390–92 (7th Cir. 1971).

The irrelevance of motive has sometimes been used for a more global argument that it should never be employed in the criminal law, however. See Susan Gellman, Sticks and Stones Can Put You in Jail, but Can Words Increase Your Sentence? Constitutional and Policy Dilemmas of Ethnic Intimidation Laws, 39 UCLA L. Rev. 333, 363–68 (1991). For the view that criminal law does—and should—use motive, see Murphy, Bias Crimes, *supra* note 45; Paul H. Robinson, Hate Crimes: Crimes of Motive, Character or Group Terror? 1992/93 Ann. Surv. Am. L. 605; Kent Greenawalt, Reflections on Justifications for Defining Crimes by the Category of Victim, 1992/93 Ann. Surv. Am. L. 617.

72. On self-defense, see LaFave & Scott, *Criminal Law, supra* note 32 at 454–59; Joshua Dressler, *Understanding Criminal Law* 199–233 (2d ed. 1995); on provocation, see chapter 8; for motive circumstances supporting capital punishment, see Calif. Penal Code sec. 190.2 subsections (1) (killing for financial gain); (5) (killing to avoid

arrest or to escape); (6) (retaliation for peace officer's performance of duties); (10) (killing of witness to prevent testimony or retaliate for testimony); (16) (killing because of race, color, religion, nationality, or country of origin).

73. On insanity, see Douglas Husak, Motive and Criminal Liability, 8 Criminal Justice Ethics 3 (1989). Michael Moore, *Law and Psychiatry* 197 (1984). On duress and necessity, see LaFave & Scott, *supra* note 32 at 432–50; Dressler, *Understanding Criminal Law, supra* at 261–92. A number of offenses usually termed "special intent" crimes also require an answer to a second "why" question and thus a kind of motive analysis. Burglary, for example, requires a knowing and unlawful entry into a structure with the further purpose of committing a crime therein. For an excellent overview of past and current criminal law doctrines that rely on motive analysis, see Martin R. Gardner, The Mens Rea Enigma: Observations on the Role of Motive in the Criminal Law Past and Present, 1993 Utah L. Rev. 635.

Even when criminal law has not explicitly required proof of motive, basic criminal doctrines have strongly suggested its importance. For example, in murder law, consider the images conjured up by traditional descriptions of the *secret* killer, the killer who *lies in wait*, or who *premeditates* his crime. In all instances the manner of killing suggests a particularly evil motive. If the killer had a legitimate grievance with his victim, he would confront him openly. The worst killings are often called "cold-blooded," a phrase that suggests not only premeditation but a radical lack of concern for others, a person who kills for purely selfish reasons. See Arave v. Creech, 113 S.Ct. 1534, 1539–44 (1993) (interpreting the phrase "cold-blooded, pitiless slayer"); Austin v. United States, 382 F.2d 129, 137 (D.C. Cir. 1967).

74. See Hall, *General Principles of Criminal Law, supra* note 71 at 100–102; MPC secs. 210.1–3, art. 6–7; *Royal Commission, supra* note 3 at 173–77; McGautha v. California, 402 U.S. 183 (1971). The current federal sentencing guidelines on murder do not make specific mention of motive as a factor to be considered, however. United States Sentencing Commission, *Guidelines Manual*, secs. 2A1.1, 2A1.2, 2A1.3.

Outside the realm of criminal law, contemporary analyses of racial discrimination under the Fourteenth Amendment and sexual and racial discrimination covered by federal statutes make broad use of motive analysis. E.g., Washington v. Davis, 426 U.S. 229 (1976) (racial discrimination under the federal constitution); Price Waterhouse v. Hopkins, 490 U.S. 228 (1989) (sex discrimination under federal statute).

75. With the significant exception of recent bias crime enactments, and some provisions in capital punishment laws noted earlier, the modern trend in American law has been away from allusive forms of mens rea that encompass motive concerns toward narrowly defined forms that do not. See Gardner, The Mens Rea Enigma, *supra* note 73.

Only a few commentators have suggested that motive should be a basic part of murder doctrine. See Tarde, *Penal Philosophy, supra* note 7 at 464–65 arguing that only economically motivated murders should be first degree); Baron Raffaele Garofalo, *Criminology* 373–83 (R. Millar trans. 1914, 1968) (arguing for distinction between purely egoistic murders from those of misconceived honor or passion). See also F. Tennyson Jesse, *Murder and Its Motives* (1924, 1954); Husak, Motive and Criminal Liability, *supra* note 73 at 147–48. Several European murder schemes, most prominently the German, utilize motivation analysis. In German law aggravated homicide is based upon a killing for pleasure (*Mordlust*), for pecuniary reasons (*Habgier*), or for sexual satisfaction. St. Gb sec. 211(2); Fletcher, *Rethinking Criminal Law, supra* note 7 at 326–27. German law provides: "Anybody who kills a human being out of murderous lust, or to satisfy a sexual urge, or out of greed or from other base motives, maliciously or cruelly, or by means of endangering the public, or in order to commit or cover up another punishable act, is a murderer." The German Penal Code of 1871 (G. Mueller & T. Buergenthal trans. 1961).

76. For general arguments about the difficulty of proving motive, see Walter Hitchler, Motive as an Essential Element of Crime, 35 Dickinson L. Rev. 105, 109–11 (1931); Hall, *General Principles of Criminal Law, supra* note 71. With respect to bias offenses or sentencing enhancements, see Gellman, Sticks and Bones, *supra* note 49; Gerstenfeld, Smile When You Call Me That!, *supra* note 46 at 268–73 (1992); Comment, The Problem of Motive in Hate Crimes: The Argument against Presumptions of Racial Motivation, 82 J. Crim. L. & Criminol. 659, 667–72 (1992).

77. Gardner, The Mens Rea Enigma, *supra* note 73 at 688.

78. See generally Gardner, The Mens Rea Enigma, *supra* note 73. In an earlier work, I proposed another definition of the motive element for aggravated murder, one that I now believe to be too broad. See Evil and the Law of Murder 24 U.C. Dav. L. Rev. 437 (1990).

79. I should add a particular caveat with regard to motive analysis and the power killing category of aggravated murder, however. The concept of a power killing is introduced here for the first time. In order for it to be successfully implemented in law, the concept must be more widely discussed and accepted than it is now. In accord with the criteria of success for American criminal law set out in chapters 5 and 6, we want criminal rules that draw on terminology and ideas that are readily understood and generally accepted by the public. At present neither is true of power killing. On the other hand, change must begin somewhere, which is why I propose a power-killing category here. And given the democratic process of criminal reform, there is little chance that any jurisdiction will adopt the power-killing concept until the concept has won acceptance in the public marketplace of ideas.

80. For other examples of hate crimes, see Jack Levin & Jack McDevitt, *Hate Crimes* (1993). As in all homicides, the crime scene and other evidence about the nature of the attack provide critical evidence. See Connie Fletcher, *What Cops Know* 68, 84–86 (1991). One related objection might be that a motive requirement would make confessions critical to conviction. The hazards of overdependence on confessions are well recognized. See, e.g., Miranda v. Arizona, 384 U.S. 436 (1966); Leonard W. Levy, *The Origins of the Fifth Amendment* (1968); Edward Peters, *Torture* 40–73 (1985). Confessions will no doubt prove useful in proving aggravated murder, but as

is true with other crimes now, they will generally provide more information about the killer's identity than his culpability. Confessions normally provide strong proof of what the offender did, but many are self-serving on the question of moral culpability. Police investigators are trained to use rationalization techniques designed to allow suspects to minimize their own culpability. E.g., David E. Zulawski & Douglas E. Wicklander, *Practical Aspects of Interview and Interrogation* (1993). Assuming they are willing to talk, some aggravated murderers, like Ted Bundy, may provide important information about why they killed. Others will be like Gary Gilmore, who could not explain his own actions. At the penalty phase of his murder case, when asked why he had slain one of his robbery victims, he said he did not know. Mailer, *The Executioner's Song, supra* note 66 at 439. In both situations the jury must make its own judgment about the reasons for the conduct.

81. The most significant change may be for police. Contrary to the portrait of criminal investigation provided in most mystery and crime novels, police rarely spend much time considering motive. See David Simon, *Homicide* 70 (1991).

82. One approach would be to permit experts to make observations about motive in homicides generally but not allow them to give an opinion about what the motive was in the particular case to be decided. The exclusion of ultimate issue testimony should also alleviate the inevitable conflict between the causal explanations of science and the moral inquiries of criminal law. This approach has been taken in several jurisdictions with mental health expert testimony bearing on a defendant's mens rea and insanity. E.g., Fed. R. Evid. 704 (b); Calif. Penal Code sec. 29; see Kevin T. Smith, The Psychiatric Expert in the Criminal Trial: Are Bifurcation and the Rules Concerning Opinion Testimony on Ultimate Issues Constitutionally Compatible? 70 Marq. L. Rev. 493 (1987). For a general theory of expert testimony in accord with this approach, see Edward J. Imwinkelried, The "Bases" of Expert Testimony: The Syllogistic Structure of Scientific Testimony, 67 N.C. L. Rev. 1 (1988). For limitations on police officer expert testimony, see Deon J. Nossel, Note, The Admissibility of Ultimate Issue Expert Testimony by Law Enforcement Officers in Criminal Trials, 93 Colum. L. Rev. 231 (1993).

83. With regard to hate crimes, courts have adopted two different rules: that the motive was a substantial factor in the offense, United States v. Bledsoe, 728 F.2d 1094, 1098 (8th Cir. 1984), or that the motive played some role in the offense, State v. Hendrix, 813 P.2d 1115, 1118 (Or. App. 1991) *aff'd.* 838 P.2d 566 (Or. 1992).

84. This question is similar to that of causation in homicide: deciding whether the accused's action made a sufficient contribution to the victim's death that the accused should be held criminally responsible. Causation questions are notoriously difficult, involving both factual and normative assessments. Courts have developed an elaborate lexicon of intervening, supervening, dependent, and independent causes that express highly fact-sensitive judgments about responsibility. In essence, jurors and judges must decide whether the accused made enough of a contribution to the victim's death that he may be justly punished for it. Similarly with regard to motive,

the decision maker must resolve that the particular bias was an important enough motivation to place the killing in the highest offense category.

85. In California, motive can be an important part of premeditation analysis. *People v. Anderson*, 70 Cal.2d 15, 26–27 (1968).

86. I would define the general murder offense as any purposeful or knowing killing or any killing that meets the criteria for extreme moral indifference set out in chapter 9. This is similar to the definition of murder in the Model Penal Code. See sec. 210.2.

NOTES TO CHAPTER 8: CRIMES OF PASSION

1. The story told here is essentially the defense version of the case, provided by defense witnesses at trial. It is the version most supportive of the jury's verdict. The prosecution's evidence told a different story of the homicide. The prosecution introduced prior statements by Nesler and other evidence indicating that Nesler had brought the gun to court herself as part of a plan to kill Driver. See Mark Arax, Jury in Nesler Trial Begins Deliberations, Los Angeles Times, Aug. 6, 1993, at p. 3; Arax, Mother Guilty of Voluntary Manslaughter, L.A. Times, Aug. 12, 1993, at p. 1; Nancy Vogel, Judge Ignores Pleas, Sentences Nesler to 10 Years, Sacramento Bee, Jan. 8, 1994, at p. A1.

2. For example, in California purposeful killings may be punished as first-degree murder, with penalties ranging from death to a sentence of 25 years to life in prison, or as second-degree murder, with penalties from 15 to 25 years to life in prison, or as voluntary manslaughter, with penalties ranging from 3 to 11 years in prison. Cal. Pen. Code secs. 190(a), 193(a).

3. A note on coverage: in this chapter I consider provocation as it relates to rational, impassioned homicides. The related doctrines of self-defense and imperfect self-defense are covered briefly later; the doctrine of diminished capacity almost not at all. This focus is in keeping with my basic project of analyzing mens rea.

Another important issue not covered in the chapter is burden of proof. Traditionally the burden of disproving provocation has fallen on the prosecution, for under the common law the state had to establish malice aforethought for murder, and provocation negates malice aforethought. See Mullaney v. Wilbur, 421 U.S. 684 (1975). Some jurisdictions, though, treat modern versions of provocation as an affirmative defense and place the burden of its proof on the defendant. Patterson v. New York, 432 U.S. 197 (1977). In close cases, the question of who bears the burden of proof may be critical. Nevertheless, serious consideration of these issues would lead us into evidentiary considerations not directly related to my main concerns.

4. See William Blackstone, 4 *Commentaries on the Law of England* 184 (1783); for a slightly different derivation, see Edward Coke, *Institutes* 57 (1628).

5. Sir James Fitzjames Stephen, 3 *History of the Criminal Law of England* 59 (1883).

6. East, 1 *Pleas of the Crown* 241 (1803). Sir James Fitzjames Stephen described

this law as "adjusted at every point to a state of things in which men habitually carried deadly weapons and used them on very slight occasions." He suggested that "[w]hen the common mischief to be guarded against is the occurrence of set fights with deadly weapons, it is natural to lay down rules which treat each party as being pretty much on a level." 3 *History of the Criminal Law of England, supra* at 59, 60.

7. See Stephen, 3 *History of the Criminal Law of England, supra* note 5 at 59–60, 71; Bernard J. Brown, The Demise of Chance Medley and the Recognition of Provocation as a Defence to Murder in English Law, 7 J.Am. Leg. Hist. 310 (1963). See also T. A. Green, The Jury and the English Law of Homicide, 1200–1600, 74 Mich. L. Rev. 414 (1976); J. M. Kaye, The Early History of Murder and Manslaughter, parts 1 & 2, 83 Law Q. Rev. 365, 569 (1967).

8. Lawrence Stone, *The Crisis of the Aristocracy, 1558–1641* 223–25 (1965), quoted in Fox Butterfield, *All God's Children* 11 (1995).

9. "[W]herever two persons in cool blood meet and fight on a precedent quarrel, and one of them is killed, the other is guilty of murder, and cannot help himself by alleging that he was (a) first struck by the deceased; or that he had often (b) declined to meet him, and was prevailed upon to do it by his importunity; or that it was his intent only to vindicate his reputation." William Hawkins, *A Treatise of the Pleas of the Crown*, bk. 1, sec. 21, 96 (1824). By contrast, if "two happen to fall out upon a sudden, and presently agree to fight, and each of them fetch a weapon, and go into the field, and there one kill the other, he is guilty of manslaughter only, because he did it in the heat of blood." *Id.* at 97. "[I]f he who draws upon another in a sudden quarrel make no pass at him till his sword is drawn, and then fight with them and kill him, he is guilty of manslaughter only, because that by neglecting the opportunity of killing the other before he was on his guard, and in a condition to defend himself, with a like hazard to both, he shewed that his intent was not so much to kill as to combat with the other, in compliance with those common notions of honor, which prevailing over reason during the time that a man is under the transports of a sudden passion, so far mitigate his offence in fighting, that it shall not be adjudged to be of malice prepense." *Id.* See also Jeremy Horder, The Duel and the English Law of Homicide, 12 Ox. J. Leg. Stud. 419 (1992); Brown, The Demise of Chance Medley, *supra* note 7.

10. For example, in Watts v. Brains, 78 Eng. Rep. 1009 (1600), the victim and defendant had maintained a dispute with words and blows off and on over the course of two days. The victim passed defendant's shop and gave him a wry smile, then kept walking. The defendant stabbed him fatally from behind. The court said: "If one make a wry or distorted mouth, or the like countenance upon another, and the other immediately pursues and kills him, it is murder: for it shall be presumed to be malice precedent: and that such a slight provocation was not sufficient ground or pretence for a quarrel."

11. Jeremy Horder, *Provocation and Responsibility* 21–92 (1992).

12. There are two reports of the case. Here I use the report of Lord Ventris, 1

Vent. 158, 86 Eng. Rep. 108 (1672). The other report is Raym. 212, 83 Eng. Rep. 112 (1672).

13. See, e.g., Joshua Dressler, *Understanding Criminal Law* 490 (2d ed. 1995).

14. 10 Mich. 212. In one sense, this attribution is misleading, for as Richard Singer has noted, the court never spoke of the reasonable man, only the average or ordinary man. The Resurgence of Mens Rea: I—Provocation, Emotional Disturbance, and the Model Penal Code, 27 B.C. L. Rev. 243, 280 n.193 (1986). Nevertheless, the court spoke at length about reasonableness being the key to adequate provocation, indicating that there was a strongly normative (reasonableness) component to comparisons between the defendant's reactions and those of the ordinary person. Succeeding courts and legislatures have combined the two concepts in the reasonable man, or reasonable person, standard. In England, the first major reasonable man case in provocation was R. v. Welsh, 11 Cox CC 336 (1869).

15. 10 Mich. 212, 218 (1862).

16. *Id.* at 219–20 (emphasis in the original).

17. *Id.* at 220. Or as nineteenth-century scholar Francis Wharton put it, following an account of cases involving mutual combat: "The indulgence which the law extends to cases of this description is founded on the supposition that a state of sudden and violent exasperation is generated in the affray, so as to produce a temporary suspension of reason, and that transport of passion excludes the presumption of passion." *A Treatise on the Criminal Law of the United States* 443 (3d ed. 1855). Cooling time was likewise a test of character. "[W]hen anger, provoked by a cause sufficient to mitigate an instantaneous homicide, has been continued beyond the time which, in view of all the circumstances of the case, may be deemed reasonable, the evidence is found of that depraved spirit in which malice resides." State v. McCants, 1 Speers 384, 390, quoted in Joel Prentiss Bishop, 2 *Commentaries on the Criminal Law* 401–2 (1882).

18. 10 Mich. 212, 221.

19. California courts, for example, spent nearly a century developing two different strands of provocation law, one hewing to the traditional, categorical view that adequate provocation had to be based on a "serious and highly-provoking injury inflicted upon the person killing." People v. Valentine, 28 Cal.2d 121, 138, 169 P.2d 1 (1946), quoting the Crime and Punishments Act of 1850, sec. 23, and another taking the Maher approach and letting juries define reasonable provocation. The earliest case setting out the traditional view was People v. Butler, 8 Cal. 435 (1857). The earliest case espousing this potentially broader view of provocation was People v. Hurtado, 63 Cal. 288 (1883). Finally, in 1946 the California Supreme Court resolved that the broader view of provocation was correct, thus permitting a manslaughter instruction in a case where none of the traditional provocation categories applied. People v. Valentine, *supra.* In that case the defendant and victim had had a verbal argument after the defendant claimed, apparently incorrectly, that the victim had trespassed onto the defendant's property to peer into the bathroom window of

defendant's house. The victim lived in the house behind the defendant's and had walked by the defendant's house along a cement path on his way to work.

20. The changes in provocation law that resulted were part of the larger movement, noted in chapter 6, away from use of explicitly moral language in mens rea to more analytic concepts of wrongdoing. For example, compare two characterizations of reasonable provocation at the beginning and end of the century. In the 1917 case of People v. Logan, 175 Cal. at 48–49 the court held that provocation must involve a "heat of passion . . . as would naturally be aroused in the mind of an ordinarily reasonable person under the given facts and circumstances. . . . Thus no man of extremely violent passion could so justify or excuse himself if the exciting cause be not adequate, nor could an excessively cowardly man justify himself unless the circumstances were such as to arouse the fears of the ordinarily courageous man." Here reasonableness is clearly infused with character judgment. In a recent Michigan case, the Court of Appeal quoted several paragraphs from the Maher decision speaking of "evil passions" and "wickedness of heart" and commented that "this language is somewhat archaic in tone," but that the court's underlying reasoning remained valid, "that to protect the public and the integrity of the judicial system, there is certain conduct that we will not allow in mitigation of criminal responsibility in the absence of findings of insanity or diminished capacity." People v. Gjidoda, 364 N.W.2d 698, 700 (Mich. Ct. App. 1985). The court was comfortable justifying the rule in terms of public protection, but not condemnation of evil. In that case the defendant had tried to claim provocation where he had killed his daughters because they were to testify against him in a previous murder case. This legal change to some extent reflects a social change in attitudes toward anger. See Carol Zisowitz Stearns & Peter N. Stearns, *Anger: The Struggle for Emotional Control in America's History* (1986).

21. People v. Borchers, 50 Cal.2d 321, 329, 325 P.2d 97 (1958) (quoting dictionary definition of passion); People v. Berry, 18 Cal.3d 509, 515, 556 P.2d 777 (1976) (quoting language with approval). American courts had often included fear as a candidate for the passion of provocation; see, e.g., Johnson v. State [2] S.W. 609, 615 (Tex. App. 1886). This was consistent with the mutual combat strand of provocation in which the passions of self-defense were implicated.

22. State v. Elliott, 411 A.2d 3, 9 (Conn. 1979). See People v. Shelton, 385 N.Y.S.2d at 717. The intensity test involves a comparison with the individual's normal emotions and decision making. "Consideration is given to whether the intensity of these feelings was such that [defendant's] usual intellectual controls failed and the normal rational thinking for that individual prevailed at the time of the act. In its charge, the trial court should explain that the term 'extreme' refers to the greatest degree of intensity away from the norm for that individual." Eliott, *supra* at 10.

23. E.g., R. v. Doughty, 83 Cr. App. Rep. 319 (1986) (England) (murder conviction reduced to manslaughter where otherwise-affectionate father smothered his crying baby; issue of reasonable loss of control due to passion should have been submitted to the jury).

24. MPC, sec. 210.3(b), Commentary, 60–63 (1980). Nevertheless, the victim's conduct—or lack of it—may well affect the jury's determination of the MPC's "reasonable explanation or excuse" element.

25. Sec. 210.3(1)(b).

26. People v. Casassa, 404 N.E.2d 1310, 1316 (NY 1980). This does not mean that fact finders actually follow this admonition. Indeed, in this same case, the court seemed to revert to traditional moral judgment of reasons for passion by affirming the trial court's decision that the defendant's jealous-obsessive slaying of a former girlfriend was "the result of defendant's malevolence rather than an understandable human response deserving of mercy." *Id.* at 1317.

27. For an extended description and critique of the psychological reading of the MPC, see Willard Gaylin, *The Killing of Bonnie Garland* (1982). Gaylin writes of a homicide case in which a psychiatrist testified that the defendant, who had killed his girlfriend when it appeared their relationship was ending, gave the following "reasonable explanation" for his extreme emotional disturbance at the time of the killing: "The reasonable explanation rests in what this girl meant to him and how dependent he became upon her for his very essence of psychic survival, having a sense of identity, self-worth, and self-esteem, and a sense of belonging to the world around him." *Id.* at 185. The prosecution argued in response that there was no reasonable explanation, that defendant simply wanted the victim exclusively to himself. *Id.* at 230. For another morally and psychologically sophisticated critique of the MPC, see Norman J. Finkel, Achilles Fuming, Odysseus Stewing, and Hamlet Brooding: On the Story of the Murder/Manslaughter Distinction, 74 Neb. L. Rev. 742 (1995).

Courts interpreting the MPC have made clear their understanding that it sought to import new psychological understandings of behavior into the law. New York's highest court explained the differences between the old and new law of provocation "by the tremendous advances made in psychology since 1881 and a willingness on the part of the courts, legislators, and the public to reduce the level of responsibility imposed on those whose capacity has been diminished by mental trauma." State v. Patterson, 347 N.E.2d 898, 908 (N.Y. 1976), *aff'd sub nom.* Patterson v. New York, 432 U.S. 197 (1977). In the same opinion, the New York court described the MPC provision in psychodynamic terms. "An action influenced by an extreme emotional disturbance is not one that is necessarily . . . spontaneously undertaken. Rather, it may be that a significant mental trauma has affected a defendant's mind for a substantial period of time, simmering in the unknowing unconscious and then inexplicably coming to the fore." *Id.* Not surprisingly, the testimony of mental health experts has become a central feature of cases involving the MPC. See, e.g., State v. Gratzer, 682 P.2d 141, 144 (Mont. 1984); State v. Elliott, 411 A.2d 3, 5 (Conn. 1979); People v. Ford, 423 N.Y.S.2d 402, 404–5 (1979); People v. Shelton, 385 N.Y.S.2d 708, 715–17 (Super. Ct. 1976). For a critical view of the use of experts here, see Singer, The Resurgence of Mens Rea, *supra* note 14 at 322.

28. MPC, Commentary to sec. 210.3 at 62.

29. See Director of Public Prosecutions v. Camplin [1978] 2 All E.R. 168 (approving an age and sex-specific standard); cf. Bedder v. Director of Public Prosecutions [1954] All E.R. 801 (rejecting defense argument that jury should take into consideration defendant's impotence in assessing alleged insult and assault by victim). For arguments against a sex-specific standard for provocation, see Stanley Yeo, Resolving Gender Bias in Criminal Defenses, 19 Monash U. L. Rev. 104 (1993); Hilary Allen, One Law for All Reasonable Persons? 16 Intl. J. Soc. of L. 419 (1988). But see Yeo, Sex, Ethnicity, Power of Self-Control and Provocation Revisited, 18 Sydney L. Rev. 304 (1996) (arguing for sex-based determination of normal reaction patterns to determine reasonable loss of self-control).

30. E.g., R. v. Ahluwalia [1992] 4 All E.R. 889, 896–98 (England) (observing that, depending on the case, some mental and personality characteristics of the defendant may be incorporated into reasonableness in provocation). In the U.S., the drafters of the MPC explained that the reasonableness of the defendant's extreme emotional disturbance will include some personal characteristics of the defendant and individual circumstances: "Thus, blindness, shock from traumatic injury, and extreme grief are all easily read into the term 'situation.' This result is sound, for it would be morally obtuse to appraise a crime for mitigation of punishment without reference to these factors." But the commentary continues: "On the other hand, it is equally plain that idiosyncratic moral values are not part of the actor's situation. An assassin who kills a political leader because he believes it is right to do so cannot ask that he be judged by the standard of the reasonable extremist. . . . An exceptionally punctilious sense of personal honor or an abnormally fearful temperament may also serve to differentiate an individual actor from the hypothetical reasonable man, yet none of these factors is wholly irrelevant to the ultimate issue of culpability. . . . In the end, the question is whether the actor's loss of self-control can be understood in terms that arouse sympathy in the ordinary citizen. Commentary to sec. 210 at 62. In non-MPC jurisdictions, at least a reasonable temper is required. See Joshua Dressler, *Understanding Criminal Law* 493 (2d ed. 1995).

31. See People v. Berry, 18 Cal.3d 509, 556 P.2d 777 (1976); Donna K. Coker, Heat of Passion and Wife Killing: Men Who Batter/Men Who Kill, 2 Rev. L. & Women's Studies 71 (1992). The Berry case represented the high-water mark for the psychological approach in California with regard to provocation. More recently the state's law has taken several steps back toward traditional analysis. For example, in the early eighties, both legislative and initiative measures restricted the scope of provocation by eliminating claims of psychological incapacity from its purview. See Cal. Penal Code secs. 25, 28. Thus defendants may not claim mitigation (as opposed to a full insanity defense) based on a mental or emotional condition that reduced their ability to reason or control action. The California legislature also eliminated expert testimony on whether a defendant was *capable* of the requisite mens rea; experts may still testify about whether the defendant actually had the requisite mens rea, however. Court decisions on provocation have focused more on victim wrongdoing than on

the psychological experience of the defendant. E.g., People v. Spurlin, 202 Cal. Rptr. 663 (Ct. App. 1984) (provocation limited to killings of person who provokes). In recent years California appellate courts also seem to treat mental health expert testimony more skeptically. See, e.g., In re Thomas C., 228 Cal. Rptr. 430, 437 (Ct. App. 1986). In Thomas C. the court rejected the argument that the defendant's depression should be taken into account in assessing the reasonableness of his emotional state at the time of a homicide.

32. For the traditional categorical approach, see People v. Chevalier, 544 N.E.2d 942, 944 (Ill. 1989); State v. Shane, 590 N.E.2d 272 (Oh. 1992). Thirteen jurisdictions have adopted some form of the MPC's provocation formulation. Victoria Nourse, Passion's Progress: Modern Law Reform and the Provocation Defense, 106 Yale L.J. 1331, 1345–46 n.88. For an overview of modern versions of the Maher approach to provocation, see Dressler, *Understanding Criminal Law, supra* note 13 at 491–92.

33. E.g., People v. Berry, 18 Cal.3d 509, 556 P.2d 777 (1976) (manslaughter instruction required where defendant said wife had provoked him with tales of her infidelity; defendant waited 20 hours in apartment for wife to return, then strangled her); People v. Ahlberg, 301 N.E.2d 608 (Ill. App. Ct. 1973) (manslaughter conviction where defendant dragged wife from house and beat, kicked, and stomped her to death after she told him, among other things, that he never satisfied her sexually, that she had found an older man who could love her and her children better, and that she was going to get a divorce). See also People v. Borchers, 50 Cal.2d 321, 325 P.2d 97 (1958) (provocation found based on mistress's admitted infidelity, her requests that defendant kill her and child, and her taunt: "Are you chicken?").

34. See Nourse, Passion's Progress, *supra* note 32 at 1352 noting that 26 percent of cases studied from MPC jurisdictions involve such departures. For exemplary cases, see *id.*; State v. Gratzer, 682 P.2d 141, 145 (Mont. 1984) (extreme emotional disturbance instruction required in case where young man, whose relationship with his girlfriend was deteriorating, fatally shot another man he had seen with her); Gaylin, *supra* note 27. Nourse also reports that in MPC jurisdictions most provocation claims based on infidelity occurred in cases where the couples were separated (37 percent) than where there was an ongoing relationship (12 percent). Nourse, *supra* at 1359.

For criminologic data showing that women are at greatest risk of being killed when contemplating separation or during separation, see Christina Rebecca Block & Antigone Christakos, Intimate Partner Homicide in Chicago over 29 Years, 41 Crime & Delinquency 496, 506, 518, 521 (1995).

35. See, e.g., R. v. Ahluwalia [1992], 4 All E.R. 889; State v. Guido, 191 A.2d 45 (N.J. 1963).

36. Commentators who agree with this view generally argue that provocation should emphasize the reasons for passion rather than the fact of loss of self-control. See Andrew von Hirsch & Nils Jareborg, Provocation and Culpability in *Responsibility, Character, and the Emotions* (F. Schoeman ed., 1987); Finbarr McAuley, Anticipat-

ing the Past: The Defence of Provocation in Irish Law, 50 Mod. L. Rev. 133 (1987) A. J. Ashworth, The Doctrine of Provocation, 35 Camb. L.J. 292 (1976). Most such commentators agree that provocation involves a partial justification of feeling. See also Nourse, Passion's Progress, *supra* note 32 at 1392–99; Uma Narayan & von Hirsch, Three Conceptions of Provocation, 15 Crim. Just. Ethics 15 (1996); Jeremy Horder, Reasons for Anger: A Response to Narayan and von Hirsch's Provocation Theory, 15 Crim. Justice Ethics 63, 66–68 (1996). See also Dan M. Kahan & Martha C. Nussbaum, Two Conceptions of Emotion in Criminal Law, 96 Col. L. Rev. 269, 305–23 (1996).

37. Along these lines many argue that provocation provides a partial excuse based on the defendant's loss of self-control. Such commentators argue that defendants should receive less punishment if they can show that passion significantly reduced their ability to make rational choices. See Singer, The Resurgence of Mens Rea, *supra* note 14; Joshua Dressler, Rethinking Heat of Passion: A Defense in Search of a Rationale, 73 J. Crim. L. & Criminol. 421 (1982); Dressler, Provocation: Partial Justification or Excuse? 51 Mod. L. Rev. 467 (1988); Dennis Klimchuk, Outrage, Self-Control, and Culpability, 44 Univ. Toronto L.J. 441 (1994); Tim Quigley, Battered Women and the Defence of Provocation, 55 Saskatchewan L. Rev. 223 (1991); Dolores A. Donovan & Stephanie M. Wildman, Is the Reasonable Man Obsolete? A Critical Perspective on Self-Defense and Provocation, 14 Loy. L.A. L. Rev. 435 (1981); Jack K. Weber, Some Provoking Aspects of Voluntary Manslaughter Law, 10 Anglo-Am. L. Rev. 159 (1981); Alec Samuels, Excusable Loss of Self-Control in Homicide, 34 Mod. L. Rev. 163 (1971).

38. 153 P. 9 (Wash. 1914).

39. See Larry Cata Backer, Raping Sodomy and Sodomizing Rape: A Morality Tale about the Transformation of Modern Sodomy Jurisprudence, 21 Am. J. Crim. L. 37, 38 (1993).

40. See Commentary, MPC sec. 210.3 at 59–60.

41. Even in earlier years courts made some allowance for persons disinclined to violence with regard to the timing of homicide in cases where the victim's wrongful action was particularly grievous. In State v. Martin, 57 S.E.2d 55 (S.C. 1949) the court held that the jury should have been instructed on manslaughter in a case where the defendant was charged with murder for fatally shooting the victim as the victim sat in a pickup truck outside defendant's home, yelling for defendant's wife. The victim Squires had on three separate occasions on earlier dates attacked and raped the defendant's wife. The opinion does not specify the time lapse between the last attack and the shooting, but presumably if there was a significant time lapse the court, which was sympathetic to the defendant, would have mentioned it. Chief Justice Baker of the South Carolina Supreme Court wrote: "The record discloses that appellant was a craven, and that it was only on this one occasion that his great fear of Squires . . . was sufficiently overcome by heat of passion to produce his drastic action. And where is the one man who can unerringly reach the conclusion that the taunt-

ing of the appellant and his wife by the deceased at the time and place he was shot and killed, viewed in the light of the great wrongs and indignities he had theretofore inflicted upon them, was not 'the straw that broke the camel's back' . . . ?" *Id.* at 59.

42. *Id.* at 11. Presumably the "weakened condition" mentioned by the court referred to Gounagias's headaches and depression.

43. For a revealing modern account of male-on-male rape, see Michael Scarce, *Male on Male Rape: The Hidden Toll of Stigma and Shame* (1997).

44. 686 P.2d 1001 (Or. 1984).

45. *Id.* at 1004.

46. *Id.*

47. Many criminologists have noted the prevalence of such "if I can't have you then no one else can" killings, usually of a woman by a man. See Martin Daly and Margo Wilson, *Homicide* 196–202 (1988); Kenneth Polk & David Ranson, The Role of Gender in Intimate Homicide, 24 Aust. & N.Z. J. Crim. 15 (1991).

For an illuminating account of a similar killing, see Jack Katz, *Seductions of Crime* 34 (1988). Katz writes of the killing of a lover by a woman named Ruth.

From within the assailant's perspective, killing a deserting lover makes sense as a way of *preserving* a relationship that would otherwise end. . . . By killing her mate, Ruth made their relationship last forever; in the most existentially unarguable sense, she made it the most profound relationship either had ever had. Then no one else could have him; no one else could develop a relationship with him that would retrospectively extinguish the special significance they shared. Killing him was her means of honoring and protecting the transcendent significance of their relationship.

48. There is another possible reading of the case which presents Ott's motivations in a different light. If the fact finder decided that Stephanie played with Ott's affections, that she deliberately gave conflicting romantic signals to him, knowing his vulnerability to such manipulation, then his anger would be more justified. (I am grateful to Anne Coughlin for raising this possibility.) Personally, I find little evidence to support this reading from the facts given in the appellate opinion, however.

49. As Jack Katz writes: "Rage is not necessarily expressed in chaotic thrusts; the common killer does not go berserk, striking at any proximate object and killing only when the victim stumbles by accident in the path of a randomly aimed blow." *Seductions of Crime, supra* note 47 at 30. But cf. Tenn. Code Ann. sec. 39-13-211(a): "Voluntary manslaughter is the intentional or knowing killing of another in a state of passion produced by adequate provocation sufficient to lead a reasonable person to act *in an irrational manner*" (emphasis added). The state's Sentencing Commission explained the latter phrase was "utilized so as to encompass a broad consideration of mental states produced by adequate provocation." Historical Notes, Tenn. Code Ann.

50. See chapters 2 and 3. Contrary arguments may be found in Laurie J. Taylor, Comment, Provoked Reason in Men and Women: Heat of Passion Manslaughter and Imperfect Self-Defense, 33 UCLA L. Rev. 1679 (1986); Note, Partially Determined

Imperfect Self-Defense: The Battered Wife Kills and Tells Why, 34 Stanf. L. Rev. 615 (1982).

51. Or as a nineteenth-century court put it, provocation doctrine presumes that as to the accused, "passion disturbed the sway of reason and made him regardless of her admonitions. It does not look upon him as temporarily deprived of intellect, and therefore not an accountable agent, but as one in whom the exercise of judgment is impeded by the violence of excitement, and accountable therefor as an infirm human being." State v. Hill, 34 Amer. Dec. 396, quoted in Smith v. State, 3 S. 551 (Ala. 1888).

52. See Hans Toch, *Violent Men* 2 (1992).

53. See Glanville Williams, Provocation and the Reasonable Man, 1954 Crim. L. Rev. 740, 751–52. Note that in the broadest sense of the phrase even killings for trivial provocations are crimes of passion. As one Chicago police officer put it: "A lot of the murders we get are crimes of passion—but you hate to use the word 'passion' because the idea of a crime of passion is the guy coming home and finding his wife in bed with another guy. In most of our murders, the passion is over who gets the last drag on a marijuana cigarette or who gets the last swig of Richard's Wild Irish Rose wine," quoted in Connie Fletcher, *What Cops Know* 63 (1991).

54. R. v. Kirkham 11 C&P 115, 119 (1837).

55. Commonwealth v. Flax, 200 A. 632, 637 (Pa. 1938).

56. See von Hirsch & Jareborg, Provocation and Culpability, *supra* note 36.

57. The rule requires good reason to believe in the victim's wrongdoing rather than complete proof of that wrongdoing. In this fashion the rule addresses the problem of mistakes about the provoking incident or the direction of violence. Mistake cases fall into four categories: (1) where the provoked defendant intentionally attacks the provoking party and kills him, but is only reckless or negligent as to causing death; (2) where the defendant purposely kills the victim because of a mistaken belief that the victim had committed a serious wrong; (3) where an adequately provoked defendant, in an effort to kill the provoker, recklessly or negligently kills another; and (4) and where the defendant, adequately provoked by one person, deliberately kills another as a means of expressing his general rage.

The first and third categories of cases are briefly covered in chapter 9. At least as to the first category of cases, I argue that if the defendant has reason for great rage at the victim, this rage should preclude a finding of the high degree of indifference required for a murder conviction. The third category of cases should be assessed individually, as the carelessness with which the attack is pursued might in some cases suffice for indifference at the murder level.

In the second category of cases, as under current law, where the defendant had good reason to believe that the victim committed a serious wrong against himself or a loved one, he may claim provocation even if it later turns out he was mistaken concerning the victim's conduct.

Courts have almost uniformly rejected provocation in cases involving the deliberate killing of an innocent party (the fourth category). See Kruchek v. State, 702 P.2d 1267 (Wyo. 1985); State v. Fowler, 268 N.W.2d 220 (Iowa 1978); R. v. Scriva, [1951] Vict. L.R. 298 [Australia]; Wayne R. LaFave & Austin W. Scott, Jr., *Criminal Law* 582 (2d ed. 1986). The reform proposal would produce the same result. Assume that a father sees his daughter run over by a carelessly driven car. As his daughter lies terribly injured on the ground, the driver speeds off. A bystander stops to help. The father, in rage and despair, kills the bystander. (For a similar scenario, see R. v. Scriva, [1951] Vict. L.R. 298 [Australia]). Here, while the father was justifiably impassioned, he had no good reason to rage at the bystander. While psychologically he might not have appreciated the victim's innocence, as a matter of morality we must. In killing an entirely innocent person, the father commits murder, not manslaughter.

58. Cf. People v. Caruso, 159 N.E. 390 (N.Y. 1927) (conviction of premeditated murder reversed where, following the death of his son, defendant strangled to death the doctor who had treated the son, apparently under the misimpression that the doctor had administered the wrong dose of medication and had smiled at news of the son's death). This is one instance where a deterrent theory of punishment would diverge significantly from one based on desert. Under a deterrent rationale, the exceptional nature of the situation would argue for minimal punishment. For another example of the consequences of a broad definition of passion, see Capps v. State, 478 S.W.2d 905 (Tenn. Ct. App. 1972) (manslaughter verdict where mother killed 20-month-old daughter reportedly after becoming distraught at child's grabbing of mother's legs and dress and running through the house).

Another example comes from police work. Many incidents of police brutality occur after a high-speed chase of a suspect. For the police officer the chase is an adrenalin rush, a roller-coaster ride with emotions supercharged by fear of the real hazards involved, anger at the suspect for defiance of legal authority, and the thrill of a hunt. When the chase ends, the hunter's passions seek dramatic expression. If the suspect resists in any fashion—and sometimes even if he does not—officers may leap to the attack. The passions inspired by the chase are normal; so is the violence which often follows. But this hardly excuses unjustified violence. Unless the officers had good, i.e., professionally acceptable, reasons for rage, they should receive no mitigation of punishment for their attack.

59. The case of the grief-stricken killer reminds us of two uncomfortable features of criminal responsibility: its tragedy and its crudity. Criminal responsibility is tragic in that it reflects the unchosen circumstances of our lives. As noted in chapters 2 and 3, the act of judging others should not make us self-righteous but humble and thankful. We should feel humble in recognizing the moral frailty of humans and thankful that our situations have not brought us the kinds of temptations (both internal and external) that caused the defendant's wrongdoing. Criminal responsibility is crude in that it judges only a small part of a person's moral conduct and character reflected in that conduct. Criminal verdicts make necessarily simplistic judgments about wrongdoing. Full moral evaluation is far more complex.

For another case where considerations of mercy push the boundaries of the reason-based approach, see R. v. Doughty, 83 Cr. App. Rep. 319 (1986) (England).

60. The other main candidate for expansion of provocation's passions is mercy. A killing motivated by pity for another's suffering may express deep love for another and respect for his or her worth as an intelligent, sentient being. Depending on the circumstances, such a killing might support especially lenient treatment by the law. Here I must invoke the author's privilege of defining his subject and declare the larger moral issues out of bounds. Questions of euthanasia, assisted suicide, and mercy killing involve sufficiently different moral questions than the cases considered here, and the dynamics of mercy killings, which usually involve extended deliberation, are likewise different enough that they merit separate discussion, and probably separate legal treatment.

61. Modern English law, for example, provides that a victim's wrongful act may constitute provocation if it is "enough to make a reasonable man do as he did." Homicide Act, 1957, 5 & 6 Eliz. 2, c. 11 sec. 3. See also LaFave & Scott, *Criminal Law, supra* note 57 at 653: adequate provocation is "a provocation which would cause a reasonable man to lose his normal self-control."

62. See Jerome M. Michael and Herbert W. Wechsler, A Rationale of the Law of Homicide, 37 Colum. L. Rev. 1261, 1281–82 (1937).

63. For a particularly strong criticism of the MPC's approach to provocation along these lines, see Finkel, Achilles Fuming, *supra* note 27.

64. Similarly, see People v. Washington, 58 Cal. App.3d 620, 624–26, 130 Cal. Rptr. 96 (1976) (rejecting defense argument that reasonable person standard should be individualized to either female or homosexual person to recognize defendant's status as servient homosexual in relationship with victim).

65. Along these lines, in Queen v. Hill [1986] 1 R.C.S. 313, 333–34, the court held that age and sex were part of the reasonable-person formula, but that this information need not be included in jury instructions. The chief justice wrote: "I have the greatest of confidence in the level of intelligence and plain common sense of the average Canadian jury sitting on a criminal case.... The accused is before them. He is male and young. I cannot conceive of a Canadian jury conjuring up the concept of an 'ordinary person' who would be either female or elderly, or banishing from their minds the possibility that an 'ordinary person' might be both young and male." In other words, the jury can be trusted to separate empirical from normative analysis without specific guidance.

66. See Horder, *Provocation and Responsibility, supra* note 11 at 186–97; Klimchuk, Outrage, Self-Control and Culpability, *supra* note 37 at 459–65 (1994); Taylor, Provoked Reason in Men and Women, *supra* note 50. Others have focused their concern with gender bias on the psychological approach to provocation. Nourse, Passion's Progress, *supra* note 32 (focusing particularly on the MPC); Coker, Heat of Passion and Wife Killing, *supra* note 31 (focusing especially on California's People v. Berry decision). The doctrine has also been criticized as homophobic, or at least per-

mitting the expression of homophobic ideas. Adrian Howe, More Folk Provoke Their Own Demise (Homophobic Violence and Sexed Excuses—Rejoining the Provocation Law Debate, Courtesy of the Homosexual Advance Defense), 19 Sydney L. Rev. 336 (1997); Robert B. Mison, Homophobia in Manslaughter: The Homosexual Advance as Insufficient Provocation, 80 Cal. L. Rev. 133 (1992).

67. See Horder, *Provocation and Responsibility, supra* note 11 at 156–85; Stephen J. Morse, Undiminished Confusion in Diminished Capacity, 75 J. Crim. L. & Criminol. 1, 33–34 (1984).

68. Morse, Undiminished Confusion in Diminished Capacity, *supra.* Morse contends that some extreme cases of provocation where the individual loses all self-control might support acquittal, but otherwise deficits in self-control should be considered only at sentencing. I reject Morse's acquittal option on the same grounds that I have argued against capacity-based responsibility throughout. We blame, or excuse, not according to assessments of psychological capacity to do otherwise, but according to assessments of the moral nature of (the reasons for) conduct. Ott may have had less control capacity at the time of killing than did Gounagias, but that should not give Ott a better excuse or mitigation argument.

69. Horder, *Provocation and Responsibility, supra* note 11 at 194–97. Horder also argues that provocation condones violence in dispute resolution by assuming that some form of nonhomicidal violence would have been an appropriate reaction to the victim's conduct. The early English common law of provocation clearly presumed the morality of lesser violence in response to a wrong: the offender was punished not because he used violence but because he used *too much.* Today provocation rests—or should rest—on different grounds: that justified passion makes self-control particularly difficult. It does not assume that some level of violent response was justified. Horder also argues that provocation as presently conceived condones patriarchy, *id.* at 186–91. The sexist tendencies of provocation are addressed in the next section of the chapter.

70. Nourse, Passion's Progress, *supra* note 32 at 1347. For more on assaults connected to romantic separation, see Martha R. Mahoney, Legal Images of Battered Women: Redefining the Issue of Separation, 90 Mich. L. Rev. 1 (1991).

71. For an example, see Gaylin, *The Killing of Bonnie Garland, supra* note 27.

72. Nourse, Passion's Progress, *supra* note 32 at 1377–80.

73. For a typical description: "The commission of unlawful sexual intercourse with a female relative is an act obviously calculated to arouse ungovernable passion, and it is well settled that the killing of the seducer or adulterer under the influence or in the heat of passion thus engendered is, in the absence of actual malice, voluntary manslaughter and not murder. This is especially true in cases of illicit intercourse with the wife of the slayer." Homicide, 40 Am. Jur. 2d sec. 65 at 358. For a good overview of the law of provocation based on adultery, see Singer, The Resurgence of Mens Rea, *supra* note 14 at 256–58, 272–75.

For criticisms of this aspect of provocation as sexist, see Coker, Heat of Passion and Wife Killing, *supra* note 31; Taylor, Provoked Reason in Men and Women, *supra* note 50; Andrée Côté, Violence Conjugale, Excuses Patriarcales et Défense de Provocation, 29 Criminologie 89 (1996) (critiquing Canadian law).

74. R. v. Mawgridge, 84 Eng. Rep. 1107, 1115.

75. *Id.* Holt even doubted whether a conviction for manslaughter was warranted in this situation. "If a thief comes to rob another, it is lawful to kill him. And if a man comes to rob a man's posterity and his family, yet to kill him is manslaughter. So is the law though it may seem hard, that the killing in the one case should not be as justifiable as the other." A similar view of adultery as provocation prevailed in this country in the South throughout the nineteenth and into the twentieth centuries. Several states provided that a killing in the heat of passion, upon discovery of adultery, was entirely excused. See Rollin M. Perkins & Ronald N. Boyce, *Criminal Law* 96–97 n.42 (3d ed. 1982).

76. See Taylor, Provoked Reason in Men and Women, *supra* note 50 at 1691–98.

77. See Polk & Ranson, The Role of Gender in Intimate Homicide, *supra* note 47; Barnard et al., Till Death Do Us Part: A Study of Spouse Murder, 10 Bull. Am. Acad. Psychiatry & L. 271 (1982).

78. Like many potential provocation situations, such cases will often present complex and difficult questions. For example, see Thornton v. State, 730 S.W. 2d 309 (Tenn. 1987) (husband shoots lover of wife in bedroom during separation period after conducting surveillance of house); People v. Bridgehouse, 47 Cal.2d 406, 303 P.2d 1018 (1956) (husband shoots man who had extended affair with wife after man appears at mother-in-law's house and wife refuses to either grant divorce or stop seeing rival).

79. *Men, Women and Aggression* (1993).

80. *Id.* at 71.

81. Campbell refers to this as the expressive model because women use violence to express their frustration. *Id.* at 7–11. See also Jane Totman, *The Murderess: A Psychosocial Study of Criminal Homicide* 9 (1978). I find this term unhelpful, since all violence is expressive. The term "explosive" also better captures what seems to be a central point of Campbell's female model, that women become violent in an unplanned and unpredictable way, as a result of overwhelming pressures.

For criminologic support for this model of violence in homicides committed by females, see Robbin S. Ogle et al., A Theory of Homicidal Behavior among Women, 33 Criminology 173 (1995).

82. *Id.* at 125–40.

83. See Elijah Anderson, The Code of the Streets, *The Atlantic Monthly*, May 1994 at 81, 92; Andrea N. Jones, They Get Right in Your Face, Utne Reader, July/August 1994, at 54–55. From 1982 to 1991, the female arrest rate for aggravated assault rose 73.7 percent and for all violent crime rose 60.5 percent. Federal Bureau of Investigation, Uniform Crime Reports, Crime in the United States 1991, 218 (1992). For

a powerful fictional account of the phenomenon, see Yxta Maya Murray, *Locas* (1997).

84. Campbell, *Men, Women and Aggression, supra* note 79 at 49.

85. For example, this is sociologist Jack Katz's description of the rage of killing. "Rage is a sophisticated incompetence. It is deaf in the sense of being indifferent to reasoned argument and dumb in the narrow sense of being inarticulate. Fury judges but without hearing arguments and it does not pause to explain its reasons, even to itself. Rage is also blind, but it is not stupid. . . . Would-be killers create their homicidal rage only through a precisely articulated leap to righteousness, which logically resolves, just for the crucial moment, the animating dilemma." Katz argues that many impassioned killers turn scenes of frustration and humiliation into a righteous rage which, in the mind of the killer, justifies the homicide. *Seductions of Crime, supra* note 47 at 30.

86. See, for example, State v. Guido, 191 A.2d 45 (N.J. 1963) (defendant, who had separated from husband and sought a divorce, killed him while he slept after repeated threats and abuse from him designed to force her to return to him).

87. The literature on self-defense and battered women is voluminous. For advocacy of significant conceptual or doctrinal change in self-defense law, see, e.g., Richard A. Rosen, On Self-Defense, Imminence and Women Who Kill Their Batterers, 71 N.C. L. Rev. 371 (1993); Phyllis L. Crocker, The Meaning of Equality for Battered Women Who Kill Men in Self-Defense, 8 Harv. Women's L.J. 121 (1985). For recent works critical of at least some suggested changes in self-defense law in this context, see, e.g., Joshua Dressler, Battered Women, Sleeping Abusers, and Criminal Responsibility, 2 Chicago Policy Rev. 1 (1997); Holly Maguigan, Battered Women and Self-Defense: Myths and Misconceptions in Current Reform Proposals, 140 Un. of Pa. L. Rev. 379 (1991); Susan Estrich, Defending Women, 88 Mich. L. Rev. 1430 (1990).

88. See Ogle, A Theory of Homicidal Behavior, *supra* note 81.

89. Cf. Klimchuk, Outrage, Self-Control, and Culpability, *supra* note 37 at 465, arguing that the traditional timing requirement may be gender-biased in battered-woman cases, but that rather than change provocation law, such cases should be handled under a modified self-defense doctrine. See also Aileen McColgan, In Defence of Battered Women Who Kill, 13 Ox. J. Leg. Stud. 508 (1993).

90. See Marvin E. Wolfgang & Franco Ferracuti, *The Subculture of Violence* 260–63 (1967). But see Kenneth Polk, Lethal Violence as a Form of Masculine Conflict Resolution, 28 Aust. & N. Zealand J. Crim. 93 (1995) (reporting use of planned violence by working-class males to resolve conflicts).

91. See Wolfgang & Ferracuti, *The Subculture of Violence, supra.*

Most homicide statistics do not distinguish between different types of purposeful, criminal killings. Therefore, racial disparities appear in the totals of purposeful homicides. In 1992 the Surgeon General noted that homicide was the leading cause of death among fifteen to thirty-four-year-old black males. American Medical Association, *Violence: A Compendium . . . from the Journals of the AMA* 21 (1992). For the year 1991, 47 percent of the murders and nonnegligent homicides known to police involved white victims; 50 percent involved black victims. Bureau of Justice Statistics, U.S. Dept. of Justice, *Sourcebook of Criminal Justice Statistics—1992* 390 (1993). In 1991, 51.8 percent of those believed by police to have committed murder and non-negligent manslaughter that year were black; 46.1 percent were white. *Id.* at 395. See, generally, *Homicide among Black Americans* (Darnell F. Hawkins ed. 1986).

92. The early English law of murder and manslaughter also reflected class differences in its doctrine. Spontaneous combats leading to death were termed manslaughter, but duels, with their delay between dispute and fight, were uniformly classified as murder by the courts. See Horder, The Duel and the English Law of Homicide, 12 Ox. J. Leg. Stud. 419 (1992). This distinction involved not only timing but social class. The premeditated duel was a gentlemanly affair. The delay between challenge and duel demonstrated a gentleman's self-control and courage: even with time for second thoughts he would not back down. By contrast, taking the field was only a step removed from the common tavern brawl. Horder quotes from an eighteenth-century writer on male honor: "When the meaner sort fall out, the Port which intoxicated them is thrown at one another's head, and they come to boxing and cuffing immediately. . . . But gentlemen . . . are not satisfied nor will put up with their differences without a duel." *Id.* at 422.

93. See Edward L. Ayers, *Vengeance and Justice: Crime and Punishment in the 19th-Century South* 9–33 (1984); Butterfield, *All God's Children, supra* note 8 at 11–18. In a fascinating and terrifying example of the transfer of violent cultures, Butterfield describes in his book how a violent white society in Revolutionary South Carolina led to continuing violence in white male society throughout the nineteenth century, when it was taken up by black male society as well, with repercussions continuing through the end of the twentieth century.

94. *Patterns in Criminal Homicide* 188–89 (1958). A fuller statement of the theory may be found in Wolfgang & Ferracuti, *The Subculture of Violence, supra* note 90. For a related approach applied to race, see Lynn A. Curtis, *Violence, Race, and Culture* (1975). For a critical overview of subculture theories, see Phillip Feldman, *The Psychology of Crime* 245–46 (1993); George B. Vold & Thomas J. Bernard, *Theoretical Criminology* 214–19 (3d ed. 1986). The subcultural approach has been particularly criticized in the racial context, sometimes on grounds that it does not explain the phenomena it purports to and sometimes for an overemphasis on cultural values as opposed to structural factors in society such as socioeconomic status and history of oppression. See, e.g., Darnell F. Hawkins, Black and White Homicide Differentials: Alternatives to an Inadequate Theory, in *Homicide among Black Americans, supra* note 90. The great danger of the subcultural approach, recognized by even its strongest proponents, is its potential for reinforcing racial, ethnic, and class prejudice. Some may take the existence of a subculture of violence as indicative of genetic or other fundamental and essentially irremediable flaws in a particular group. Subcultures of

violence develop in reaction to larger social structures, however. Outcast groups develop outcast values. See William B. Harvey, Homicide among Young Black Adults: Life in the Subculture of Exasperation, in *Homicide among Black Americans, supra.*

95. See Anderson, The Code of the Streets, *supra* note 83. Phillipe Bourgois, In Search of Masculinity: Violence, Respect and Sexuality among Puerto Rican Crack Dealers in East Harlem, 36 Brit. J. Criminol. 412 (1996).

96. For other arguments in favor of group-based pluralism in provocation, see Stanley Yeo, Sex, Ethnicity, Power of Self-Control and Provocation Revisited, 18 Sydney L. Rev. 304 (1996); Bernard Brown, The "Ordinary Man" in Provocation: Anglo-Saxon Attitudes and "Unreasonable" Non-Englishmen, 13 Int'l & Comp. L.Q. 203 (1964); Colin Howard, What Colour is the "Reasonable Man"? [1961] Crim. L.R. 697.

97. See David C. Baldus, George Woodworth, & Charles Pulaski Jr., *Equal Justice and the Death Penalty* (1990). For general commentary on the devaluation of black lives in the criminal justice system, see Randall L. Kennedy, McCleskey v. Kemp: Race, Capital Punishment, and the Supreme Court, 101 Harv. L. Rev. 1388 (1988); Stephen L. Carter, When Victims Happen to Be Black, 97 Yale L.J. 420 (1988); Hawkins, Black and White Homicide Differentials, *supra* note 94 at 114–18.

98. See Harold M. Rose & Paula D. McClain, *Race, Place, and Risk: Black Homicide in Urban America* 226–27 (1990) (detailing homicide convictions in Atlanta, St. Louis, and Detroit). See also Randy E. Barnett, Bad Trip: Drug Prohibition and the Weakness of Public Policy, 103 Yale L.J. 2593, 2595 (1994) (detailing wholesale reductions of murder charges to manslaughter in Chicago in the mid-'70s). Statistics for the state of California in 1988 indicate a similar trend. Of those arrested for murder and convicted of an offense, nearly as many were convicted of manslaughter (40.2 percent) as were convicted of murder (43.1 percent). Of whites arrested for murder, 49.9 percent were convicted of murder; 31.1 were convicted of manslaughter. By comparison, of blacks arrested for murder and convicted of an offense in that year, only 38.4 percent were convicted of murder and 48.3 percent were convicted of manslaughter. Calif. Bureau of Criminal Statistics, *Homicide in California, 1988* at 94. A Justice Department survey of cases involving defendants charged with murder or voluntary manslaughter in the seventy-five most populous counties in the nation revealed that in cases disposed of in 1988, 19 percent of defendants were convicted of first-degree murder, 22 percent of second-degree murder, and 22 percent of voluntary manslaughter. Approximately 98 percent of these defendants were originally charged with either first- or second-degree murder. Bureau of Justice Statistics, Murder in Large Urban Counties, 1988 (1993).

Researchers looking at the same data for spousal homicides concluded that race had no significant impact on race in conviction or sentence. Patrick A. Langan & John M. Dawson, Bureau of Justice Statistics, Spouse Murder Defendants in Large Urban Counties 24 (1995). Nevertheless, some of the statistics on race suggest at least a need for more research. The conviction percentages based on race of the victim were very close: 81 percent in cases with white victims, 79 percent in cases with black victims. In terms of sentences, of those convicted for first-degree murder (a small minority of the total of those convicted), average sentence in white-victim cases was twenty-nine years versus thirty-two years in black-victim cases. For second-degree murder, however, average sentences were: nineteen years in white victim cases, thirteen years in black victim cases and for voluntary manslaughter, eight years in white victim cases and six years in black victim cases. *Id.*

I should add one important caveat concerning overall amount of prison time for homicide convictions. My concern here is with relative sentences—comparing punishment between homicide cases. My concern is that defendants who commit similar offenses may receive dissimilar sentences due to the different social statuses of the victims involved. I make no argument about how much time any particular defendant should serve. To the extent that American prison terms are generally set higher than they should be, as many liberal critics maintain, then the inequity in outcome suggested here should be alleviated not by increasing the time served by those who now receive lesser sentences, but by reducing the time served by those who receive higher sentences.

99. See Independent Commission on the Los Angeles Police Department, Selected Messages from the LAPD Mobile Digital Terminal System 8 (1991): "This is a definite NHI [no human involved]. Do have to make an arrest . . . I dont want to I want to make a rpt."

100. Psychologists note two different ways of thinking: propositional thinking, which follows the abstract, formal, logical analysis common in law; and narrative thinking, which is highly contextual, concrete and based on interpersonal interactions; in other words, stories. To the extent decision makers use narrative thinking rather than propositional, stories are more important than rules. See Finkel, Achilles Fuming, *supra* note 27 at 775.

101. See Bishop, 2 *Commentaries on the Criminal Law, supra* note 17 at 394. Later in his commentaries, Bishop was even more explicit about the insufficiency of rule statements to explain the law of provocation.

> The reader perceives that the foregoing discussions, if such they may be called, contain but little of *doctrine*; being in the main enunciations of what the courts have found, sitting, almost like jurors, in determination upon particular facts. If, below this outward seeming, there lies a science, harmonizing, in the nature of a rule, these several determinations, it would be pleasant to uncover the rule, and present it, in words, to the reader. Perhaps it would be, that, when the facts evince a certain degree of culpability, they constitute the "malice aforethought" of the old statute, and the killing is murder; while, when they come short, it is manslaughter. But there are no words, other than these obscure ones of the old statute, to express the degree; therefore it can be shown to the reader only by such illustrations as are set down in these pages.

Id. at 706–7.

102. E.g., State v. Grugin, 47 S.W. 1058 (Mo. 1898) (defendant kills son-in-law, who reportedly raped defendant's sixteen-year-old daughter, when son-in-law responds to rape accusation by saying, "I'll do as I damn please about it"); State v. Flory, 276 P. 458 (Wyo. 1929) (defendant kills father-in-law who raped defendant's wife). See also State v. Martin, 57 S.E.2d 55 (S.C. 1949).

103. See also Taylor v. Mississippi, 452 So.2d 441 (Miss. 1984) (fourteen-year-old pregnant girl shoots social worker after social worker states that mother will not only be barred from visiting her first child that had been removed from the mother's care, but the mother would lose custody of her unborn child once it was born).

104. For the same reason we need to rid the law of phrases such as "sudden quarrel" and "mutual combat," for these phrases conjure up images of conflicts that should no longer represent classic instances of provocation. Cf. Calif. Pen. Code sec. 192(a) (sudden quarrel); People v. Parker, 632 N.E.2d 214, 218 (App. Ct. Ill. 1994) (mutual combat).

In a number of ways, modern courts have already altered traditional provocation doctrine to accord with the new proposed paradigm of serious physical harm to the victim. In jurisdictions where the judiciary continues to regulate the categories of provoking conduct, minor physical assaults will not support provocation. See LaFave & Scott, *Criminal Law, supra* note 57 at 574. Likewise those jurisdictions that recognize mutual combat as legal provocation have required that the defendant be blameless in starting the fight and have used only proportional violence in an absolutely fair physical contest. See People v. Austin, 549 N.E.2d 331 (Ill. 1989); People v. Whitfield, 66 Cal. Rptr. 438 (Cal. App. 1968).

NOTES TO CHAPTER 9: CRIMES OF INDIFFERENCE

1. The doctrine is also known as depraved mind murder and extreme indifference murder. For articles specifically focusing on the doctrine, see Bernard E. Gegan, More Cases of Depraved Mind Murder: The Problem of Mens Rea, 64 St. John's L. Rev. 429 (1990); Gegan, A Case of Depraved Mind Murder, 49 St. John's L. Rev. 417 (1974); Note, Defining Unintended Murder 85 Col. L. Rev. 786 (1985).

2. *Commentaries on the Laws of England* 192 (1769, 1979).

3. *Id.* In Colorado today this mens rea is described as universal malice and serves to distinguish first and second degree murder in unintentional homicide. See People v. Zekany, 833 P.2d 774, 776 (Colo. 1991). Most jurisdictions make no legal distinction between recklessness that endangers one person versus that which endangers many and categorize such murders as second degree. E.g., Marasa v. State, 394 So.2d 544 (Fla. App. 1981).

4. As one California court put it, the definition of depraved heart murder traditionally has been "more visceral than intellectual." People v. Love, 168 Cal. Rptr. 407, 410 (Cal. App. 1980).

5. Commonwealth v. Drum, 58 Pa. 9, 15 (1868).

6. On depraved heart murder as a wanton act, see Rollin M. Perkins & Ronald N. Boyce, *Criminal Law* 60 (3d ed. 1982); Jenkins v. State, 230 A.2d 262, 266 (Del. 1967) ("cruel and wicked indifference to human life"); People v. Love, 168 Cal. Rptr. 407, 411 (Cal. App. 1980) ("there is an element of viciousness—an extreme indifference to the value of human life."); Calif. Penal Code sec. 188 ("when the circumstances attending the killing show an abandoned and malignant heart").

7. For articles focusing on particular modern interpretations, see sources cited *supra* note 1. See also Jeffrey F. Ghent, Validity and Construction of "Extreme Indifference" Murder Statute, 7 A.L.R.5th 758; Dale R. Agthe, Validity and Construction of Statute Defining Homicide by Conduct Manifesting "Depraved Indifference," 25 A.L.R.4th 311.

The categorization of offenses has changed somewhat, however. In most United States jurisdictions depraved heart murder is no longer a capital offense. But see Tison v. Arizona, 482 U.S. 921 (1987) (holding that extreme recklessness causing death is constitutionally sufficient to support the death penalty). Depraved heart murder is usually a form of second-degree murder, punished less severely than first-degree murder. See, e.g., Calif. Pen. Code secs. 188, 189. Some jurisdictions classify a form of depraved heart murder as first-degree murder, however. See People v. Zekany, 833 P.2d 774 (Colo. 1991).

8. See Hyam v. Director of Public Prosecutions [1974] 2 All E.R. 41. For a proposal to alter English murder law by removing the murder mens rea of intent to do great bodily harm and replace it with a mens rea of subjective recklessness toward risk of death and proof of culpable indifference, see Barry Mitchell, Culpably Indifferent Murder, 25 Anglo-Amer. L. Rev. 64 (1996). This proposal would make English law similar to American, but with more content given to the concept of indifference.

9. See Wayne R. LaFave & Austin W. Scott Jr., *Criminal Law* 620–22 (2d ed. 1986). To illustrate the range of approaches, California requires actual awareness of "life-threatening conduct." See People v. Dellinger, 783 P.2d 200, 202–3 (Cal. 1990); New York requires recklessness: subjective awareness of a substantial risk, plus an objective determination that the conduct demonstrates indifference to life. See People v. Register, 457 N.E.2d 704 (N.Y. 1983). See Gegan, More Cases of Depraved Mind Murder, *supra* note 1; while Maine requires only an objective determination of indifference. See State v. Woodbury, 403 A.2d 1166 (Me. 1979); Note, Louis B. Butterfield, Maine's Unintentional Murder Statute: Depraved Indifference on Trial, 40 Maine L. Rev. 411 (1988).

10. Secs. 2.02(c); 210.1; 210.2(1)(b).

11. Sec. 2.02(2)(c).

12. That is, in most cases, a defendant who realizes his actions pose a certain level of risk to others will be found reckless if a decision maker later deems that level of risk to be unjustifiable in the circumstances. The MPC seems to permit the argument that recklessness should not be found in this situation where the defendant realized the level of risk but did not realize its lack of justification. For example, assume a po-

lice officer fired his weapon in trying to restore order in a bar. Assume the officer believed firing the weapon was dangerous, but necessary; assume a jury later disagreed about its necessity. The statutory language suggests the officer should be acquitted of recklessness here. The problem with this result is that it seems to base acquittal (at least for recklessness) not on lack of perception of risk but on the accused's *normative* judgment about that risk. The criminal law generally does not grant excuses based on an accused's normative disagreement with the law or a decision maker's judgment about a legal standard.

In one important sense, even the awareness approach does not require full realization of the risks involved. A person who purposefully, knowingly, or recklessly kills another acts with intellectual awareness of the legally significant consequences of his conduct. He may not realize the moral meaning of these consequences, however. This may seem like a trivial distinction, but it is not. A person who kills, knowing only that killing is illegal, misses the moral dimension of killing, a dimension arguably far more important to both notice and culpability than understanding of legal prohibitions. Only if we imagine what a violent death would mean to the victim and the victim's loved ones can we say that we understand the meaning of killing.

13. See Roy Moreland, *The Law of Homicide* 99–182, 235–39 (1952).

14. See Joshua Dressler, *Understanding Criminal Law* 478 (2d ed. 1995).

15. *Id.* For those jurisdictions following the MPC, involuntary manslaughter requires proof of a lesser degree of recklessness than for murder. Sec. 210.3. The MPC defines a further lesser offense, negligent homicide, based on a negligence mens rea. Sec. 210.4. For an overview of current English law, see see J. C. Smith & Brian Hogan, *Criminal Law* 218–27 (7th ed. 1992).

16. Dressler, *Understanding Criminal Law, supra* note 14.

17. The MPC creates a third level of punishment for negligent homicides where the offender was not actually aware of an unjustifiable risk of death but a reasonably careful person would have been. Sec. 210.4 (1).

18. Sec. 2.02(2)(d).

19. Commentary to sec. 2.02 at 242.

20. See Richard Singer, The Resurgence of Mens Rea: I—Provocation, Emotional Disturbance, and the Model Penal Code, 27 B.C. L. Rev. 243 (1986); Glanville Williams, Recklessness Redefined, 40 Camb. L.J. 252 (1981), and The Unresolved Problem of Recklessness, 8 Legal Studies 74 (1988); Jerome Hall, Negligent Behavior Should Be Excluded from Penal Liability, 63 Colum. L. Rev. 632 (1963); Note, Negligence and the General Problem of Criminal Responsibility, 81 Yale L.J. 949 (1972).

21. See R. A. Duff, *Intention, Agency & Criminal Liability* (1990); Robert Goff, The Mental Element in Murder, 104 L.Q. Rev. 30 (1988); Gerald H. Gordon, Subjective and Objective Mens Rea, 17 Crim. L.Q. 355 (1974–75); D. J. Birch, The Foresight Saga: The Biggest Mistake of All? [1988] Crim. L. Rev. 4; John Stannard, Subjectivism, Objectivism, and the Draft Criminal Code, 101 L.Q. Rev. 540 (1985); James

B. Brady, Punishment for Negligence: A Reply to Professor Hall, 22 Buff. L. Rev. 107 (1972–73); P.J.T. O'Hearn, Criminal Negligence: An Analysis in Depth, 7 Crim. L.Q. 27 (1964–65); Simon Gardner, Reckless and Inconsiderate Rape [1991] Crim. L. R. 172. See also George Fletcher, The Theory of Criminal Negligence: A Comparative Analysis, 119 U. Pa. L. Rev. 401 (1971).

For thoughtful articles that critique the understanding of culpability and linguistics underlying the awareness approach, see Brenda Baker, Mens Rea, Negligence and Criminal Law Reform, 6 Law & Phil. 53 (1987); Alan R. White, Carelessness, Indifference and Recklessness, 24 Mod. L. Rev. 592 (1961).

Kenneth Simons argues that awareness and indifference are in a sense incommensurable because they represent different kinds of mens rea. He argues we should differentiate mens rea belief-states such as knowledge from desire-states such as purpose or reckless indifference. Simons argues that reckless indifference, with its emphasis on callousness, may serve an important role as a mens rea in criminal law, equal protection doctrine and other areas of law. Rethinking Mental States, 72 Bos. U. L. Rev. 463 (1992).

Related issues are also involved in the mens rea of willful ignorance, which can substitute for knowledge. See Robin Charlow, Willful Ignorance and Criminal Culpability, 70 Tex. L. Rev. 1351 (1992).

22. Morisette v. United States, 342 U.S. 246, 250 (1952) ("The contention that an injury can amount to a crime only when inflicted by intention is no provincial or transient notion.")

23. For collections of exemplary cases, see Rollin M. Perkins & Ronald N. Boyce, *Criminal Law* 59–60 (3d ed. 1982); People v. Love, 168 Cal. Rptr. 407, 411 (Cal. App. 1980).

24. R. v. Caldwell [1982] A.C. 341, 354 (Lord Diplock); R. v. Lawrence (Stephen) [1982] A.C. 510; R. v. Reid 1 W.L.R. 793 (1992). Many academic commentators have criticized this view of recklessness, arguing it should require actual awareness of the risk. Others have supported the notion of recklessness independent of awareness, although not necessarily the English court's formulation. See sources set out in notes 20 & 21 *supra*.

25. There is one other argument in support of awareness that may work in the background. Although I have found no commentator who makes the argument explicitly, support for the awareness approach in criminal law may also stem from the liberal political principle that the government may only punish individuals for aggressive harms to others. Political liberals have long argued that government may punish individuals for affirmative wrongs done to others, but government may not force individuals to act in a morally good fashion. In criminal law, this argument is used to support the common law doctrine that a person has no legal obligation to rescue another in peril unless she was herself responsible for the peril or had a special relationship with the victim. Similarly, a wealthy person need not give to the poor, even if some may starve as a result. Liberal theory holds that although such con-

duct may be immoral, the government may not intervene unless the individual affirmatively harms another. Lesser harms must be handled by the individual. Any alternative approach would give government too much power over individuals and violate the social contract, in which government's power is limited to maintenance of a minimal order among individuals. See John Kleinig, Good Samaritanism, 5 Phil. & Pub. Aff. 382 (1976). A similar argument might be used to support the awareness approach to criminal culpability. Government may punish harmful acts where the individual sees the dangers involved and acts regardless because here the individual consciously chooses to put others at risk. Government may not require persons to look out for harms to others, however. An affirmative obligation of concern for others—a requirement that the individual carefully consider all consequences before acting—would ignore the vital distinction between private morality and public wrongdoing.

The obvious retort to this approach is that the hazards of modern technology preclude easy distinctions between recognizing risk and looking out for it. Even an ordinary activity such as driving a car involves risks so great that we have incorporated affirmative perception obligations into our definition of basic wrongdoing. A driver may not claim exemption from a red light on grounds that he "just didn't see it." He must have a good reason why he did not fulfill his affirmative obligation to see and obey all traffic signals. This indicates that the debate about awareness and indifference will not be resolved on grounds of political theory. At least in some circumstances we agree that the government may punish failures to look out for others.

26. Ulric Neisser, *Cognition and Reality* 84 (1976).

27. Some forms of perception, especially basic sense perception that requires little mental processing, can be unaware, however. In fact, the study of unaware perception has been a staple of psychology in recent years. E.g., Lawrence Wiskrantz, Search for the Unseen, in *Attention: Selection, Awareness and Control* 235 (A. Baddeley & L. Wiskrantz, eds. 1993); Dianne Berry, Implicit Learning: Reflections and Prospects, in *id.* at 246; Larry L. Jacoby, Diane Ste-Marie & Jeffrey P. Toh, Redefining Automaticity: Unconscious Influences, Awareness, and Control, in *id.* at 261.

28. See Owen Flanagan, *Consciousness Reconsidered* 46 (1992).

29. See Neisser, *supra* note 26.

30. For introductions to the psychology of attention, see David LaBerge, *Attentional Processing* 1–17 (1995); William N. Dember & Joel S. Warm, *Psychology of Attention* (2d ed. 1979). For a philosophic and spiritual account, see James S. Hans, *The Mysteries of Attention* (1993).

31. For the psychology of selective attention and the value of denial—of avoiding certain realizations—see Daniel Goleman, *Vital Lies, Simple Truths* (1985).

32. Matthew Hugh Erdelyi, Hyperamnesia and Insight, in *Consciousness in Contemporary Science* 211 (A. J. Marcel & E. Bisiach eds. 1988). As Ulric Neisser put it: "The fact that people do not notice something is no evidence that they could not have noticed if they had tried." *Supra* note 26 at 91. Or as James Hans observes: "Our

principles are always manifested in that to which we choose to attend." *Supra* note 30 at 21.

33. E.g., Daniel C. Dennett, *Consciousness Explained* 112–13, 126, 138 (1991) (arguing that consciousness is what we get when we self-consciously probe our own stream of consciousness; therefore the difference between the unconscious and conscious depends entirely on when and how we choose to introspect).

34. E.g., Marcel Kinsbourne, Integrated Field Theory of Consciousness, in *Consciousness in Contemporary Science, supra* note 32 at 239, 245–46; E. Roy John, A Model of Consciousness, in 4 *Consciousness and Self-Regulation* (Gary Schwartz & David Shapiro eds. 1976); William H. Calvin, *The Cerebral Symphony* (1989).

35. See Neil Stillings et al., *Cognitive Science: An Introduction* 48–49 (2d ed. 1995); Donald A. Norman & Tim Shallice, Attention to Action: Willed and Automatic Control of Behavior, in 4 *Consciousness and Self-Regulation* (R. Davidson, G. Schwartz, & D. Shapiro eds. 1986).

36. People v. Protopappas, 201 Cal. App.3d 152, 246 Cal. Rptr. 915 (1988). At trial Protopappas claimed Andreassen was not put under general anesthetic, but a medical assistant testified to the contrary. *Id.* at 917, n.3.

37. *Id.* at 924, n.9.

38. *Id.* at 927–28. Another example cited by the appellate court of how the doctor reacted to warnings involved his treatment of 31-year-old Cathryn Jones. Important to the context is that one of the signs of respiratory failure is poor circulation, as shown by purple lips or fingernails.

About one and one-half hours into the operation, the dental assistant told Protopappas Jones's lips were turning blue. Protopappas testified he looked at her lips but they were not blue. He did not take her pulse because bright red blood was squirting in her mouth indicating to him that she was properly oxygenated. A short while later the assistant again told Protopappas Jones's lips were turning purple. He became angry and told the assistant she did not know what purple was. Comparing Jones's lips to a purple syringe cap he held up, Protopappas said, "Goddamn it, this is purple," and pointing to her lips, "this is not." The assistant warned him of Jones's deteriorating condition a third time, this time pointing out that her fingernails were blue. Protopappas insisted they were pink.

The assistant left the patient to get more drugs. When she returned, Jones did not appear to be breathing. Her hands were cold and her fingernails were purple. Finally acknowledging Jones needed oxygen, Protopappas finished suturing before giving her three short breaths through an oxygen mask.

Patient Jones never regained consciousness. She died two days later. *Id.* at 920.

39. See Gordon, Subjective and Objective Mens Rea, *supra* note 21 at 366. Gordon quotes Barbara Wooton, a British magistrate and criminal law commentator, on proving that the defendant in a receiving stolen goods case knew that the goods were stolen:

There is little doubt that convictions have often been reached on the basis that, even if knowledge cannot be proved—any reasonable man must have known—a practice which has always appeared to me to be a violation of the scrupulous regard for the letter of the law which normally characterizes legal procedure. (Admittedly, very few charges of "receiving" would otherwise have succeeded.)

Quoted from The Changing Face of British Criminal Justice, in *Law and Crime* 116 (N. Morris & M. Perlman eds. 1972).

40. The possibilities for confusion caused by the use of both methods of awareness analysis are illustrated by the following situation. The offender, who carries a sawed-off shotgun in a canvas bag, is stopped by a police officer and questioned about the bag's contents. The offender "panics" and kills the officer with a shotgun blast. Assuming that "panic" is an accurate description of the defendant's mental state, does this mean he did not realize the risk involved, or does it just describe his motive for the action? See People v. Rose, 548 A.2d 1058, 1069–73, 1109, 1110–18 (N.J. 1988). Here the majority held that the defendant must have been aware of risks of a point-blank shot while the dissenters argued that the defendant's statement about panicking and evidence about his emotional reaction to the shooting indicated that he may not have been aware of the risks involved.

In order to avoid such problems, some jurisdictions emphasize the objective aspects of carelessness: the obvious and unnecessary dangers of conduct, often with a cursory nod toward the idea of indifference. See State v. Crocker, 435 A.2d 58 (Me. 1981); People v. Register, 542 N.E.2d 704 (N.Y. 1983). The problem with such approaches is that indifference is not clearly defined; it works as a place-holder for decision maker intuition, which may or may not track the reasons-for-perceptive-failure analysis suggested here.

41. People v. Moquin, 142 A.D. 347, 536 N.Y.S.2d (1988).

42. J. Caher, Moquin to be Paroled after 5 Years for Fatal DWI, Albany Times Union at C1, Dec. 8, 1992.

43. See Stanley Beck & Graham Parker, The Intoxicated Offender—A Problem of Responsibility, 44 Can. Bar Rev. 563, 570–73 (1966); Monrad Paulsen, Intoxication as a Defense to Crime, 1961 U. Ill. L. Forum 1, 1.

44. A nineteenth-century court used a particularly colorful dualist metaphor to express the same responsibility idea: the drunk "must be held to have purposely blinded his moral perceptions, and set his will free from the control of reason—to have suppressed the guards and invited the mutiny." Roberts v. People, 19 Mich. 401, 418 (1870).

For arguments that addiction to intoxicants does not preclude moral responsibility, see Herbert Fingarette, *Heavy Drinking* (1988); Douglas Husak, *Drugs and Rights* 108–17 (1992); United States v. Moore, 486 F.2d 1139 (D.C. Cir. 1973).

45. See sources cited at note 43 *supra*. Some argue that as long as we do not become caught up in dualist confusions about mens rea, intoxication requires no spe-

cial legal treatment, because intoxication will rarely negate any form of mens rea, including recklessness. See Roger Shiner, Intoxication and Responsibility, 13 Intl. J. Law & Psych. 9 (1990).

Assuming intoxication does affect awareness of risk, we have to ask whether we can really separate perception of risk from the personality changes that intoxication induces. Here again we may be attempting the impossible task of distinguishing perception and decision making. The intoxicated driver experiences problems with sight and mechanical (speed, distance, direction, etc.) judgment, not just because alcohol interferes with the brain processes necessary to these activities, but because he takes a different attitude toward risk. The drunk driver feels more invulnerable, therefore he devotes less processing resources to signals of danger. Evidence that a car is coming in the opposite lane may be, in a sense, willfully ignored. The closest we could come to separating these two aspects of intoxication is if we believed the driver fought the effects of intoxication by making every effort to drive safely.

46. See, e.g., People v. Watson, 637 P.2d 279, 285–86 (Cal. 1981).

47. See Jerome Hall, *General Principles of Criminal Law* 556 (1960); Beck & Parker, The Intoxicated Offender, *supra* note 43 at 609; Law Commission Consultation Paper No. 127, Intoxication and Criminal Liability (1993) (England); Graham Virgo, The Law Commission Consultation Paper on Intoxication and Criminal Liability [1993] Crim. L.R. 415.

48. See MPC sec. 2.08 and Commentaries at 357–59. The Anglo-American common law makes a similar distinction in a rather crude and haphazard fashion by permitting intoxication as a potential defense to "specific intent" crimes: generally those involving purpose and knowledge, but not those of "general intent" that are often satisfied by recklessness. See, generally, LaFave & Scott, *Criminal Law, supra* note 9 at 387–94; People v. Majewski [1976] 2 All E.R. 142; but cf. Ill. Rev. Stat. ch. 38 sec. 6–3; R. v. O'Connor [1980] A.J. L.R. 349 (Australia).

49. For arguments supporting what I have called the intoxication exception, see Simon Gardner, The Importance of Majewski, 14 Ox. J. Leg. Stud. 279 (1994); Paulsen, Intoxication as a Defense to Crime, *supra* note 43.

50. *Criminal Law: The General Part* 122–23 (2d ed. 1961), quoted in Sanford H. Kadish & Stephen J. Schulhofer, *Criminal Law and Its Processes* 451 (6th ed. 1995).

51. Negligence, Mens Rea and Criminal Responsibility, in *Punishment and Responsibility* 136–57 (1982).

52. State v. Williams, 484 P.2d 1167 (Wash. App. 1971). Walter Williams was not the natural father of the boy but assumed responsibility for his care and acted in all ways as a loving parent. *Id.* at 1170.

53. *Id.*

54. The state legislature has since modified its law of unintentional manslaughter. Washington law now provides for two degrees of unintentional manslaughter, one based on recklessness and the other based on gross negligence. See Wash. Rev. C. sec. 9A.32.060, 9A.32.070; State v. Norman, 808 P.2d 1159, 1164 (Wash. App.

1991). Most jurisdictions base involuntary manslaughter on gross negligence. E.g., State v. Everhart, 231 S.E.2d 604, 606 (N.C. 1977); People v. Oliver, 258 Cal. Reptr. 138, 142–44 (Ct. App. 1989). For an overview, see MPC sec. 210.3 Commentary at 83–84.

55. *Id.* at 1171.

56. *Id.* at 154.

57. *Id.* at 1170, 1172, 1173. The court's references to the parents' love are curious in an opinion purporting to analyze only negligence in treatment of the sick. The references illustrate the underlying tension in the case between intuitions about indifference and the formal analysis of negligence. The court also noted that the defendants were young native Americans with limited educations, factors relevant to capacity analysis, although irrelevant to the negligence standard set out by the court.

58. See Indian Child Welfare Act of 1977; Hearing on S. 1214 before the Senate Select Committee on Indian Affairs, 95th Cong. 1st Sess. (1977); Russel Lawrence Barsh, The Indian Welfare Act of 1978: A Critical Analysis, 31 Hastings L.J. 1287 (1980).

The importance of this motive is made clear by a comparison of *Williams* with other manslaughter or murder convictions based on child neglect, where the failure to care for the child forms part of a pattern of callousness toward the child. See, e.g., People v. Burden, 72 Cal. App.3d 603, 140 Cal. Rptr. 282 (1977); People v. McNeeley, 77 A.D. 205, 433 N.Y.S.2d 293 (1980).

59. Under current law, individual mental skills are relevant to recklessness determinations, because a person of low intelligence may not be aware of risks that others would have been aware of in the same situation. See R. v. Sheppard [1981] A.C. 394 (England) (conviction of young, poor parents of low intelligence of willful neglect of children reversed); R. v. Wallett, 2 Q.B. 367 (England) (murder conviction reduced to manslaughter based on sixteen-year-old defendant's low intelligence, that his strangulation of girl during sexual attack did not show intent to do great bodily harm). But cf. Elliott v. C. 1 W.L.R. 939 (1983) (England) (defendant held guilty of reckless arson where gave no thought to risk of property damage and where her age [14] and low intelligence indicated she would not have realized the risk had she thought about it). In negligence cases, the law judges by the standard of a person of average reasoning powers, apparently making the defendant's mental defects irrelevant. See Commonwealth v. Pierce, 138 Mass. 165, 171–76 (1885); O. W. Holmes, Jr., *The Common Law* 53–59 (1881). Nevertheless, some courts invest the reasonable person with the defendant's reasoning powers in order to individualize the standard of liability. E.g., State v. Everhart, 231 S.E.2d 604 (N.C. 1977) (reversing involuntary manslaughter conviction of low-intelligence girl who accidentally smothered newborn infant she believed to have been stillborn).

60. Often youth is a factor in combination with low intelligence. See cases cited above. See also People v. Roe, 542 N.E.2d 610, 614 (N.Y. 1989) (rejecting argument based on youth of fifteen-year-old) but cf. People v. Michael B., 197 Cal. Rptr. 379

(Cal.App. 1983) (insufficient evidence of gross negligence for involuntary manslaughter conviction of nine-year-old boy who shot playmate at close range with a rifle). The defense of infancy, which applies to much younger individuals, should be distinguished. See LaFave & Scott, *Criminal Law, supra* note 9 at 398–400.

61. In this respect an indifference definition would not change the law in most jurisdictions. Under the common law, proof that the defendant was actually and reasonably provoked by the victim negated the malice necessary for murder, resulting in conviction for the lesser offense of manslaughter. E.g., Martinez v. State, 360 So.2d 108 (Fla. 1978); Ramsey v. State, 154 So.2d 855 (Fla. 1934); See LaFave & Scott, *Criminal Law, supra* note 9 at 653. Most United States jurisdictions adhere to this rule structure, but several now make an exception for reckless murder, holding that provocation or provocation-type arguments are irrelevant here, reasoning that provocation implies an intentional killing and should not apply to reckless or negligent offenses. People v. Wingate, 422 N.Y.S.2d 245, 245–46 (App.Div. 1979) (state's extreme emotional disturbance variant of provocation unavailable as basis for reducing extreme indifference murder to manslaughter); State v. Grunow, 506 A.2d 708, 709–14 (N.J. 1986) (holding that aggravated manslaughter—equivalent to second-degree murder in other jurisdictions—may not be reduced to simple manslaughter by proof of provocation).

62. See, e.g., State v. Juinta, 541 A.2d 284 (N.J. Sup. 1988) (in case where defendant stabbed girlfriend to death, defendant may use mental disease or defect to negate the mens rea of recklessness in homicide offenses). Linda R. Reece, Comment, Mothers Who Kill: Postpartum Disorders and Criminal Infanticide, 28 UCLA L. Rev. 699 (1991). See also People v. Spring, 200 Cal.Rptr. 849 (Cal.App. 1984), where a delusional defendant punched a priest once in the face, a blow which caused a fatal subdural hematoma. Defendant was convicted of second-degree murder. The Court of Appeal reduced the conviction to involuntary manslaughter, finding in part that the blow was not a severe one and did not involve the degree of risk necessary for depraved heart murder. *Id.* at 853. To this extent, the decision did not rely on defendant's mental disease. The court also found the defendant's delusional state relevant to mens rea. Prior to the fatal blow, the priest had barred defendant's entry to a rectory, where defendant believed a Ms. Suggs was being held against her will. "[G]iven Springs bizarre delusional state, it cannot be said his spontaneous striking out sprang from an abandoned and malignant heart as opposed to an irrational frustration stemming from the quixotic pursuit of the elusive Ms. Suggs." *Id.* In its diminished-capacity analysis, the court followed a California Supreme Court decision that was later overturned by legislative enactment. See *id.*; People v. Conley, 411 P.2d 911 (Cal. 1966); Cal. Pen. C. sec.28. See, generally, Miguel A. Mendez, Diminished Capacity in California: Premature Reports of Its Demise, 3 Stan. L. & Pol. Rev. 216 (1991) (tracing changes in the doctrine).

63. Walker v. Sup. Ct., 763 P.2d 852 (Cal. 1988).

64. *Id.* at 137, quoting People v. Watson, 637 P.2d 279 (Cal. 1981).

65. *Id.* at 136–38.

66. See *id.* at 118, n.1.

67. It is important to note that criminal law is not society's only tool to combat the dangers to children posed by religious beliefs like those of Laurie Walker. If a child's illness becomes known to others, the government can legally force medical treatment over the mother's objections. The only question for the criminal law is whether Laurie Walker deserves punishment for causing her child's death.

68. For example, in a recent case in Los Angeles, two ministers were convicted of involuntary manslaughter for causing the death of a woman during a violent exorcism allegedly conducted according to Korean religious norms. During the five-hour ritual, three men pinned the woman down and took turns pushing on her abdomen with fingers, knuckles, and feet. She suffered fatal injuries as a result, including sixteen broken ribs and crushed internal organs. The trial court, ruling against depraved heart murder on a recklessness theory, stated: "These men, misguided as they were, did not act with a conscious disregard for the victim's life, but with a real, possibly tunnel vision-regard for it." One of the state's witnesses testified that the exorcism had been conducted because the victim had become "spiritually arrogant" and had refused to obey her husband, evidently signs of demonic possession. Michael D. Harris, Judge Imposes Prison in Fatal Exorcism Case, Los Angeles Daily Journal, April 25, 1997, at 1. See also State v. Norman, 808 P.2d 1159 (Wash. App. 1991).

69. F. Scott Fitzgerald, *The Great Gatsby* 180–81 (1925, 1988).

NOTES TO APPENDIX

1. See Theodore Eisenberg & Martin Wells, Deadly Confusion: Juror Instructions in Capital Cases, 79 Cornell L. Rev. 1 (1993); Peter Tiersma, Reforming the Language of Jury Instructions, 22 Hofstra L. Rev. 37 (1993); Geoffrey Kramer & Dorean Koenig, Do Jurors Understand Criminal Jury Instructions? Analyzing the Results of the Michigan Juror Comprehension Project, 23 Mich. J. L. Ref. 401 (1990); Edward Imwinkelreid & Lloyd Schwed, Guidelines for Drafting Understandable Jury Instructions: An Introduction to the Use of Psycholinguistics, 23 Crim. L. Bull. 1325 (1987); Laurence Severance, Edith Greene, & Elizabeth Loftus, Toward Criminal Jury Instructions That Jurors Can Understand, 75 J. Crim. L. & Criminol. 198 (1984); A. Elwork, B. Sales, & J. Alfini, *Making Jury Instructions Understandable* (1982).

2. Here I refer to mens rea despite my believe that juries should not be instructed in terms of legal jargon. The other alternative is to use an ordinary language term such as intent, which must be redefined to make it more precise. In this instance, the dangers of ordinary language meanings blurring the legal definition are so great that employing a uniquely legal term is needed to ensure clear thinking about reasons for action.

3. This instruction should be given only when warranted by the facts of the case.

Index

About the Author

A former journalist and federal prosecutor, Samuel H. Pillsbury is Professor of Law and Williams Rains Fellow at Loyola Law School in Los Angeles, California.